Murray Stein

This book provides a comprehensive introduction and overview of the work of Murray Stein, beginning with a unique psychobiography of Stein's life, followed by a systematic, chapter-by-chapter presentation of all of Stein's seminal contributions to the field of analytical psychology.

Herrmann offers an in-depth examination of all nine volumes of Stein's *Collected Writings*, including his most recent contributions to the Jungian field—his books, plays, and literary works—which brings his review up to date. Each chapter is dedicated to a specific topic area of Stein's varied theories, including Solar/Lunar conscience, Jung's treatment of Christianity, the psychology of men, four pillars of analytical psychology, individuation, transformation, analytical training, and Jung's *Red Book*, all of which provide a foundation for a psychology of the present and future.

Providing readers with an accessible and holistic understanding of Stein's impact on Jungian psychology, this book will be of interest to Jungian scholars, students, and all who want a better understanding of Jung's psychology from a unique perspective.

Steven Herrmann, PhD, MFT, is a Jungian analyst, poet, teacher, and analyst member of the C.G. Jung Institute of San Francisco. He is the author of ten books, including his recent publication *Meister Eckhart and C.G. Jung: On the Vocation of the Self* (2024). He has an analytic practice in Oakland, California.

Routledge Introductions to Contemporary Analytical Psychology and Neo-Jungian Studies
Series Editor: Stefano Carpani

This collection invites readers to explore the influential work and scholarship of contemporary Jungian thinkers, recognized as contemporary classics in the field, as well as key themes and topics associated with analytical psychology. Each volume delves into significant contributions and theoretical frameworks of these thought leaders, and key concepts of Jung's psychology, enhancing your understanding of this dynamic and evolving discipline. Ideal for seasoned clinicians, academics, students, or simply enthusiasts of analytical psychology and neo-Jungian studies, this series will deepen one's appreciation of the discipline's ongoing evolution and contemporary relevance.

Titles in this series:
Murray Stein: Individuation, Transformation, and the Ways to the Self in Jungian Psychology
Steven Herrmann

Forthcoming:
Andrew Samuels: Loyal Critic of Jungian Analysis and Psychotherapy
Ruth Williams
Verena Kast: Bringing Jung Down from Heaven to Earth
Konstantin Rößler

Murray Stein

Individuation, Transformation, and the Ways to the Self in Jungian Psychology

Steven Herrmann

Routledge
Taylor & Francis Group
LONDON AND NEW YORK

First published 2026
by Routledge
4 Park Square, Milton Park, Abingdon, Oxon OX14 4RN

and by Routledge
605 Third Avenue, New York, NY 10158

Routledge is an imprint of the Taylor & Francis Group, an informa business

For Product Safety Concerns and Information please contact our EU representative GPSR@taylorandfrancis.com. Taylor & Francis Verlag GmbH, Kaufingerstraße 24, 80331 München, Germany.

Trademark notice: Product or corporate names may be trademarks or registered trademarks, and are used only for identification and explanation without intent to infringe.

British Library Cataloguing-in-Publication Data
A catalogue record for this book is available from the British Library

ISBN: 978-1-041-12291-3 (hbk)
ISBN: 978-1-041-12290-6 (pbk)
ISBN: 978-1-003-66402-4 (ebk)

DOI: 10.4324/9781003664024

Typeset in Times New Roman
by codeMantra

This book is lovingly dedicated to my wife,
Lori Goldrich

Contents

Series Editor Introduction

"Who exactly are today's Jungian ancestors?" asked Andrew Samuels in his endorsement of my book *Breakfast at Küsnacht* (2020). His answer was both provocative and illuminating: "really Jung, von Franz, Wolff, Neumann, Jacobi, Hillman, Fordham, etc., etc. Well, of course we all read them—but ancestors change. The analysts who studied under those giants are, if not today's giants, then at least already ancestors in their own right."

This insight became the point of departure for my editorial vision behind the *Anthology of Contemporary Classics in Analytical Psychology: The New Ancestors* (Routledge, 2022)—and it continues to shape the present book series.

Routledge Introductions to Contemporary Analytical Psychology and Neo-Jungian Studies emerges from the same generational reflection: a recognition that analytical psychology is not a closed canon, but a living tradition shaped by new voices, new contexts, and new ancestral figures.

Who are the (new) ancestors for my generation of newly certified analysts? The term ancestor is, of course, a provocative one—and perhaps even controversial in the context of contemporary psychoanalysis. It may be helpful, then, to distinguish between mentors and ancestors.

Mentors, I propose, are personal. The mentor-mentee relationship is based on mutual attraction and reciprocal growth. Without this dynamic, such a relationship cannot truly exist. Think of Plato and Socrates, or Jung and Freud—undoubtedly a mentoring relationship, while it lasted. For Jung, Freud only became an ancestor after his death, when the personal transformed into the symbolic and collective.

Ancestors, by contrast, are not chosen—they are collective. They belong to the entire community, to the psychological family. We do not select them; they are already present, exerting their influence. And yet, we must tread carefully when using the term. The Cambridge Dictionary defines an ancestor as "a person related to you who lived a long time ago"—a definition too narrow for our purposes. I prefer the Collins Dictionary definition: "your ancestors are the people from whom you are descended." This phrasing allows for a symbolic lineage—not necessarily biological or distant in time, but deeply formative nonetheless. This symbolic descent is what I seek to map out in this book series.

The words forefather/mother, predecessor, precursor, or forerunner all point to the same idea: someone who came before you, influenced your thinking, and helped shape who you are—whether directly or indirectly. In this light, the central question of this series becomes: Who are the ancestors of my generation—the neo-Jungians—and of the next generation(s)? Who are our new ancestors? This book series offers an attempt to answer that question.

Routledge Introductions to Contemporary Analytical Psychology and Neo-Jungian Studies is a new and essential book series I have developed and curated for Routledge, designed to introduce readers to the thinkers, theories, and concepts that have shaped analytical psychology over the past three decades.

Despite the vast and growing body of literature in Jungian and post-Jungian studies, there remains a significant gap: a curated, accessible, and conceptually rigorous series that highlights the contemporary evolution of the field. This series seeks to fill that gap. Each volume provides a critical, yet accessible introduction to the life's work of key authors and to foundational and emergent themes in analytical psychology. The series acts as both a reference and an invitation—to reflect, debate, and further develop the legacy of C.G. Jung in our time.

Envisioned as an encyclopedic yet approachable collection, this series focuses on individual figures or concepts, illuminating their major contributions, theoretical frameworks, and enduring influence. These are not exhaustive tomes but focused and insightful introductions—each book concise, rich in substance, and limited to 80–100 pages.

Every volume offers:

- A critical discussion of the chosen author or concept;
- The historical and theoretical background underpinning their development;
- A clear exposition of their main features and innovations;
- An analysis of their relevance within the broader context of analytical psychology and contemporary thought;
- A chronological narrative that traces the evolution of the author's work or concept over time.

Our authors are distinguished clinicians, scholars, and educators—each deeply familiar with the terrain they map. Their task is to offer both specialist insight and general accessibility, making this series ideal for clinicians, academics, trainees, and informed readers across disciplines.

While written primarily for an English-speaking readership, the international scope and resonance of the series is intentional. Whether in Berlin, Buenos Aires, Boston, or Beijing, readers will find these books to be valuable companions in their psychological, academic, and clinical inquiries.

Why This Series Now?

As analytical psychology continues to evolve, it becomes increasingly important to revisit, reassess, and re-present its most influential figures and ideas. This book series will serve as a foundational resource for today's Jungian studies and a springboard for tomorrow's innovations.

This is a series for anyone interested in how Jung's legacy is carried forward—critically, creatively, and with a view toward the future.

I am deeply grateful to Steven Herrmann, the author of this inaugural volume on the work of Murray Stein, for taking on the task of distilling the legacy of one of analytical psychology's most influential living figures. His commitment to capturing the essence of Stein's thought is a gift to our field and to this series.

My own relationship with Murray Stein has been marked by guidance, collaboration, and intellectual kinship. As a guiding presence in my development as an analyst and scholar, he has helped shape my understanding of what it means to think and live analytically in the contemporary world.

I would also like to express my sincere thanks to Routledge for their confidence in this project. Their support in approving this series affirms a shared recognition that analytical psychology continues to evolve—and that it deserves a contemporary canon that reflects its living, breathing tradition.

Dr Stefano Carpani
Berlin & Trieste, October 2025

Acknowledgments

My first debt of acknowledgment goes to the Jungian analyst John Beebe, MD, who connected me to Murray Stein's work in 1997 when he asked me to review Murray's books for *The San Francisco Jung Institute Library Journal*. I titled my essay, "Murray Stein: The Transformative Image." After that, John introduced me to Murray in person, at a History Symposium organized by the Jungian analyst Thomas (Tom) Kirsch. We shook hands. Murray thanked me kindly for my review and I nodded to him with a smile. Later on, in 2002, I approached Murray myself, during a break at another conference held in San Francisco. I let him know of my idea for a paper I had been thinking about writing about Herman Melville's *Moby-Dick*, following the events of September 11, 2001. Murray, who had just assumed the presidency of the International Association for Analytical Psychology (IAAP), told me to finish the essay up and he would publish it on the website.[1] Yet if John had not made the initial connection, I am not sure whether our two destinies would have crossed in quite the way they did after the turn of the new millennium. So, first, a warm thank you goes to John. Second, I want to thank my dear old friend, Tom Kirsch. After I published my essay, "Melville's Vision of Evil," in 2003,[2] Tom invited me to join him for lunch at the Evvia Estiatorio restaurant in Palo Alto, California, near his office and home. This sparked a friendship that lasted for 14 years until his death in 2017. During this time, I learned a great deal from Tom about the history of the Jungian movement. Third, I want to thank Stefano Carpani for inviting me to write this book. It was Stefano's original vision to propose a book series to Routledge that would honor our Jungian ancestors. So hats off to him for that. Fourth, I want to acknowledge textual editor, Valerie Appleby. And Fifth, I want to bow publically to Murray for having given us his essential teachings, now in nine handsomely printed blue volumes of his *Collected Writings*. As anyone who opens the pages of this book will detect, Murray's works have been a boon and a blessing to me, in so many ways. He has been my only consistent post-Jungian teacher since 1997 and I truly value his books—all 17 of them, which I review herein. I see Murray as a transpersonal mentor-friend of sorts. He has disseminated and distilled Jung's wisdom into practical and universally relevant teachings, and his works are among the best ever penned by a Jungian. He has no competitors. He stands in a genre all of his own, and he is perhaps our foremost teacher in the field of Jungian psychoanalysis. Thus, to have been asked to write this book was a great honor. Finally, I want to thank my wife, Lori Goldrich, for reading through the manuscript and offering excellent editorial comments and feedback. I hope that this book will contribute to the legacy project that is currently building momentum for Murray in his 81st year. Thank you, all five of you!

I would also like to express my sincere thanks to Routledge Editor Katie Randall and Editorial Assistant Manon Berset for their fine work preparing this book for publication and to the Production team at Routledge as well. It was a pleasure working with them!

Quotations from Murray Stein's *Collected Writings* are reprinted with permission from *The Collected Writings of Murray Stein*.

Notes

1 Herrmann, S. "Melville's Vision of Evil." Expanded ed. International Association for Analytical Psychology (IAAP), 2005. Available at iaap.org.
2 Herrmann, S. "Melville's Vision of Evil." *The San Francisco Jung Institute Library Journal* 22, no. 3 (2003): 14–36.

Introduction

The summer Murray Stein stepped into his new role as President of the International Association of Analytical Psychology, I was preparing to apply to the C.G. Jung Institute of San Francisco for analytic training. It was 2001, and I was planning to begin training in the fall of 2003. This would be 30 years after Stein earned his diploma in Zürich, at the age of 30. My first contact with Stein was a very brief conversation during the 2002 North American Conference of Jungian Analysts and Candidates in San Francisco. The conference was taking place not long after the September 11 attack on America, and the papers presented addressed the phenomenon of terror in the world and psyche. At the time, this terror was manifesting in violent outbreaks on the world stage, in dreams of nuclear disaster, in frenzies of fright about a possible apocalypse, and in dire political warnings about an escalating crisis between the United States and Middle East. Against this backdrop, the presenters addressed themes of destructiveness and evil emerging in their clinical work.

In the 24 years since then, Stein has been busy advancing new postulates in analytical psychology that have taken our field out of the clinical setting and into the world of global affairs, through various forms of social activism. He did not make a formal presentation at the 2002 conference, but his presence was palpable. In 1998, I had the honor of reviewing his books for *The San Francisco Jung Institute Library Journal*. It would not be an exaggeration to say that, in the process, I projected part of my spiritual Self onto him and formed with him what he describes as a "transformative relationship." Subsequently, he became an internalized Self-figure for me, representing the highest attitudinal values that a Jungian analyst can possibly embody. He became an imaginary figure in my psyche—someone I could look up to and idealize in my youth, admire, seek to follow, and even bow to in fantasy. To me, he was more than a Jungian analyst; he was a sage of the world field, an internationally esteemed teacher.

I continue to be inspired by Stein, and since I am an introverted intuitive feeling type by nature, I cannot help but show my feelings as William James said we must, if we are to be true to our callings as radical empiricists or natural scientists of the human psyche.[1] I have been a vocational dream researcher for 44 years,[2] and in this book, I will take a grounded theory approach to organize my thoughts about what I

DOI: 10.4324/9781003664024-1

find most extraordinary about Stein's life and works, and his enduring contribution to the field of analytical psychology. I feel a bit like a librarian's assistant in this assignment, helping to arrange and catalogue his many books. At least, that is my working fantasy.

Today, Stein is living peacefully in Goldiwil (Thun), Switzerland with his wife, Jan, enjoying a view of the Swiss Alps and teaching occasionally at the International School of Analytical Psychology Zurich (ISAPZURICH). Working on his *Collected Writings* and some new works, he spends time contemplating the future of analytical psychology as a nascent science with tremendous possibility for further development. Jung never meant for his theories to become Procrustean, and he rightly recognized that clinical analysis was only in its infancy a century ago. What excites me most about this series spearheaded by Stefano Carpani is its focus on what is new, original, and innovative in our expanding field of Jungian psychoanalysis. This is what originally astonished me when I first read and reviewed the books by Stein that I was selected to critique in 1998. Every one of them carried an unmistakable stamp of originality. There was no imitation of Jung in them. They were all authentic Stein. Even in Stein's most popular book, *Jung's Map of the Soul*—perhaps the most lucid presentation of Jung's ideas in a single volume—his personal voice broke through. This was true of every volume I read. They showed the most eloquent grace in style and had the effect of lifting my spirits.

Since the beginning of my career as a published Jungian author in 1997, I have written under the mantle of a Jungian scholar and analyst/psychotherapist-researcher, and I maintain this perspective in the present work. In the pages ahead, my task will be purely psychological and, thanks to Stein's breakthroughs, also somewhat theological, as it must be to subsume his entire oeuvre.

Stein has served the international community of Jungian analysts and scholars devotionally for 50 years. Ever since he first picked up a copy of *Memories, Dreams, Reflections*—which he found by happenstance on the shelves of a Washington, D.C. bookstore—he has been gripped by a fascination with depth psychology. As he writes, reading this book changed his life, leading him to a new vocation. Thirty years later, when reading Stein's book *Transformation: Emergence of the Self,* something similar happened to me. His masterful style captured me, and I experienced his reading of Jung's works as deeply enriching, profoundly illuminating, and divinely inspiring.

The question for all Jungians today is whether the human soul can ever be plumbed to its deepest depths, and whether its vast territory will ever be diagrammed empirically in a single book. Such a work would need to encompass the complete contributions of the early classically trained Jungians, as well as those of the more critically focused, psychoanalytically informed theorists. Stein is an explorer of new dimensions of the soul and innovative directions in Jungian psychoanalysis, and it is my endeavor here to illuminate his most memorable marks of singularity. True to his name (Stein means "stone" in German), he has left no stone unturned in his consideration of the contributors to analytical psychology following Jung's seminal works.

When I spoke with Stein at the Myako Hotel in 2002, he was at a turning point. A decade later, he would publish what San Francisco analyst John Beebe, MD, described as his "masterpiece" on individuation—a slim but profound volume titled *Minding the Self: Jungian Meditations on Contemporary Spirituality.* Stein concluded this work in a Zen-like fashion, asserting that "minding" the Self in one's full maturity requires a shift in one's personality from a personal center of ego consciousness to a "plural consciousness." This plural consciousness, impersonal in its foundation and marked by experiences of Oneness, reflects the awakened individual's awareness of a plurality of selves and the cosmic consciousness that surrounds us. This theme became one of the leitmotifs in his writings on individuation.

In his later years, Stein began to speak of a dimension of soul that Jung called the psyche-like (or quasi-psychic) territory that will always remain unmapped: the vast, eternal, psychoid depths of the Universal Self as the origin of human consciousness and being. This is the inner/outer space through which psyche extends into non-psychic regions of the world and matter, including "all around us." While the ego is the center of individual awareness, becoming aware that this ego revolves around a greater psychic entity, the Self, led Stein to a deeper reverence for the embodied experience of the great mystery of life, which limits us to time to the utmost.

Writing a century after Jung's discovery of complexes—showing that the human psyche contains multiple centers of consciousness, each revolving around a central point or nucleus of supreme meaning—Stein postulated that the Self represents the pinnacle of our being, encompassing the entirety of who we are, from birth to the grave. The question is: How can we allow the Self to emerge from its rhizome state into the light of consciousness? How does it grow from a germinal seed into its fullest blooming potential during midlife and beyond? Is there a living symbol for the process Jung termed individuation? If so, what might that be? For Stein, this symbol was the metamorphosis of a caterpillar into a butterfly, which was shown to him in a woman's dream. I saw the same symbol emerge in the dreams of a six-year-old girl in my practice and a middle-aged woman in transit through a painful separation and divorce, leading to a rediscovery of her calling as a poet.[3] The butterfly is a universally recognized symbol for the soul (*psyche* in Latin) in its spiritually transformed state, and thus an apt image for the Self. Indeed, it is what I call the nuclear symbol of Stein's hypothesis in his book *Transformation: Emergence of the Self.*

Stein took careful note of the shifts occurring in the field of Jungian theory and practice following Jung's death, and he began to apply his insights to his own developing hypotheses about the healing potential of depth psychotherapy. Building on Jung's original thoughts about human destiny, he explored the question of what directs psychic energy along particular pathways toward specific vocations and social endeavors. A key insight he received from his studies of Jung's oeuvre was that certain symbols possess the power to transform and direct the libido, guiding consciousness toward its ultimate destination within an acausal vertex of organized symmetry.[4] From Jung, he also learned that psychic energy progresses toward states of equilibrium, moving prospectively to a final goal in the future. To Stein, these ideas seemed to shed significant light on problems pertaining to our personal destiny.[5]

Moreover, Stein found that complexes are not only reactive, problematic, and disruptive to consciousness—though these characteristics are most obvious to any analytically attuned researcher—but they also have the potential to become creative, as also described by Jung's most brilliant student, Erich Neumann.[6] Complexes can be purposive and even transparent, allowing the Self to shine through. They may also produce energetic effects that radiate outward into the environment, fostering healing. One might even live out a mother or father complex from one's family of origin and become a theologian! In fact, this very thought crossed Stein's mind as a young scholar at Yale: "I am Murray Stein, born on such-and-such a date, with this particular [Protestant] history."[7] Yet, such autobiographical reflections, alone, would have left out the archetypal dimension of his awareness of pure "I-ness." Had Stein merely followed in his Baptist father's footsteps as a minister, he would not have emerged as the master teacher and international leader in Jungian affairs that we recognize today. Nevertheless, his personal father complex was part of the providential design that shaped his life, endowing him with one of his most admirable gifts as a Jungian. This is what we mean by the purposive nature of the complexes: To realize his fullest potential, Stein needed to tap into the core of his Christian inheritance to awaken the nuclear symbol of his vocation. Only this could allow him to fulfill his calling, leading him to energize the field of Jungian analysis and bestow upon us his best teachings.

The core of Stein's identity—his calling as a Jungian analyst—was first evoked during his time at Yale, where he encountered Jung's work. This sent him on a quest to discover the "Holy Grail" of Jungian scholarship: the Self and its relationship to metaphysical dimensions of existence. This concept, central to analytical psychology, had remained a constant over time. However, Stein's distillation of Jung's work on it would undergo many transmutations, influenced by the shifting intellectual climate of post-Jungian studies (shaped by, among others, Michael Fordham in London, Erich Neumann in Tel Aviv, and Joseph Henderson in San Francisco).[8]

Stein's persona has served him as a "bridge into the world," and it is difficult to trace its evolution, marked by American and Swiss inflections, without employing an archetypal-developmental model that deeply honors his profound integrity. My attempt to capture an authentic reflection of this remarkable man will hopefully offer readers a meaningful encounter with an esteemed ancestor of our field. Furthermore, Stein's anima has produced a symbolic child, representing a synthesis within his personality reconciling the opposites at play in the symbols of the Self he has so vividly depicted in his clinical portraits. This "child" signifies a dynamic unity of a narratives, enriched by the transformative images that form the colorful spectrum of his consciousness—from the infrared to the ultraviolet dimensions of the psychoid continuum—grounding his ego firmly in reality.

My examination of Stein's life journey, from his birth in 1943 to his later years (2025+), will culminate in the capstone of Jung's psychology of individuation, postulated by Stein's theory of the Self as the "Ground of Being"—encompassing the subject's interconnectedness with the world and the foundational structures of empirical and ontological being/Being, the *unus mundus*.[9] The evolving conception of the self/Self, as reconceived and reconfigured by contemporary Jungians, has pulled the compass needle of Stein's ego toward true north. What he could not yet see clearly during his early engagement with Jung's works at Yale became more fully realized over time, particularly after his relocation to Zürich in 2003.

What Stein has consistently taught us throughout all of his works is that Jung wore many masks, or personae, during his lifetime. Yet, the singular identity he ultimately embraced, following a now-famous dream recounted in *Memories, Dreams, Reflections*, became his guiding star, illuminated by the natural light of an archetypal image of the natural scientist. As a wise analyst once told me around the time I first reviewed Stein's books, "Jung was the Einstein of the human soul." I believe this to be true. Much like William James, Jung frequently spoke of the limits of psychology and his role as an empiricist, and he also stressed the importance of our relationship with the infinite. In Stein's work, however, these boundaries are not always so clearly delimited by science, since Stein is also a religious thinker and theologian. This dual perspective enables him to straddle the fields of psychology and religion in a non-dualistic manner, enriching our understanding with theological insights.

Someone in our field needed to clarify that Jung had not been constructing a new theology of God, but articulating a new God image for the Age of Aquarius. This destiny fell to Stein, who, during his time at Yale, shifted his focus from theology to psychology. Thankfully for us, he later redirected the stream of Jungian thought toward a more unified worldview—one inclusive of the metaphysical foundations that Jung had pointed to, awaiting further research.

Convinced that Jung's concept of the Self was not that dissimilar from the model of the Self that had been postulated in America by William James, Stein steered his course toward furthering the unfinished project of bridging Eastern and Western perspectives that Jung had initially pioneered in his collaboration with Richard Wilhelm. Recognizing Jung's assertion that the Self is infinite, as James had posited before him, Stein extended the notion of individuation to the farthest reaches of human consciousness—those that open the doors to the Self—so as to broaden its scope in therapeutic practice. While Jung had expressed this same idea in numerous places across his works, he consistently refrained from touching metaphysics. In contrast, Stein has embraced metaphysical principles with clarity and confidence. In 2014, he expanded his conceptual framework with a few deft strokes of the pen, like a skilled Zen master, showing his readers that no fundamental differences exist between *satori* or *samadhi* and the highest states of spiritual awakening possible within Jungian analysis. This contribution was indeed a brush stroke of pure genius.

In *Jung's Map of the Soul*, Stein showed that the sage of Küsnacht had postulated that a fourth stage of consciousness is within the range of possibility in empirical psychology. This stage represents a state of mind characterized by the radical extinction of projections and illusions, whether rooted in psychological, theological, or ideological abstractions. Such annihilations, Stein argued, can lead an individual to the "creation of an empty center," which Jung associated with modernity. This fourth stage was emblematized, Stein argued, by the "modern man in search of a soul."[10] Moreover, Stein, interpreting Jung, suggested the potential for a fifth stage of consciousness transcending and superseding the modern—a stage characterized by a postmodern attitude acknowledging the psychic reality inherent in projections and positing that the psyche, itself, can serve as an object of scrutiny and psychoanalytic reflection. The challenge, Stein described, lies in capturing and engaging with these projections in psychoanalytic practice, especially when investigating dreams, relational phenomena, and the imagination through the lens of the transcendent function. This, he argued, represents Jung's vision of a possible question for postmodernity.[11]

However, Stein further postulated that, while Jung officially concluded his framework at stage five, his writings suggest the possibility of a sixth, and perhaps even a seventh stage of consciousness. Stein situated these stages within Eastern traditions, surpassing the boundaries typically recognized in the West. In particular, he pointed to Jung's seminar on Kundalini yoga in 1932 as a key source for this intuition. The superconscious awareness Jung identified in Kundalini yoga, Stein argued, could be considered a potential stage seven. He also proposed that stage six could be recognized in Jung's theory of the Self, which envisioned a unity of psyche and matter, connecting physics, metaphysics, and cosmology.[12]

Expanding on Jung's notion of the psychoid, Stein posited a conceptual bridge between time and eternity. In particular, he drew insights from Jung's relationship with the Nobel Prize–winning physicist Wolfgang Pauli to explore the theory of synchronicity, revealing Jung's implicit identity as a metaphysician—a persona that Jung, himself, denied.[13] Nevertheless, Stein openly affirmed this dimension of Jung's work, asserting its legitimacy. And this affirmation carried weight, given his academic credentials (including a Master of Divinity from Yale and a doctorate from the University of Chicago Divinity School).

With Jung's hypothesis of the potential unity of Self and God,[14] Stein mindfully questioned whether Jung's theories could hold validity for both psychology and theology in a non-dual manner. Recognizing Jung's efforts to forge a link between science and religion, similar to William James's at Harvard, Stein set out to investigate whether Jung's theory of synchronicity might serve as a unifying symbol. He posited that synchronicity could integrate the psyche's opposites by revealing a hidden order: an orchestration of chance events in time by unseen organizers or "architects," imbuing synchronistic moments with meaning and significance.[15]

This hunch led Stein to explore ideas that Jung had left for further development, including his speculation of an "unknown knower" within us—a figure who transcends the categories of space and time while remaining simultaneously present in our personal histories. Stein identified this knower as the Self, envisioning it as a "destiny factor" with a unique purpose or calling to actualize specific potentialities in a uniform way, while touching upon transcendental mysteries.[16]

That the human psyche and personal psychology participate in the interplay of order and chaos inherent in the universe at its most profoundly psychoid levels of experience makes possible the unity of causality, teleology, and trans-causality. By attending to dream imagery, engaging in active imagination, and observing synchronicities as they unfold within human relationships, individuals can come to recognize the foundational structure of the universe and psyche as interconnected and potentially ordered cosmos within them.

In this book, I will provide an overview of Stein's published writings and trace his personal journey from infancy to his current age of 81, speculating on where his insights might lead and what his contributions mean for us today. I will not offer a verse-by-verse review of Stein's entire oeuvre but will preserve his words as he has written, inviting readers to ponder his theoretical innovations. While not all of Stein's novelties align strictly with Jungian thought, they represent a distinctly Steinian perspective, if I may be permitted to modestly claim. Accordingly, I will not endlessly reference Jung's *Collected Works* and published letters, as my focus will instead be on Stein's own writings.

What I aim to provide herein are Stein's words as faithfully as possible. To get at the hidden essence behind the persona of the man—who once humorously referred to himself as C.G. Jung's "missionary"—I will take a pragmatic approach, grounding my observations in fact. This method aligns with how Jung taught us to conduct scientific research into the nature of the psyche. Thus, I will strive to allow Stein to speak for himself.

We need a theologian like Stein to help us navigate the *blitzkrieg* of Jung's numerous writings. My intention with this book is to step aside sufficiently to allow the sage of Goldiwil to articulate, with some assistance from one of his "Green Men,"[17] who he truly is and what his body of work is all about. In the next chapter, I will introduce you to Stein the child hero, then Stein the young man at Yale, followed by Stein the man in midlife in Chicago and, later, Stein the world sage. This development will lead us to his current self—a more evolved man dedicated to advancing our field of Jungian studies.

How This Book Came into Being

On July 11, 2024, I received an email from the Berlin-based Jungian analyst Stefano Carpani, informing me about a book series he was editing dedicated to our Jungian ancestors, with the potential for publication by Routledge. Carpani believed that such a series was missing in our field and expressed that he and Stein had agreed that I would be the ideal candidate to author a volume on Stein's work. I replied that same day, thanking Carpani deeply for considering me for the book project, which, without question, was a great privilege and honor! I expressed my delight at the opportunity to author such a distinguished title, especially with Carpani serving as series editor. By then, I had read most of Stein's major works, some of which I had reviewed in 1998. However, I had yet to read his *Collected Writings,* aside from Volume 6: *Analytical Psychology and Religion,* which I had made good use of while writing some of my own books.

I shared with Carpani that I could not think of an ancestor in our field who had influenced me more profoundly than Stein. His work had quite literally changed my life as both a writer and an analyst, just as it has so many others. Yet, after some reflection, I confessed to Carpani that I was unsure how to wrap my mind around such a monumental task. While John Beebe had generously provided me with seven of Stein's books for me to write my essay "Murray Stein: The Transformative Image" in 1998, in the 16 years that had elapsed, Stein had produced an extraordinary number of new publications. I knew I would need to approach this project with diligence and focus. I resolved to acquire a complete set of Stein's *Collected Writings* and get to work. I had read *Minding the Self: Jungian Meditations on Contemporary Spirituality*, but given Stein's prolific output, I could not help but feel momentarily overwhelmed by the enormity of the project. Nevertheless, I assured Carpani that I could likely have the book written by the spring or summer of 2025.

There was so much to read and assimilate in order to present readers with an aerial view of Stein's work, representing the best thinking in our field. I was humbled by this calling, which demanded my serious concentration and commitment—perhaps more than any other book I had written. The relatively short timeline of less than a year added to the challenge, pushing me to the utmost. To assist with this effort, Stein arranged for Chiron Publications to send me his *Collected Writings*, along with the book *Outside Inside and All Around: And Other Essays in Jungian Psychology*. I began by reading the latter while awaiting the arrival of the *Collected Writings*, giving me a head start.

From there, I drafted the structure for this book, based largely on intuition. I chose to begin with a psychobiography of Stein's life, followed in Chapter 2 by an exploration of his *Four Pillars of Jungian Psychoanalysis*, laying out what I believe to be the basic model for the future of analytical depth psychology. Beginning in Chapter 3, I would review each of the volumes in Stein's *Collected Writings,* following their numerical order from Volumes 1 to 9, with the exception of Volume 2, which I omitted from my purview. The final three chapters would provide an overview of *Outside Inside and All Around: And Other Essays in Jungian Psychology*, my reflections on a seminal paper in Volume 4 titled *Four Modalities of Temporality and the Problem of Shame*, and a review of *Ways to the Self: Five Conversations*. It occurred to me as an afterthought that Stein's paper in *The Practice of Jungian Psychoanalysis* could provide a conceptual link between the psychobiography presented in Chapter 1 and the thematic developments of Chapters 11 and 12. In this paper, Stein writes:

I clearly remember that I was 4 or 5 when my father taught me to tell time. It was an Easter Sunday morning, and before going to church, my pastor father gave me a lesson in time. He took a clock about the size of his hand and showed me how the pointers moved, could be moved on the face. The small pointer showed the hour, he said, and the large pointer showed the minute. The numbers pointed to indicate the time. I knew enough about time to understand these words... Proudly, I announced to my Sunday School friends that I could tell time now! It was a breakthrough in learning for me, and it is a moment in time I have never forgotten. It is a permanent and constant part of my life's narrative. Ever since I have felt that time was my friend, and I rarely lose track of time and am almost never late for meetings. If I slip up, I feel ashamed... Perhaps by coincidence, my earliest memory of experiencing shame dates from about this same age.[18]

After I read this memory, and just as I completed the first draft of the manuscript, I realized that the essay on the four types of time was actually best suited for the Afterword, or my final summary and conclusion, linking Chapter 1 with Chapter 11 and providing the missing thread to complete the tapestry of overarching meaning. In the chapters that follow, I will review eight of the nine volumes of Stein's *Collected Writings* (excluding Volume 2) in chronological order of their publication. My review will not offer a consecutive overview of all of Stein's works from A to Z, but will more modestly cover select books, essays, and lectures as presented in the natural progression of the *Collected Writings*. I will also touch on a few works currently being prepared for publication. In addition, my study of Stein's life and work will cover some previously published books that have not yet been incorporated in the *Collected Writings*. Finally, I will provide readers with a brief overview of Stein's present projects.

Structure of This Book

I will begin the book with a brief biographical study of Stein's early life and childhood, offering readers a bird's eye view of the familial and ancestral influences that helped shape his unique contributions to Jungian psychoanalysis, his personality, and his colorful array of psychological types. This opening psychobiographical chapter will be followed by an overview of the main features of Stein's theoretical contributions to Jung's seminal works, including his innovations on individuation, conscience, midlife, transformation, the Bible, Christianity, evil, spirituality, wholeness, Zen, the Tao, love, and synchronicity. Subsequent chapters will provide an in-depth examination of Stein's substantive contributions to analytical psychology, as presented in the nine volumes of his *Collected Writings* and several of his best books not yet incorporated into this series.

Notes

1 Herrmann, S. *William James and C.G. Jung: Doorways to the Self.* Oberlin, OH: Analytical Psychology Press, 2020.
2 Herrmann, S. *Vocational Dreams: Calling Archetypes and Nuclear Symbols.* USA/Singapore: Strategic Book Publishing, 2024.

3 Herrmann, S. *Swami Vivekananda and C.G. Jung: Yoga in the West.* USA/Singapore: Strategic Books Publishing and Rights Co., 2022.
4 Stein, M. *Jung's Map of the Soul: An Introduction.* Chicago, IL: Open Court, 1998, 69.
5 Stein, 71.
6 Stein, 73.
7 Stein, 114.
8 Stein, 120.
9 Stein, 152.
10 Stein, 183.
11 Stein, 186.
12 Stein, 187.
13 Stein, 200.
14 Stein, 206.
15 Stein, 210.
16 Stein, 212.
17 I mean this in an imaginative sense, as one of the many individuals attuned to the archetype of the Green Man, or Verdant One. Additionally, this interpretation plays on his wife Jan's dream of a younger man helping an older man swiftly organize his bookshelf—a dream that will be discussed in later chapters. Suffice it to say that the Green Man represents what Stein refers to as a "transformative image" within the human psyche—one that can be accessed through meditation or creative engagement.
18 CW4, 275.

Chapter 1

Beginnings

A Brief Psychobiography

In an essay called "Light in the Shadow of Death," written during his 81st year in 2024, Stein writes:

> From my father and mother, I inherited the indefatigable sense of service. My father was a pastor, and the last words I heard him speak as he lay dying and some fellow pastors were visiting him in the hospital was: "I would still like to be of service!" He said this with tears in his eyes. I have had the same sense of willing obligation to serve a community, and in my life, it has been the community of Jungians worldwide. In the past, this was carried out partly through working in various institutions such as training institutes and the International Association for Analytical Psychology, and now I do this primarily by writing and teaching.[1]

This pretty much says it all. For well over 50 years, Stein has been busy bringing together various viewpoints in the field of analytical psychology, infusing them with a spiritual attitude and the fragrance of a flower for our butterfly-souls to drink. Following Jung, whom he affectionately refers to as the "Master," he has consistently emphasized the centrality of the "religious attitude" in healing the psyche. To Stein, this attitude extends beyond mere individuals in Jungian psychoanalysis, including those in all walks of life, across all vocations, whom he reaches through his ever-growing readership.

In addition to being an internationally recognized scholar and author of many Jungian texts reaching a worldwide audience, Stein has been in ceaseless service to analysts and training candidates by helping them find their life callings or steering them toward successful careers. Stein has literally transformed the ways in which we typically think about Jung's concept of individuation and the problem of embodied evil that is the task of human incarnation to realize and transform. He has done so especially through his theories about the psychology of religious experience from childhood to midlife and into old age. The religious problem is one of his specialties. He has taken Jungian psychoanalysis out of the clinical setting and into the workplace, from sacred places of worship into the realms of pure psychological experience.

DOI: 10.4324/9781003664024-2

Stein has been consistent in his teachings and writings on adult individuation about the pivotal role played by the spiritual function of the psyche in Jungian analysis and how we might reimagine psychology through a theological lens. This includes his response to Jung's exploration of evil in Volume 7 of his *Collected Writings* (*The Problem of Evil*), as well as the theoretical essays that appear therein, such as his own "Answer to Evil."[2] As I will clarify in the chapters ahead, Stein has radically altered the ways in which Jungians have typically thought about Jung's views on evil. I hypothesize in what follows that based on his early childhood experiences and his visionary experiences of the Risen Jesus as a living symbol in his psyche from the age of four onwards, Stein performs a therapeutic function of providing a medicine to Jung's one-sided views on Christianity, making Jung's reflections more theologically grounded with sound criticism, based on overlooked Biblical facts. Stein reshapes Jung's writings on God and evil, rendering Jung's works more accessible for both theologians and therapists and Christian readers alike. Stein's vision of Divinity is shaped by his own distinct postulates as a theologian and Protestant minister. His reading of the Bible is compelling and affirms my own research, particularly because Jung's obsessive need to engage in polemics with theologians over the problem of evil distracted from his broader aims as a psychologist of a non-dual theory of the Self. The relationship between Stein's work on conscience and the perennial problem of evil is fully engaged with in the following pages. Evil, Stein will assert, is not an inherent property of nature or the universe, but an essential category of human thought, a product of the human mind—a judgment, rather than an objective metaphysical reality. This is vitally important for Jungian analysts to realize because we all have a moral responsibility and an ethical duty to work with evil in the consulting room as well as in society. This is an essential aspect of Jungian work, particularly with respect to observing our own countertransference responses during analytic treatment. Stein offers a shamanistic remedy—a medicine for evil in humans and the problem of violence. Stein will give significant attention to Jung's relationship to the Dominican priest Victor White, for whom the idea of a God embodying good and evil would have been a calamitous theological aberration—one hostile to his position as a Blackfriar, a member of the Dominican Order and the tenets of his faith. Unlike critics who have been defensive of Jung's positions on evil, Stein gives White generous credits for having inspired one of Jung's most important works. This is an attitude that I find commendable in Stein's work.

No one has done more than Stein to illuminate the central importance of transformative relationships, dream work, and active imagination in psychotherapy, literature, art, and spiritual practice throughout the lifespan. His contributions can be found virtually everywhere in the International Association of Analytical Psychology (IAAP) and the International Association of Jungian Scholars, as well as countless other contexts where the name C.G. Jung is mentioned.

Today, Stein is more focused on late-stage individuation and the prospect of "enlightenment," though his hypotheses continue to account for infancy, childhood, and adolescence.[3] Indeed, his *Collected Writings*, published by Chiron Publications in nine handsome volumes, cover all life stages. However, throughout his analytic career, Stein's primary interest has not been the early stages of development, but "what actually happens to people inwardly when childhood, with its well-known 'stages' and its scars and complex formations, is completely outgrown, not only chronologically but psychologically."[4] By this, he means transformation in the broadest sense as a "cosmic" experience bound simultaneously to the finite, the body-self, and the ego complex. Throughout his works, Stein has continued to build upon the same bridge Jung constructed, seeking to unite Eastern and Western spiritual traditions. His aim is to deliver a message of hope, healing, and visionary consciousness to a global audience, helping cure "the disease of the modern, namely the lack of connection to the religious function and to the symbols that bring the ego into a more conscious relationship to the Self."[5]

Stein's contributions have augmented Jung's efforts, enriching the developmental and symbolic approaches of Jungian analysis. His synthesis of postmodern Jungian thought and spirituality has offered a contemporary framework that, when viewed as a whole, seems essentially seamless.

Early History

An individual's life and contributions to society are critically shaped by their personal biases and interests. Therefore, it is important to know something about the personal background that influenced Stein's unique contributions to Jungian analysis during the early Age of Aquarius. To fully engage with the sacred atmospherics of this book and give sound to the spirit of the depths within the man it celebrates, we must first explore his distinct perspectives, upbringing, and worldview. The admission of personal bias is basic to the attitude of analytical psychology and resonates with the psychology of William James. James's "pragmatism" and "pluralistic" views of the subconscious began to influence European dynamic psychiatry in 1890, following the publication of *The Principles of Psychology*—a work that C.G. Jung first encountered during his studies at the University of Basel. In his writing, Stein frequently acknowledges James's impact on Jungian thought, as in the following: "[William] James collected and studied the religious experiences of ordinary individuals and analyzed them without judgment from a psychological perspective. Jung wholeheartedly embraced this return to the study of primary religious experience and its effect on the individual psyche."[6]

Religious experience and pluralism lie at the heart of Stein's *Weltanschauung*. Jungians, by nature, are both pragmatists and pluralists. Stein's vision of interconnection in Jungian psychoanalysis is "based on a realization of a network of relations that ties all peoples together into one pluralistic unity. It requires almost unimaginable tolerance of differences and acute consciousness of interdependence among all the parts."[7]

The Nuclear Symbol of the Bible

The King James Bible was a constant in Stein's childhood and formative years. Throughout this time, his mother, Jeanette Stein, regularly read selected passages aloud before meals, while his pastor father read it from the pulpit three times a week. As a boy, Stein memorized long passages from the Bible, developing an ear for poetry and the musicality of language through the power of its English prose. The mythopoetic verses of the King James edition accompanied his family wherever they went, serving as their steadfast companion. Thus, it formed the nuclear symbol of Stein's vocation during his childhood and latency, later shaping his literary style. Its influence is evident in his prose, which is unmatched in eloquence, depth of wisdom, and erudition.

Like Jung, Stein grew up in a Protestant parsonage. His father, Walter Stein, was born in Gerstungen, near Eisenach, Germany, where the family had owned a lumber mill since the 1500s. Walter emigrated to Canada in 1930, at the age of 18. Although baptized Lutheran—the dominant religion of his ancestral region—his father was an outspoken atheist. Thus, as a youth, Walter was religiously indifferent, and perhaps agnostic. However, this changed when he traveled to Canada with a group of fellow students on a study exchange program.

As the youngest of four brothers, Walter had no claim to the family business and sought a different path for his livelihood. His father, a harsh German *Vater* type, ensured that the family mill passed to the eldest son. (Following World War II, this son became a ranking Communist Party official in Soviet-occupied East Germany.) In his youth, Walter trained in fine carpentry and cabinetmaking, which seemed a suitable vocation at the time. After arriving in Canada, however, he befriended a group of Baptists who encouraged him to pursue higher education and eventually enter the ministry. It turned out that Walter did have a strong spiritual side, which flourished under their guidance. After leaving home, he never saw his mother again and had only occasional contact with his brothers. In the 1950s, he met his father once at the border between West and East Germany, but the war and its aftermath ultimately separated him from his family of origin, for good.

As a young pastor, Walter married Jeanette, a bright schoolteacher from the small village of Ebenezer, Saskatchewan. Jeanette's family had emigrated to Canada in the 1890s, together with their entire Baptist village from Prussia (now Poland), in an attempt to keep their sons out of the Prussian army. They settled as pioneers in the wilderness of Saskatchewan, clearing the land granted to them by the provincial government and surviving the harsh winter months in hand-built houses and barns, alongside their children and livestock. Jeanette was born in a log cabin in 1916, the middle of three children. Her older brother became a schoolteacher and eventually served as the Head of the Department of Education for the Province of Saskatchewan. Her younger brother inherited the family farm and spent his life on the homestead. Jeanette, herself, earned a Teacher's Certificate from the Normal School of Education in Yorkton, Saskatchewan, and went on to teach grades 1–12 in a one-room schoolhouse in Ebenezer. It was during her time as a teacher that she met Walter, who had been called to the Ebenezer Baptist Church as a pastor in 1940. People said that she resembled Princess Elizabeth, who later became Queen.

Jeanette and Walter married in 1942, and Stein was born the following year, in 1943. Later in life, Jeanette earned a Master's degree in Mathematics from the

University of North Dakota in Grand Forks. A natural teacher like her elder brother, she devoted much of her life to education, including teaching the Bible in Sunday School until the end of her life. Jeanette was known for her wonderful sense of humor, and Stein has many fond memories of her laughter, along with his father's, around the dinner table as she mimicked the heavy German accents of the local townsfolk. Walter also had a strong accent, but he could laugh at himself and took part in the playful banter. They had a lot of fun together as a young family. Theirs was not a stern, religious household. However, Jeanette also possessed a darker side that occasionally revealed itself. Stein recalls moments when her sense of humor turned toward the topic of death. At the end of her life, as she lay dying, Stein asked her which of the biblical writers was her favorite. Without hesitation, she named Paul, the theologian. When Stein subsequently inquired about her faith, her candid response surprised him: "Even if it's not true, it's a good way to live." Jeanette's pragmatic, rational nature had shaped her role as a pastor's wife—a persona she maintained for the church community while keeping any personal doubts to herself. She confided in Stein that, in her later years, she had experienced many important dreams. This revelation surprised him, as dreams had never been discussed within the family. When Stein asked her about these dreams, she could not recall specifics, only that the dreams felt "very important." Stein never heard his mother and father argue or exchange a harsh word. They always functioned as a team—Walter as the pastor and Jeanette as the pastor's wife. Within the church community, Stein, of course, took on the persona of the ideal PK ("preacher's kid"), precociously performing his role to meet the expectations of the congregation and its elders. For the Stein family, fulfilling these prescribed duties and vocational scripts was not only a calling, but a necessity for their collective survival.

The small village in Saskatchewan, Ebenezer, lies near Stein's birthplace of Yorktown, a railway hub and regional center for agricultural trade. He arrived around noon on September 2, 1943, weighing a remarkable 11 pounds! That's a large baby. Named Murray after a celebrated Scottish Admiral—honored by Canadians at the height of World War II—he was a challenging infant, plagued by colic and frequent crying fits. Caring for such a demanding newborn proved overwhelming for Jeanette, his newly minted mother. So, to recover from what may have been a period of postpartum depression following the physically traumatic birth, she entrusted Murray to the care of her mother for several months. This arrangement provided Murray with additional maternal care and nurturance, fostering a deep and lasting bond with his grandmother. Jeanette, an introverted thinking type with extroverted sensation as her secondary function, needed time and space for her recovery, which limited her ability to engage with Murray in such an intimate manner. Walter, on the other hand, was an extroverted feeling type with intuition as his secondary function. Gregarious and much loved by the congregants of the churches he served, he balanced Jeanette's introspective nature. Together, they formed a complementary pair from the standpoint of psychological types and attitudes.

Stein's attitude and typology might be best positioned somewhere between those of his parents, though he has noted, "I am not a feeling type." From this admission, we might gather that his natural disposition aligns more closely with the thinking type, like his mother, Jeanette. However, Stein has also reflected that, in his opinion, "the real test of individuation, in the sense of maturity, comes from relationship. This means to love."[8] Relational love, then, has served as an inspiration for his transformations later in life.

What about his grandmother, Rose? What was her personality type? Stein describes her as warm and loving, sharing more in common temperamentally with Walter than with Jeanette. Rose loved flowers and colorful clothing and was more outgoing and cheerful than her daughter. By contrast, Stein's grandfather, John, was kind but taciturn, a typical farmer type. It seems likely that Rose was an extroverted feeling type, contributing to the strong bond she formed with Stein during his infancy. He reportedly cried whenever he had to leave her home after their visits. Interestingly, Stein later discovered that his grandparents' roots were ancestrally Swiss—a realization that only came to light in his 60th year, following his relocation to Zürich.

As we shall see, Stein seems to have been drawn to Switzerland by a mysterious lodestar rooted in his maternal ancestry—a giant hand guiding him to establish roots in this beautiful country. This hand, as he perceives it, is the spiritual hand of his master and the ancestral father of his destiny, C.G. Jung. It was only in his sixth decade, after he and his wife moved into their apartment in Zürich, that he came to recognize the profound role of divine providence in preparing him for his destiny as a Jungian analyst, since infancy.

As recounted in various places in his *Collected Writings*, Stein stumbled upon this revelation during an exhibition at the glorious Grossmünster church in Zürich. At the time, the church was commemorating the 500th anniversary of the birth of Heinrich Bullinger, successor to the Reformer Huldrych Zwingli. One of the displays chronicled the Swiss Reformers' vicious history, including their persecution of a small sect of Christians known as "*Taüfer*" (Anabaptists), who had lived in the parish of Zollikon, near Zürich. While studying the exhibited materials in the ancient stone hallways of the church, Stein was struck by a sudden realization. Among the names inscribed on the historical records, he recognized "Reiman," his mother's maiden name. It dawned on him that the Swiss Anabaptists were, in fact, his maternal ancestors. At that moment, he felt as though a centuries-old circle had been closed—a "return" to Switzerland that had taken 500 years to complete.[9] As Stein stood quietly in the Grossmünster, contemplating his family history, he experienced this discovery as a miracle of meaningful chance.

Appearance of the Anima and the Importance of the Bible

At the age of four, Stein underwent a hernia operation. While recovering in the hospital, he delighted in the smiling face of a nurse on the ward who tended to him caringly at his bedside. This encounter marked his first conscious impression of the anima—the doorway to the collective unconscious in the Jungian lexicon. It was such a memorable experience for him that, to this day, Stein remembers her face and the insignia on her white uniform. Since then, the anima has been a frequent visitor in his life.

As a young boy, Stein attended church with his family three times a week, where his father was engaged with preaching and teaching Scripture. At home, daily routines began with Bible story readings from a large picture book. Reflecting on this formative period, Stein wrote:

> Sunday mornings for an hour of Sunday School and an hour of worship; Sunday evenings for an hour of hymn singing and a sermon; Wednesday evenings for an hour of Bible study. Bible School, which took place during summer vacations went on for three weeks.

Biblical education, he noted, "was a given."[10] As a child, Stein memorized extensive passages from both the Old and New Testaments, often reciting them in front of his father's congregation. His prodigious memory earned him numerous prizes and accolades. Within the parish community, children were awarded medals for their impressive feats of memorization, marking them as fledgling students of Scripture.

Stein's early years also included several moves throughout Canada and the United States, as his father's pastorates typically lasted between two and five years. The family resided in parsonages either next door to or near the churches his father served. These homes often included vegetable gardens, which were meticulously tended by Stein's father, an expert gardener. His efforts ensured the family enjoyed fresh produce throughout the year.

At the age of eight, Stein was baptized by his father through total immersion in water. This baptism, which followed a conversion experience, signified both his confirmation of Christian faith and his partial spiritual alignment with his father. Although Stein felt a natural urge to identify with his father, his mother had a way of "unconsciously undermining" his "separation from herself,"[11] creating an internal conflict. This conflict between the two loves of his early life—his father and his mother—was likely psychologically significant during Stein's developmental years. We may even be thankful for it, today, as this dynamic may have contributed to Stein's eventual struggle to supersede his father and his vocational choice *not* to become a Protestant minister but to instead become a Jungian analyst. This would be the reductive interpretation. Alternatively, a prospective view might support the hypothesis that being a minister would have been far too limiting for Stein's personality.

When Stein was ten, his sister was born. At the time, the family was living in the small town of Tyndall, South Dakota. His sister's arrival may have encouraged him to become more independent of his mother's influence, fostering a more self-reliant identity as he transitioned into adolescence.

During Stein's junior high and early high school years, the family lived in Grand Forks, North Dakota, home to the University of North Dakota. In the "Preface" to his book *Men Under Construction*, Stein recounts the humorous story of an inspirational science teacher he had during junior high school in Grand Forks. This teacher—a single, sturdily built 30-year-old woman—was totally dedicated to her work as an educator. She fascinated Stein and his classmates with her introduction to the wonders of modern physics and astronomy, and she also had the gift of humor. One day, Stein recalls, she came into the classroom with a story to share with the students. She told them that, over the weekend, she had been driving on a monotonous highway in North Dakota and decided to take a quick stop for coffee. On her way into the coffee shop, she noticed a car marked with an insignia designating it as a military vehicle. It had a sign on the back that read: "U.S. Marines. We build men!" As the teacher entered the shop, she saw the Marines sitting at a table and boldly called out to them: "Hello! Please build me a man!" The class of spellbound students laughed out loud when she told them this charming anecdote. The metaphor stayed with Stein, later inspiring the title of the book in which this anecdote appears. This work, based on a series of lectures Stein delivered at the C.G. Jung Institute of Chicago in 1988, is included in Volume 3 of his *Collected Writings*, titled *Transformation: Emergence of the Self.*

High School in Detroit and Departure for Yale

During the middle of Stein's third year of high school, the family relocated to Detroit, Michigan, where he completed his secondary education. As part of his studies, Stein read Victor Frankl's inspiring book, *Man's Search for Meaning*, which left an indelible impression on his mind. Earlier, he had read Freud's *Interpretation of Dreams*, which fascinated him but made less of an impact, as it was beyond his intellectual reach at the time. These works marked his first encounters with psychotherapy and psychoanalysis.

In 1961, Stein left home for Yale with a scholarship in hand. His proud parents drove him to New Haven, Connecticut and said goodbye to him at the gate to the Old Campus dorms. They would never again live together under the same roof. As a freshman, Stein had no idea what to study, and so he enrolled in a diverse set of courses to fulfill the distribution requirements: classical Greek (for the language requirement), American history, English (a required course), the New Testament, and Political Science. It was an odd combination of courses for a freshman at Yale. However, this eclectic combination hinted at two potential paths of study: English literature or religious studies.

Stein describes that his life has been guided by an unconscious *spiritus rector*. In the biblical tradition, the *spiritus rector* represents guidance by the grace of the Holy Spirit, as an indwelling presence of the Word of God in an individual soul.[12] In the years to follow his time at Yale, Stein would grow to embody the roles of not only language maker, but also mythmaker and meaning maker. As an undergraduate, he was introduced to the art of "deep reading"[13] by the renowned literary critic Harold Bloom. As he explains:

> Deep reading can become a meditative and imaginative engagement with figures, images, and ideas that effectively transform one's mind. It can result in metanoia, a transformation of mind and heart. This is a kind of alchemical process that brings intense stimulation and nourishment to soul and spirit, even therapeutic healing, as Bloom testifies autobiographically.[14]

Stein is fundamentally a therapist and healer of professional, social, and organizational illnesses. He fulfills this role primarily through his prolific writings and work as an analyst. His calling as a writer was cultivated through formative experiences at home, in the parish, and later at Yale, guided by the *spiritus rector* that awakened within him there. For instance, in his lectures on "The Gospel According to John," Stein invites readers to reflect on the Christ pattern at its best. He writes:

> this archetypal constellation presents us with a person who is able to put others ahead of his own needs when necessary, who is able to be generous and to share, who has mastered narcissism and envy for the sake of relationship, and who is directed by a purpose that Erik Erikson named generativity and Jung spoke of as the constellation of the transcendent function.[15]

This passage aptly describes Stein's sense of presence for me as a warm, generative man in service to others.

While Stein briefly considered becoming an English professor under the tutelage of Bloom, he was also strongly influenced by another mentor in Yale's Religious Studies Department, the theologian Hans Frei. Frei played a pivotal role in resolving Stein's uncertainty about his future path in graduate studies. Ultimately, his guidance led Stein to choose Yale Divinity School over other options on the table at the time.

Another item to perhaps add to this mosaic of Stein's life occurred to him on Christmas morning in 2024, when he recalled (in a personal email communication to me) that his senior essay at Yale had focused on George Herbert's *The Temple*. Although he remembers little of what he wrote in this piece, the project occupied much of his attention during his senior year and played a role in his eventual decision to pursue divinity school rather than graduate studies in English literature. In some ways, the essay bridged these two paths. During the summer between his junior and senior years, Stein traveled to Europe and had the chance to visit Bremerton, England, the parish where George Herbert had served. This visit left a profound impression on him. Reflecting on it later, on the day celebrating the birth of Jesus—both a poet-shaman and rabbi (for many, the Messiah)—he recognized its deeper significance, describing it as "another step on the Way." Herbert, similar to John Donne, his better-known contemporary, served as a model of the Christian life, embodying both poetic brilliance and devout ministry.

During his second year at Yale Divinity School, Stein was still uncertain about his future. To seek clarity, he took a year-long break from academic study, enlisting in an internship program at the Church of the Savior in Washington, D.C. At the time, one of the staff members, Elizabeth O'Connor, was a well-known author and teacher. At a spring garden party one Sunday in 1968, amidst a backdrop of protests against the Vietnam War, O'Connor mentioned the name C.G. Jung during a discussion about the causes of war. Why, she asked, do human beings repeatedly engage in war, and what underlies this deeply ingrained historical propensity? O'Connor, who had recently published her book *Journey Inward, Journey Outward*, which used the writings of Jung as a guide for the inner journey, asked if those gathered had read Jung's work on the projection of the shadow. Perhaps, this could help to answer the questions being discussed.

Stein had heard brief mentions of Jung during his time at Yale, but he had rarely encountered Jung's ideas in any depth. His familiarity with psychoanalysis stemmed primarily from his earlier reading of Freud's *The Interpretation of Dreams* during his high school days in Grand Forks and his short browse through Jung's *Psychology and Religion* in a library in Detroit. Similar to most American students in 1968, Stein had not studied Jung in any formal academic setting. However, O'Connor's suggestion at the garden party piqued his curiosity. The following day, he visited a local bookstore to see what he could find by Jung. In what seemed a meaningful coincidence and a stroke of good fortune, a single copy of *Memories, Dreams, Reflections*—Jung's autobiography written with Aniela Jaffé—was available on the shelf. Stein purchased the book, and as he began to read it that evening, he became immediately enthralled. Something profound began to stir within him as he turned its pages. The power of destiny's hand descended upon him, and this marvelous book became transformative and life-changing.

For Stein, reading *Memories, Dreams, Reflections* must have been like rediscovering the Bible. However, Jung's book was highly psychological, rather than theological or overly philosophical. Stein was fascinated by Jung's integration of dreams into his life narrative and construction of a personal myth. He was also captivated by the book's discussion of the problem of evil, which Stein had been pondering in relation to the Vietnam War, racism in America, and other societal challenges. The book was intimately subjective and focused intensely on Jung's early childhood dreams and other numinous experiences. The timing of Stein's discovery of this book in 1968 was unmistakably synchronistic, since it helped to clarify what Stein felt had been missing in his study of theology—namely a sense of mystery and the numinous. For the young man with a minister father and a restless search for his vocation, *Memories, Dreams, Reflections* offered not only answers, but a spiritual father in Jung. During his final year at Yale Divinity School, Stein held fast to this newfound treasure, which would become the key to unlocking the secrets of his future vocation.

Stein's identification with his personal father had been partial—loving, yet paradoxical—and Jung provided what was missing in unexpected and unprecedented ways. Both the book and the personality of Jung gripped Stein like no other work or figure he had encountered. He was astonished that such a book even existed. He wondered: How could he possibly comprehend the entire corpus of such a man's works, and still find his own authentic voice? Could he ever be equal to such an intellect as Jung's? Could Jung help him understand how "men might be built" in the context of postmodernity? Though it was still vague, Stein felt his future destiny calling him, summoning him toward something as-yet-intangible and beyond his grasp.

As a boy of eight, Stein's first master had been Jesus Christ—a human figure, a healer, and a god of love for the innocent lad. His second master, found later in life, was unequivocally C.G. Jung. In an interview, Stein even referred to Jung as his "Mahatma." Stein's quest for the ancestral Swiss grandfather he needed to guide him into postmodernity found its resolution in the father of analytical psychology. Jung's focus on the inner world of the imagination, numinous dreams, parapsychological phenomena, alchemy, religious experiences, good and evil, theological ideas, poetry, philosophy, world literature, mythology, and synchronicity was like manna falling from heaven for Stein. It was as though this rich intellectual nourishment fell directly into his hands, distilled in the pages of a single book.

Jung's focus in *Memories, Dreams, Reflections* was not merely literary or theological, but deeply and intimately experiential and human. The book's impact on Stein's sense of vocation was extraordinary. It was akin to first love—far more than an intellectual fascination or the detached appreciation of printed words on a page. *Memories, Dreams, Reflections* struck to the very core of Stein's Swiss ancestral psyche, awakening a sense of divinity in his DNA that his alma mater had not instilled in such an intimately *felt* way.

Jung had opened a doorway to regions of Stein's psyche that he had not known existed. A vivid dream world began to unfold, infused with inner significance, and synchronicities seemed to abound. The earlier conversation with Elisabeth O'Connor began to take on new significance. Things started to make sense—within, without, and all around him. When Stein stepped back onto the Yale Divinity School campus in the fall of 1968, the first person he encountered was Professor Russell Becker, Head of the Department of Pastoral Counseling. Becker had just returned from a sabbatical year at the CG Jung-Institut Zürich, and was brimming with enthusiasm for Jung's ideas. Recognizing their shared interest, Becker invited Stein to meet with him twice a week to discuss Stein's dreams. These sessions became formative, with both teacher and student learning about Jungian work together. Through this process, Stein experienced the true meaning of the word "transference." In Becker, he found both a mentor and a path that would eventually lead him (also) to Zürich to study at the CG Jung-Institut Zürich.

While working as a psychiatric aide at Yale's Community Mental Health Center, Stein wrote to the Director of the CG Jung-Institut Zürich, James Hillman, to inquire about whether he might pursue training there after completing his graduate studies. To his delight, he soon received an encouraging reply from Hillman, who warmly invited Stein to Zürich. Thrilled by the opportunity, Stein packed his worldly belongings (including his copy of *Memories, Dreams, Reflections*) into a few bags and set sail on his quest.

Stein's education as a classically trained Jungian analyst came about through a series of remarkable serendipities. These began accumulating during his mid-20s, one after another, as though the three Fates were busy at work with their hidden purposes—spinning, measuring, and cutting the threads of destiny. In retrospect, Stein feels that the Self was directing his life, step by step, along an unfolding path. His calling began to take shape as he immersed himself in studies at the Yale libraries and the Divinity School. It seemed as though, from the very beginning, a secret design was orchestrating his path, guided by an unseen hand above his head. Synchronicities continued to appear as he pursued his analytic training in Zürich.

Analytic Training in Zürich and Return to the United States

After living in New Haven for eight years and studying intensively at Yale, Stein traveled to study at the CG Jung-Institut Zürich from the ages of 26–30. While there, he worked for a period as a managing editor for James Hillman's Spring Publications. After becoming certified as an analyst, he moved to Houston, Texas, where he lived for three years. However, he found life in Houston unpleasant due to its extroverted culture and excessively hot and humid climate. Approaching midlife, Stein experienced a period of depression. He had to find the "corpse within" himself and bury it there, as he teaches we all must do at critical turning points in our lives, which we can learn to recognize from our dreams.

Stein's happiness grew significantly when he and his wife, Jan, relocated to Evanston, Illinois, just outside Chicago. There, they settled near the newly established Jung Center. June Singer, the center's founder, was of great assistance in helping Stein establish himself there as a training analyst. In 1980, the C.G. Jung Institute was founded and officially recognized as a Member Group of the IAAP, with Stein elected as its first president. He also served as President of the Chicago Society of Jungian Analysts from 1980 to 1985, and he co-organized and ran the Ghost Ranch Conferences with Nathan Schwartz-Salant from 1983 to 1992. Together, Stein and Schwartz-Salant co-founded Chiron Publications.

In 1983, the San Francisco Jungian analyst Thomas Kirsch invited Stein to join the Program Committee for the 1986 IAAP Congress in Berlin. Later, Kirsch selected Stein to serve as his Honorary Secretary during his IAAP presidency from 1989 to 1995. During this period, Stein traveled and lectured widely, including in China, Mexico, Europe, South Africa, and Japan. Kirsch and Stein often traveled together, developing a close friendship. In 1993, Heyong Shen, a Visiting Professor from South China, came to visit Stein in Chicago. Following this visit, Stein experienced a reverie in which the idea emerged that he and Kirsch should visit China to explore the growing interest in analytical psychology there. In August 1994, they traveled to Normal University in Guangzhou and continued on to Beijing, accompanied by Professor Shen. There, they engaged with mental health professionals and delivered lectures on analytical psychology, exploring its resonance with Taoism.

While teaching at the C.G. Jung Institute of Chicago, Stein realized that, despite years of diligent work with dreams, he had not taken sufficient time to experiment with active imagination to truly grasp its transformative potential. In 1995, he began practicing this method, incorporating it into his walks as a kind of ambulatory meditation. As the process deepened, he experienced a sudden and vivid vision: Jesus Christ as a symbol of the union of time and eternity. This vision revealed to him that love transcends temporality, belonging to both the temporal and the eternal, non-temporal realms. The numinous experience occurred on the pedestrian streets of Wilmette, Illinois, and it has remained with him ever since. In that moment, Stein realized that Christ was, for him, the ultimate symbol of the divine mystery. He also understood that he was truly a Christian—not by adherence to creed or doctrine, but through lived experience. From that point onward, active imagination became a daily discipline, and a practice he continues to this day during his walks in the hills of Goldiwil. This experience convinced him of the profound healing power of active imagination and its functional utility in transforming lives. A brief glance at his portfolio and the books he references demonstrates how integral this practice has become to his work and thought. As Stein notes, active imagination was, for Jung, a form of prayer. Although Jung wrote very little about prayer and its clinical relevance to individuation and Jungian psychoanalysis, Stein's writings, beginning in 1995, reflect its great significance to Jungian practice and thought.

In 2013, Kirsch and Stein served as honorary co-presidents of a conference in Taiwan that brought together speakers from Japan, Korea, and China. Around this time, Stein was also co-editing a book with Kirsch's wife, Jean Kirsch (my analyst at the time), titled *How and Why We Still Read Jung*. The East-West conference and Stein's collaboration with Thomas and Jean highlighted the fusion of spiritual connections between East and West at the time. My own occasional exchange of letters with Stein, alongside insights from Thomas and Jean, made it clear to me that it was time to take down the walls between Jung's empirical science and world religions—an early interest of mine during my studies at the University of California, Santa Cruz. Stein's trips with Thomas and Jean to China symbolically earned him his "Taoist stripes." By touching Chinese soil, he seemed to emerge like an aquatic plant from a rhizome in the muddy depths into a lotus flower in full bloom.

Stein helped to clear up some of my confusion about Jung's dualism between empiricism and metaphysics. For example, during a Zoom communication with me on August 16, 2024, he remarked:

Jung needed to have experience: What is your experience of God? This was Jung's approach to religion. Jung was not good at mathematics because math is so abstract. That's why he needed Wolfgang Pauli to help him with the theory of synchronicity. Meaning was present for Jung in the external world of the Cosmos, and it is the individual's job to figure out what it means impartially, as an objective reality. If one misses the meaning of an experience of synchronicity, it does not attain any personal significance in one's practical and personal life.

Regarding Jung's personal problem with metaphysics, Stein added: "Jung could not understand high-level abstraction. He preferred the study of symbols. That was his specialty, his genius was symbolic thinking and amplification, dreams and their interpretation."

To my knowledge, not enough has been written about faith in the field of analytical psychology from an archetypal perspective. This may, in part, stem from Jung's personal struggles with faith—his father's and his own—a struggle that seems to have cast a shadow over the subject in the field. However, not everyone shares Jung's difficulties with faith or with organized religion, be that of the church or the synagogue, the temple or the mosque. Stein openly accepts his faith in his work. This acceptance appears to have emerged at some point in his development as a Jungian analyst, particularly during a major turning point in midlife. It was at this stage that Stein seemed to fully embrace his fate and himself, without needing to alter the facts of his life as the son of two Christian missionary parents in Canada and the United States. This embrace of his faith had a profound effect on me, helping me heal my connection to my Lutheran roots in Germany.

As I mentioned earlier, Stein has, on occasion, referred to himself as a "Jungian missionary." The more deeply I engage with him and his books, the more I see that he truly means these words. For Stein, the word "missionary" is not a pejorative. It is a word to take pride in! In his book *Men Under Construction*, for instance, he describes the fourth stage of a man's life as the "missionary" stage. By this, he means having a sense of *mission*—a calling or vocation in life—not "missionary" in the traditional Christian sense, which might carry negative connotations, particularly for Indigenous peoples in the Americas or Africa. For Stein, being on a post-Jungian mission has meant serving as an arbiter of a post-Jungian vision of Oneness across the many schools of psychotherapy and psychoanalysis. His visionary scope is really that big.

One thing for readers to keep in mind as they progress through the remaining chapters is the question of what role Stein's ancestry has played in shaping his vocation as a teacher, writer, and international ambassador of Jungian affairs. If Jung's ancestors were predominantly Zwinglians and Stein's were Anabaptists, then a shared cultural trauma may lie in the background of both men's psyches. Stein appears to have been called, at the age of 60, to confront and heal this legacy when he returned to the Swiss side of his ancestral motherland. One hypothesis is that Stein's personal mother complex, alongside the affectionate attachment he experienced with his maternal grandmother, may have allowed him to embrace Jung as a second father figure—one he needed for his own individuation. However, internalizing Jung as a Self-figure also required a capacity for healthy detachment and a willingness to critique Jung's ideas, when necessary. Here is what Stein has to say about this:

> The return to Zurich in 2003 inaugurated a return to the source and core of Jungian psychology. Since then, I have been focused on a return to basics... Age intensifies one's focus on the center and brings the essential matters and values more clearly to fore, renders them less clouded over with extraneous matters and ancillary interests. It is a return to the Self... This *opus* calls for patience and concentration, selection and discrimination, rejection of the extraneous and steady attention to the essentials. It is a work in progress as I enter my ninth decade.[16]

For a long time, this book was also a work in progress, constantly undergoing editing, cutting, trimming, and the removal of extraneous matter. Stein expressed it so well! In the next chapter, I will begin with one of Stein's later works, which provides a useful structure for his major thesis: the metaphor of the "Four Pillars." While reviewing this work, I found it useful to imagine an architectural structure with four marble columns of equal width and height, supporting an arched dome and resting on a solid foundation.

Stein's Vision for the Future

Stein's oeuvre fulfills Jung's prediction that the way forward for humanity lies in making the historical God image conscious of itself in as many of its varied aspects as possible within a lifetime—a task that begins and ends with the integration of the human shadow and evil.

Stein offers the best of analytical psychology in a postmodern framework that is both healing and nourishing, providing sustenance for those hungry for analytical psychology at its finest. In my view, it does not get any better than his work—that is my personal bias. His vision for the future places the greatest importance on the ego as the carrier of consciousness of the Self, faith in one's fate as pivotal to individuation, and transformation on both personal and transpersonal levels. Today, Stein's interests lean increasingly toward experiences of transcendence, such as *satori, samadhi,* and being-in-Tao. "Now the prospect of becoming 'enlightened' attracts my attention and interest more than it did in than past," he remarked at the age of 80.[17]

Notes

1 CW8, 137.
2 CW7, 197–208.
3 CW8, 135.
4 CW3, 14.
5 CW4, 198, 199.
6 CW3, 234.

7 MS, 91.
8 CW8, 137.
9 CW8, 139. Zwingli initiated the Swiss-German Reformation from his pastoral office at Grossmünster in 1520.
10 CW6, 2.
11 CW4, 181.
12 CW6, 11.
13 CW8, 141.
14 CW8, 142.
15 CW6, 145.
16 CW8, 140.
17 CW8, 135.

Chapter 2

Four Pillars of Jungian Psychoanalysis

In one of his recent pieces of writing, Stein asks us to consider: "What makes the Jungian approach to psychoanalysis and psychotherapy unique and different from the others?" His answer: "I've boiled it down to four essential features that, when combined, are central to the Jungian approach and set it apart from the others. They are what I am calling the Four Pillars of Jungian Psychoanalysis."[1]

In Stein's *Collected Writings,* the number four appears time and again, functioning almost as a leitmotiv to transmit his message that four is an integer of wholeness. Stein uses the Four Pillars as a springboard for his vision of hope in the future of analytical psychology. Ideally, this future consists of a four-phase growth process leading optimally toward a clearly defined goal—a destination that, as Stein sees it, builds upon the classical foundation of Jung's original understanding, grounded in archetypal images and their energies. He argues that this approach provides the most pragmatic pathway for students in training to absorb into their hearts and minds the way of individuation and its ultimate aim: the realization of the Self. This stupendous essay appears toward the end of Volume 4 of his *Collected Writings*, titled *The Practice of Jungian Psychoanalysis*. The first of the Four Pillars is individuation, which Stein writes about as follows:

> If Jung has one big idea around which he circles incessantly in his abundant writings, it is the notion of individuation. Reading and studying Jung's writings over the course of more than 50 years, I am impressed by the timeless numinosity of this theme. Its symbols forever fascinate and lure one into ever deeper reading and consideration. My conclusion is that such transformation as Jung writes of is the great mystery of life.[2]

During the process of individuation, events often transpire that are so uncanny and inexplicable that they simply boggle the mind. Moments of transcendence, such as the spot of time when Stein read the name Reiman in the "Great Minister" (Grossmünster church), serve as temporal intersections in which the finite and infinite converge, opening the doors to the Self. As already noted, this significant moment of meaning occurred in 2003, following Stein's relocation to

DOI: 10.4324/9781003664024-3

Zürich. Thirty years earlier, Stein had graduated from the training program at the CG Jung-Institut Zürich, following four years of intensive analysis and study under the guidance of distinguished teachers and training analysts, many of whom had worked with Jung, himself, as part of his immediate circle. Stein feels blessed to have been able to attend lectures by luminary figures such as Marie-Louise von Franz lecture on fairytales, Heinrich Fierz and Adolf Guggenbühl-Craig on psychiatry, Barbara Hannah on animal symbolism in dreams, and Jolande Jacobi on analytic theory. And further, he feels very fortunate to have been able to study with James Hillman and Raphael Lopez-Pedraza as they formulated the basic features of what would later become archetypal psychology.[3] This rich intellectual and analytical background ultimately bore fruit during Stein's later years in Chicago. Yet, this was only the start. Once he left his mentors behind, he discovered his unique voice and unmistakable authenticity.

Central to Stein's philosophy is his conviction in the importance of grounding students in the invisible world of the archetypes. This preference reflects his commitment to a classical mode of training emphasizing relatedness, dreams, and active imagination. "It is hard to conceive of a Jungian psychoanalysis worthy of the name," he writes, "that does not include extensive consideration of dreams brought in regularly by the analysand.... Dreams are the *via regia* to the Self."[4]

As we have seen, Stein trained to become an analyst in Zürich from 1969 to 1973. He entered training at the age of 26 and completed it four years later, at the age of 30—a timeline that, to my knowledge, is virtually unheard of today. At that time, it was standard practice to bring a written record of one's dreams to every session of analysis. For Stein and his fellow candidates, these sessions occurred twice weekly. Their training was not only aimed at preparing them to become analysts, but also at developing their ability to remember and write down their dreams in meticulous detail. They were also taught how to elicit dreams from their clients and how to work analytically with patients, even in the absence of dreams.[5] Over the years, training programs have undergone significant changes, with new requirements introducing greater responsibilities and pressures for students to adapt to the spirit of the times. Nevertheless, it remains common practice for Jungian analysts to encourage clients to keep a dream notebook or journal as part of their analytical work. Through this practice, a dream series may begin to emerge in the analytic relationship. Stein explains:

> As clients get more involved with their dream life and begin recording the dreams regularly, sometimes they remember earlier dreams from childhood or recurrent dreams that have repeated themselves over and over again, and these, too, become part of the dream series.[6]

Moreover, he emphasizes an important consideration in the analytic process: the decision to interpret dream imagery objectively or subjectively: "*Objective* interpretation refers meaning to actual relationships in the surrounding world; *subjective* interpretation refers meaning to the inner world of the psyche."[7]

In the analyst training program at the International School of Analytical Psychology Zurich (ISAPZURICH), where Stein served as president for four years, students are required to write a "symbol paper" to demonstrate their proficiency in employing the method of amplification while working with their own and their clients' dreams, as well as the products of their active imaginations.[8] This assignment serves as an exercise in active visioning on a chosen archetype, such as the mother or father archetype. Stein openly acknowledges his bias toward the classical school of analysis associated with the Zürich tradition in which he was trained. Thus, it is not surprising that he returned to Zürich 30 years later to live, love, and work as a prominent figure in the Jungian community. When Stein left Chicago, he brought with him the discipline of active imagination as an integral practice.

For Stein, "imagination is the key to rebirth and transformation" because, as he explains, "it generates and secures an 'intermediate realm' wherein the encounter with transcendence and the mystery can take place and be accepted as valid and real."[9] By "rebirth," Stein means a second birth arising from the deepest levels of the collective psyche—the "spirit of the depths"—a process of transformation whose ultimate aim is complete individuation. According to Stein, the Four Pillars of Jungian psychoanalysis are as follows:

1   individuation—a *way of thinking* about psychological development;
2   the analytic relationship;
3   dream work; and
4   active imagination.

The first pillar, individuation, is covered in Volume 1 of Stein's *Collected Writings*, titled *Individuation*. In Chapter 3, I will review Stein's thoughts on individuation in depth. More immediately, however, I will focus on the second pillar, which Stein considers primary. According to Stein, the analytic relationship is the *sine qua non* of Jungian analysis. As he writes:

> When researchers have asked psychotherapists of the many schools that are in existence today what they regard as the single most important factor for a successful outcome in treatment, the answer is almost always the relationship between therapist and client.... Relationships are critically important for psychological development from the moment of birth, all the way through life until the very end.[10]

Throughout the remainder of this book, I will emphasize the analytic relationship as the most pivotal of the Four Pillars. It is perhaps the primary focus of analytic training at the San Francisco Jung Institute with which I am affiliated. Analysis cannot occur in a vacuum. Rather, it takes place within an analytic container, in the field between analyst and client. Thus, analytic work is, first and foremost, relationally focused. As a licensed marriage and family therapist in the State of California, my training has primarily centered on relationships—specifically, the ruptures that occur in both children and adults, and how the psyche produces healing imagery and emotions to assist in repair. Stein, too, is a relationally focused analyst who works in the deep field of depth psychology. He provides numerous examples of client dreams to demonstrate his process of working with symbolic material in the context of transference/countertransference dynamics, and in close relationship to analysands. In doing so, he offers clear insights into the unique archetypal images that emerge in the shared space between him and his patients. Stein describes analytical training as a form of initiation "into a dedicated vocation with clear ethical standards and a collective persona." He identifies four areas of focus that, in his view, should be addressed by all Jungian training institutions:

1 training for clinical practice;
2 training in research methodology and theory development;
3 preparation for organizational participation; and
4 persona considerations for public representation.[11]

Stein's reflections on the interactive processes of Jungian analysis have led him to describe three types of countertransference attitudes and their respective positive and negative potentials for analysis. He sees this work as an ongoing project for all Jungians—to refine, clarify, evolve, and augment Jung's hypotheses, as he himself has been doing for more than 50 years. Stein defines countertransference attitudes as stable and enduring, in contrast to countertransference reactions, which are momentary and triggered (typically) by the patient's transference. Countertransference attitudes serve as the fundamental positions on which analysts rely in their approach to all patients, shaped by the analyst's character and training. The three countertransference attitudes are as follows:

1 power-oriented (paternal and patriarchal);
2 maieutic (maternal); and
3 shamanic (hermetic).

The first two attitudes are familiar to psychoanalysts of all persuasions, as they reflect mother and father projections and relational dynamics within the transference, rooted in complexes and their nuclear cores, or archetypes. The maieutic attitude, derived from the Greek word referring to a nursemaid who assisted women in childbirth, reflects a nurturing, facilitating approach. An analyst who is visited by this feminine spirit of gestation and birthing becomes a midwife to the emergence of a new, more expansive identity within the patient. While the analyst does not "give birth" to the patient's transformation, he or she acts as a facilitator and participant in the fertilization process that nurtures the patient's individuation process. The shamanic attitude is governed by a hermetic archetype, personified by the Greek god Hermes, the creative daimon of liminality. This archetype—and the reflective awareness it inspires in analysts, often during states of reverie—focuses on transformations of consciousness and creative playfulness. It corresponds with archaic vestiges of the shaman archetype, which represents the primordial healer in human history. Shamanism lies at the foundation of all healing and artistic professions, and it may manifest as an archaic function in the dreams or sandplay activities of children, adolescents, or adults, as well as within the transference/countertransference dynamics between analyst and analysand. The origins of the shaman archetype can be traced to the era of the Great Mother religions, representing the archaic roots of human consciousness. Even today, we retain access to this archetype through our reveries, fantasies, and dreams. Stein will have much more to say about this countertransference attitude and its significance in later discussions.

It is important to note that analysts do not take credit for changes in their patients' analytic processes. Rather, they serve as witnesses to transformations and transmutations of consciousness; they work as aids, attendants, or assistants. Typically, an analytic process takes years to culminate in the birth of a fully transformed identity. Yet, Stein recounts a remarkable story once told to him by an 18-year-old French woman, speaking of her friend. This woman had undergone a single analytic session with Jung, and from that brief encounter, experienced a profound metamorphosis in her personality. What had happened? This could scarcely be considered analysis in the traditional sense. Well, after listening to the patient for only 30–40 minutes, Jung had told her that she had a calling to become a psychiatrist. This insight, alone, opened the pathway to her individuation. Here, we can see that individuation can also be initiated through influence: Jung had intuitively recognized the archetypal source of her vocation, and this recognition had been enough to catalyze her individuation process. She became "pregnant" with a new God image—a living symbol of her vocation to psychiatry. Through her medical studies and eventual licensure, she fulfilled this calling, becoming both a psychiatrist and a psychoanalyst. Stein describes this encounter as a maieutic session, because Jung served a very brief role as a midwife, assisting in a process that the client then pursued on her own to fulfill her calling from the Self.

I mention this case to illustrate that the development of the personality is not a new phenomenon introduced by Jungian psychoanalysis. Rather, it has been part of the human experience since time immemorial. What distinguishes Jungian psychoanalysis are the methods Jung developed and taught to those in his inner circle. One such method involves giving analytical attention to the inner voice, or *vocatus*—a Latin term Jung engraved above the front doorway of his home in Küsnacht. In many cases, a calling naturally arises within the analytic conversation, and hearing this inner voice can open a channel to the patient's anima or animus and, through these figures, the Self. Stein has significantly expanded our understanding of the anima and animus through his deep reading of Jung. For Stein, all individuals possess both an anima and an animus, and these are not always rigidly gendered. They can even be transgendered. The soul image is evoked within the relational field, which forms the second pillar in Stein's four-part framework.

While I am on the topic of relationships, I want to stress the special significance Stein places on "transformative relationships." This concept is one of my personal favorites among his newer hypotheses. It is an original research idea of Stein's that I wrote about in my review in 1998, and I have since incorporated into several of my case studies and books. I have not encountered it articulated with such clarity elsewhere in our field. Although I will explore this notion of transformative relationships in greater detail in the chapters ahead, I will briefly introduce it here.

Stein's theoretical work has ventured into new territory in our field, charting fascinating ideas that have arisen from his analytic investigations, personal experiences, relationships, and broad intellectual pursuits in scientific, religious, biographical, literary, and artistic domains. One of these fascinating concepts is what Stein calls a "transformative relationship" in his book *Transformation: Emergence of the Self*. Transformative relationships, as he describes, are rare yet universally resonant. They are extraordinary in nature and not exclusive to Jungians.

For instance, in fields such as science, technology, or art, a mentor encountered in early adulthood or midlife may completely transform one's life through their influence. By projecting the Self onto an external personage—someone with prominence or prestige within the field of one's vocation—one can eventually take back the Self and internalize it in an imaginary way. Stein himself experienced this phenomenon when, for instance, he purchased and read *Memories, Dreams, Reflections* at Yale, took classes with von Franz, and read Erich Neumann and Wolfgang Pauli's letters to Jung. These experiences became transpersonal transferences onto classically trained analysts and scholars, who became transformative figures in Stein's own individuation into an analyst, writer, theorist, and lecturer. To this day, Stein extensively quotes von Franz on time, Pauli on synchronicity, and Neumann on the ego-Self axis—demonstrating how these figures have held his projection of the Self in a transpersonal sense, despite the absence of a personal relationship. Many of us have engaged in similar transpersonal transferences onto Jung.

In analytic work, the analyst frequently serves as a vessel for the patient's projection of the Self. However, the transference of an analysand onto an analyst during analytical work is more of a personal type of transformative relationship, which differs somewhat from the projection onto a master figure, yet overlaps in important ways. In training analysis, for example, as candidates work with Jungian analysts, the analysand cannot help but project the Self, to some extent, onto their analyst, as long as the analyst presents the "right fit." In serving this temporary function as a transference figure, an analyst may initiate their analysand's individuation process. This process unfolds gradually, as the idealizing transference of the Self fades and loses some of its original numinosity, allowing it to be replaced by a deeper connection to a transformative image within—one that the Self intended to make conscious from the very beginning. Such transformative connections do not always require a personal relationship. For instance, they may arise through reading a book, viewing a work of art, or listening to a symphony. When the voice of the Self speaks, through whatever person or medium, it can be life-changing, depending on one's attitude toward fate and whether one chooses to accept or refuse the call.

Once a person has had such an experience, they are never the same. They are fundamentally altered at the deepest levels of human experience. In later chapters, I will explore Stein's *Transformation: Emergence of the Self*. However, I mention these experiences here to reach readers who may not feel called to the field of depth psychology. Perhaps, their vocation lies in music, science, theology, art, computer technology, or astronomy. These, too, are valid pathways for individuation. Everyone has the potential to experience deep structural change. The key is to develop the capacity to recognize transformative moments when they are constellated relationally, whether within or beyond the analytic setting.

As we have seen, Stein has been an English literature major at Yale, an ordained Protestant minister with a doctorate in Religion and Psychological Studies from the University of Chicago, and a practicing Jungian analyst with multiple callings as an editor, teacher, and writer. Today, writing, teaching, and supervision are his primary ways of serving the community. His books, which are lacking in pretention, are carefully crafted to make readers more Self-aware. Healing is his main business. Stein writes prolifically for analysts, candidates-in-training, and a global audience, and his writings are read by professionals across many nations, in various languages. He extends an open invitation to everyone to become their fullest potential by championing the unity of the Self in all individuals. There is a practice gap in analytic training about work with calling dreams. In order to become analysts, candidates-in-training need to understand, be able to apply and work with this Jungian concept and learn that vocational dreams are central to analytical treatment. Vocational dreams are important in recognizing where a patient's motivation lies, in what areas of work their sense of significance is, to harmonize their material and social drives in movement toward increasing spiritualization, physical and emotional health, self-esteem, and the crystallization of their personal and cultural identities. Such experiential knowledge is essential learning in the practice of analytic psychotherapy with patients.

In analytical psychology, the goal of individuation is not perfection but the "practice of wholeness." *Practicing Wholeness* is, in fact, the title of one of Stein's books. To practice wholeness means to serve the Self by allowing it to be of service to others. Wholeness may be approached in a relativistic manner. There are no absolutes in analytical psychology and no final, definitive experience of the Self, even during or after analysis. Individuation is a lifelong process—one that continues until one's final breath. The closest one may come to achieving wholeness might be through relationships that temporarily open an individual to transcendence. Such relationships connect individuals to the deepest and highest levels of their being/ Being, in relationship to both time and eternity. Consciously transformative relationships are essential for living out one's destiny as fully as possible. This is what analysis can offer: an ideal of transformation and a striving toward one's goal, in emotional attunement with the Self and in partnership with an analyst.

The aim of individuation, Stein explains, is "the birth of transcendence in consciousness," symbolized by the Risen Christ.[12] This stage of individuation is not limited to the approach of death or the Beyond. Rather, it transcends the materialistic realm of ego awareness. Stein gives special attention to all 20 illustrations of the *Rosarium philosophorum,* the famous alchemical text that Jung explored in "The Psychology of the Transference." However, Stein ventures further than Jung. While Jung's commentary on the transference concluded with image 10 in the series, Stein saw the need to extend the theoretical framework beyond this point. In several of his essays, he includes and analyzes images 11–20, with the final image depicting the Risen Christ—a symbol of the highest stage of individuation. As Stein writes: "The theme of divinization is continued in the final picture of the series... the image of the risen and triumphant Christ."[13]

What Stein means by this is non-denominational and universal. It represents the realization of transcendence in one's life through the mystery and miracle of Oneness. "Ultimately," Stein writes,

> there is a birth of transcendence in consciousness that rises above all divisions created by the psyche, and a person enters into a space of supreme Oneness, beyond even the division between time and eternity, where Samsara and Nirvana are one and the same.[14]

This clearly surpasses the ordinary teachings of psychotherapy, though it resonates with contemporary practices such as mindfulness meditation, which has become *de rigueur* in the United States.

Now, let us take a closer look at the third pillar. We will return to the analytical relationship in the chapters ahead. The third pillar of Jungian psychoanalysis centers on intensive dream work. As we have seen, dreams are welcomed by Jungian analysts. They are actively sought as pathways to the personal, cultural, and collective levels of the unconscious, reaching below even the basement, where the ancestral spirits reside. This is the realm of ancestral worship, inhabited by snakes and animal spirits. In Stein's *Collected Writings,* he offers numerous examples of dreams, illustrating how transformation unfolds within the human psyche and how he works with dreams and their interpretations. Dreams reveal how symbols emerge in the analytic matrix, particularly when the analytic relationship reaches profound depths.

Much like a temple built in antiquity to honor the ancestors, all of Stein's Four Pillars are equally essential. If anyone is neglected, the entire structure risks collapse. The field itself could succumb to the surrounding cultural trends of superficiality, quick symptom reduction, cognitive behavioral therapy, and other quick fixes. At its best, analysis sounds the depths of the psyche, where one's deeper callings are located.

The Jungian method of dream work is unique, requiring extensive knowledge, experience, and experimentation with Jung's methods of amplification and circumambulation. These methods differ fundamentally from free association. Jungian dream work demands research, careful reading, and a focused inner concentration on a center of meaning—one that moves beyond a mere circling around psychological blockages (or complexes). What is most essential is not technique, but a *relational presence* to activate the energy source within. As Stein asserts, "'Leave your theories and techniques at the door when you enter the consulting room!' was the Master's advice."[15] The "Master," of course, refers to Jung.

Among the Four Pillars, the fourth—active imagination—is the most spacious and least constrained by imitation, as it is unique to Jungian psychoanalysis. No other form of psychotherapy approaches active imagination in the way that Stein does. For Stein, active imagination holds greater importance than dreaming, because it is the only method capable of constellating what Jung termed the "transcendent function." The transcendent function supersedes other psychic functions, because it is not built on outer relationships, but through interaction with figures from the inner world. Dream images and fantasy figures, native to the depths of the psyche, can be actively engaged in dialogue. This practice may be performed in the presence of an analyst or during solitary creative processes, such as sitting at an easel, chiseling stone—as Jung often did —or vigorously hiking or trekking in the mountains. Stein, himself, is a daily hiker.

Stein's Theological Contributions

Jung is widely regarded as the first psychologist to develop a comprehensive lifespan perspective, and Stein has contributed significantly to his framework by diagramming Jung's map of the soul. While Jung's psychology was predominantly grounded in empirical theory, Stein has extended it by incorporating a theological foundation. He asserts that we can never fully integrate the totality of the Self, for the following reasons:

> It is because our consciousness is not big enough to integrate the whole self. We can only partially integrate the whole self. Certain aspects of the self, even after a long development of individuation, remain unconscious, beyond the reach of consciousness. The self as a whole is made up of many archetypal potentials, but an individual can realize only a few of these possibilities. An individual is a specific combination of these many archetypal possibilities. That specific combination is what the individual is responsible for realizing and manifesting as their personal life history.[16]

Such humility relieves humans of the pressure to imagine that they can ever fully incarnate the Self, thereby puncturing the bubble of our naïve sense of divinity. We are not gods. Even Jesus was merely an image of God. All we can ever incarnate of the Self is our own image of it, which is always shaped and limited by our vocation. Even Jung did not get everything right. "To be fair," Stein writes,

> one must admit that Jung was right about the dogmatic Christ image, the image of the perfect man in whom there was no sin; but he was off the mark with respect to the image of Jesus in the Gospels.
>
> (Matthew, Mark, and Luke)[17]

Jesus, as presented in the four Gospels, was not perfect. This marks a rare example of Stein crossing swords with Jung on a theological issue that was deeply important to him. Stein's point is well taken and provides a necessary correction, as Jung overlooked significant aspects of how the Christ story relates to analysis. For this reason, Stein included the last ten illustrations of the *Rosarium philosophorum* in his commentaries, arguing that these further stages of transformation must be integrated into our understanding of what is possible in analysis.

"Is every human soul potentially Christ-like?" Stein asks readers to consider. "Are we all Christian at some unconscious level?" His answer: "Presumably so... [since] the archetypes are universal and belong to the general human inventory."[18] Thus, whether one loves Christ or not, Christ loves them just the same, as he resides within everyone. Stein encourages readers to test this truth for themselves, even if they are not Christian. The same could be said of the Buddha, Moses, or Mohammed. Each is embedded within archetypal patterns of the objective human psyche. But how does one realize one's Christ-nature? Are there stages of evolution involved?

Stein describes the stages of individuation as proceeding sequentially from the mother to the father and, finally, to the mature, self-reliant individual. In the third stage, the ego adopts a modest position in relationship to the Self. One does not become Christ, but one may imagine or feel oneself to be Christ-like. Stein writes: "Jungians have called this *relativization of the ego*—putting ego consciousness in a secondary position within the psyche rather than a primary place. The ego is displaced by this and no longer holds absolute authority over decision-making."[19] Instead, one serves the Self via the humble human vehicle of one's vocation, whether that calling involves marriage, parenthood, science, or art.

Stein reports a number of dreams with both personal and archetypal significance. To illustrate his point and provide a more practical understanding, I will summarize one particularly Christ-like dream.

> The sky around her was almost iridescent blue. As she ascended into the sky on a cloud, an older Japanese man dressed in silk gently extended a ring to her of very high value with precious jewels. She put it on her ring finger. Then she noticed that it had a number 8 stamped sideways into the metal, making it appear as an infinity symbol.[20]

Stein explores this dream with careful precision, paying close attention to every detail. After a lengthy exegesis of the dream's content, he explains:

> In the dream of the golden ring (above), the feeling function would consider how the dreamer will need to grow into the relationship implied by receiving the ring, namely to take up the ethical task of love. The dream offers vocational direction.[21]

The ethical task of love, in this case, involves the dreamer entering a Christ-like feeling connection with the Japanese man who gives her the ring.

Here, we can observe a maieutic attitude in Stein the analyst—the midwifery role he takes toward the dreamer's vocation. Stein helps the dreamer "birth" the love within her heart, guiding her toward the particulars of her calling through human relationship and within the analytical matrix. The entire scene of the dream takes place in what Jung referred to as the ultraviolet end of the psyche, in a vast, sky-wide atmosphere of the Self above her. This superconscious dimension of the psychoid continuum extends into cosmic realms, where the old Japanese figure from the East lives in harmony with the infinite, as a sage-like envoy of transcendence. This figure represents a path within the dreamer's psyche toward the infinite—a vision that emerged in the intersubjective space shared between herself and Stein, her analyst. The vision pertains to her potential calling, which she needed to grow into over successive stages.

This dream serves as an instructive example of how Stein navigates the interplay between Jung's empirical psychology and his own theological perspective. Infinity, he reminds us, is without measure. One can only catch a glimpse of it during moments when the Self awakens within us, evoking a sense of mystery and wonder. We enter into this realm whenever we open ourselves to transcendence. Experiences of the Self, often accompanied by meaningful coincidences, are at least potentially Christ-like openings into Oneness. Dreams such as this must be actively engaged—worked with, amplified, and circumambulated. This particular dream is an excellent example of an archetypal dream that guided the dreamer toward individuation through a calling to compassion.

Notes on Analytic Training

Before I go over a few additional points from Stein's overview of the third pillar, I will turn to his lecture, "On Training Jungian Psychoanalysts Today," delivered in September 2020, during the height of the COVID-19 pandemic. As previously noted, Stein is both a reader of the Bible and an interpreter of *The Red Book*. Engaging with such texts through deep reading demands in-depth meditation—a practice that stands in stark opposition to the shallowness and distraction characteristic of the spirit of the times. In his intuitive vision, Stein perceives a "virus of superficiality" that has taken hold in postmodernity. This contagion, he warns, threatens to infect at least some Jungian institutes and training programs with triviality, unless steps are taken to quarantine it and prevent its further spread. The danger of postmodernity, Stein writes, lies in its paltriness:

> We live in postmodern times. The changes brought about in world culture during the last several decades, and especially since the introduction of the computer and the internet into common usage worldwide, have profoundly affected all cultures, and this has had an impact also on our profession of psychotherapy. Everything goes faster, speed and efficiency are paramount, and superficiality as the signature of the times is a result.... We might fear that the postmodern world has been infected with the virus of superficiality.... Perhaps now is the time to listen more intently to the spirit of the depths.[22]

Stein is delivering a clear and urgent message here: we risk losing the invaluable inheritance passed down from our ancestors—the way of the dream and the practice of active imagination. What is at stake is the stability of the fourth pillar, which becomes precarious if it is not in harmonious alignment with both the inner Self and the external world. Stein further elaborates:

> At the outset I have to admit a bias in favor of the classical approach to training, in that it was and continues to be grounded in the archetypal and "eternal" rather than in the personal and "transitory".... This grounding has the best chance of ensuring that Jungian psychoanalysis will continue to be a viable and culturally relevant profession in the long run.[23]

He continues: "Training/formation [transformation] is also a kind of initiation process into a dedicated vocation with clear ethical standards and a collective persona."[24] After stressing the importance of dream research and the advancement of theory, Stein transitions to underscore the importance of balanced symmetry among all of the Four Pillars. Regarding the third pillar, dreams, he states: "The Self is the dream-maker, and the Self intends individuation. So, dreams are in the service of individuation."[25]

Stein's vision—like Jung's—is a dream of wholeness. To achieve wholeness, we require relationships, dream work, and the practice of active imagination. It is interesting to reflect on the fact that Stein only began rigorously practicing active imagination in 1995—well after completing his Jungian and academic training and following 20 years of practice as an analyst and teacher. What emerged from this practice, both surprisingly and vividly, was an inner world populated by archetypal figures, culminating in a numinous vision of Christ as the answer to the pressing question: "Is love sustainable, or does it inevitably fade and die, or even turn into its opposite, hate?" The answer that came to Stein was: Love never ends! While love lifts us into a transcendent dimension within the body and within time and space, its sustainability is assured by Christ, who embodies both the temporal (love incarnate) and the eternal (divine love). For Stein, this active imagination experience forged a permanent connection between time and eternity.

Regarding the fourth pillar, Stein observes: "Active imagination is the pillar of Jungian psychoanalysis that has fallen into neglect in the recent post-Jungian generation, which has seen a strong increase in the emphasis on the relational part of the analysis."[26] It is important to remember Stein's earlier assertion: "Relationships are critically important for psychological development from the moment of birth, all the way through life until the very end."[27] This statement should be taken as an example of his activism, as he does not underestimate the value of relationships, which are central to the second pillar. On the contrary, Stein views relationships as indispensable for individuation, both within and beyond the consulting room. Intimate connection and dream analysis, in particular, demand a close union between client and analyst. However, Stein stresses the transformative quality of relatedness, which analysts must embody in their therapeutic engagements. Therefore, Stein emphasizes that active imagination "should be an essential feature in every training analysis. It is the surest way to build up the transcendent function."[28] Here, he speaks directly from his own experience as a training analyst:

> For candidates in training, the experience of active imagination will not only put them in contact with their own *prima materia* and with the Self, but it will qualify them to speak about the psyche with conviction based on personal experience. Active imagination takes the individuation process to another level and gives it a solid foundation in the depths of the psyche. The candidate has to discover the "inner analyst" in the depths of the psyche; otherwise only a professional persona will be formed in the process of training.[29]

Stein sees Jungian training programs as fertile ground for generating creative ideas and pioneering directions, propelled by research discoveries that can guide analytical psychology into the 21st century. For this vision to materialize, he emphasizes the necessity of conducting dream and imaginal research while continuing to build theoretical frameworks. As a relatively young discipline, just over a century old, analytical psychology remains in a nascent stage of development. Stein stresses that, regardless of the outcomes of our experiments with individuation in postmodernity, active imagination must play an essential role if Jungian institutes are to remain vibrant, healthy, and whole. According to Stein, the seedbeds of the future lie in engaging in dialogue with our inner analyst.

I find it heartwarming to read Stein's vision for Jungian training institutions in the present and future:

> Training programs are the seedbeds of creative new ideas and directions for the field of analytical psychology. Students are encouraged to write papers, theses, and later publishable articles and books as a part of their core activities as Jungian psychoanalysts. And training institutes take pride in the publication of their faculties and graduates. It is a mark of prestige. Jungians are known worldwide as authors and researchers.... Consequently, it is incumbent upon training programs to foster and encourage research and writing amongst their students.[30]

In his concluding remarks, Stein asks: "What archetypal image claims us as analysts? The answer to this might offer guidance for how to proceed in our training programs." An important component of this, Stein notes, is encouraging candidates to consult their inner analyst. This approach calls for a more modest sense of equality, or what might be described as a participatory democracy, within the educational practices of our training institutes.

Stein further prompts us to reflect: "What archetype did Jung incarnate so powerfully that his influence continues to impress people worldwide in increasing numbers?" He answers:

> I would venture to say that it was something to do with the shaman, that Jung became through his experiences recorded in *The Red Book* a shaman. A shaman

is a "medicine man" and someone who has contact with the spirit world.... This, I think, is the main work of training: to engage with that dialogue with the Self.[31]

In other words, the archetype of the shaman (or medicine man/woman) is a central imprint in our profession—a nuclear symbol of our Jungian vocation. The shaman, as a wounded healer, takes in the illness of the tribe, the infection, or whatever might be limiting growth toward higher levels of consciousness—perhaps, the very virus Stein identified: superficiality. The shaman metabolizes the poisons of an individual, collective, or culture within their own psyche and produces an antidote—a psychic antibody[32]—to offer as a healing force. Writing, Stein suggests, can serve as a pathway to wholeness through active imagination, as evidenced in his reflections on the importance of deep reading.

Thus, I am on board with Stein's vision for Jungian training institutions, which calls for a collaborative effort to strengthen the Four Pillars, pillar by pillar, stone by stone. Stein emphasizes: "And we as a Jungian community are in a good position IF the rulers in our midst are strong and build temples, if they honor the Self."[33] Honoring the Self, in this context, means reverencing the shaman and analyst within, without being captured by their inflationary proclivities—what Jung referred to as being possessed by the mana-personality.

Only when the Self is truly honored in a candidate's individuation process and their inner analyst is welcomed into the lineage of ancestors following their initiatory journey to the source of their own wisdom—the wisdom of the elders—will the Four Pillars be stable enough to support the entire theoretical and practical edifice. At the C.G. Jung Institute of San Francisco, a number of analysts teach dream work and active imagination to candidates in training—a tradition sustained for many years through the abiding influence of our founding fathers, including Joseph L. Henderson. The importance Stein attributes to these pillars should, it is hoped, continue to enhance and build upon what is already established at this institute, as well as numerous others.

Stein's vision for future Jungians resonates deeply with Jung's broader project of aligning the spirit of the depths with the spirit of the times through the ego-Self axis. This alignment entails recovering what has been lost due to excessive conformity to the virus of superficiality—a cultural illness exacerbated by the overwhelming influence of media and television. Such a virus calls for an antitoxin or healing antibody, which can only be found in the Self—not in the persona, shadow, or the fragmented specters of ego consciousness. The latter lack the visionary capacity provided by the transcendent function, while the former embodies the way of wisdom, as taught throughout history by sages, cultural healers, and tribal shamans.

In his seminal essay "The Four Pillars," Stein leaves us with essential teachings. Here again, Stein speaks directly to us today and for the future:

It is time to put aside superficial persona identities and ego interests, and rather to go to the temple and to make sacrifice to the "ancestor spirits" (that would be Jung and his best students, and beyond them, the alchemists, the Gnostics, the ancient Greeks, the Bible, the Upanishads, the Chinese Taoist sages). This would lead us into a contemplative place, which could bring us to a vision of action, to take up new projects and to engage in collective action, as Jungians.[34]

Jung, who felt a deep kinship with ancient philosophers, Gnostics, and alchemists, may well have been the most shamanistic of all Jungian ancestors. The wisdom given in Stein's passage is truly astounding, given that it was written in 2020. In this rare piece, Stein puts his finger on the very prize Jung had his eye on for our future, although he never articulated it so succinctly as Stein does here. Jung was the trailblazer, and Stein is one of his emissaries. For me, this exquisite passage stands out as one of the rarest jewels I have encountered in the entire corpus of Jungian and post-Jungian thought, offering a direction for what I have coined "spiritual democracy."[35]

Using Stein's model, we might be inspired to engage with the same sources Jung studied and, through their meditative quiet and wisdom, find the uniting spirit and courage to build together in peace, rather than war. Stein's leanings toward the most positive potentials in the human psyche aim at the highest spiritual principles. What would it be like if we were trained to move toward a more contemplative place—a place that Stein tells us could bring us to a vision of action, inspiring new projects and collective actions as Jungians? This is truly visionary writing—the kind I admire most in Stein. It is precisely why I continue to read him to this day, long after I was first gripped by his book *Transformation: Emergence of the Self.* Twenty-six years later, after having read most of his *Collected Writings*, I am more convinced than ever of Stein's ability to lead us into the 21st century with a vision of renewed hope for our profession.

Fortunately, Stein regards all Four Pillars as equal in their contribution to the hopeful structuring of the temple that continues to be built. His vision for the future aligns closely with my own, though he expresses it with far greater articulation and wisdom—a testament to his lifelong engagement with these ideas and the insights that come with age.

I also want to highlight the value Stein places on the work of post-Jungians following Michael Fordham in London, particularly their focus on infant observation, affect attunement, trauma theory, attachment theory, and neuropsychology. Stein covers all of these developments comprehensively, yet he goes further by stressing the importance of returning to the writings of the early Jungians and finding peace through the study of the ancient sages. He remains deeply engaged with the ongoing publications of his colleagues, and his influence is evident in the countless books he has edited.

Stein also critically examines whether Jung's early assumptions about transference still hold water in contemporary Jungian psychoanalysis. Reflecting on Jung, he writes:

[Jung] preferred to work with dreams and active imagination in sessions that were relatively free of transference. But is this really possible? He knew well enough that it is not, and he did go on to deliver a substantial lecture on the subject of transference.... 'On the Psychology of the Transference.'[36]

As we will see, Stein undertook a major revision of this foundational essay by Jung, updating it to reflect the latest theoretical contributions on LBGTQ issues, gender, and the anima/animus. Stein recalls: "Henderson told me that it was inconceivable to work with Jung and not be engaged in active imagination. It was a basic method for analysis."[37]

In his characteristic manner, and despite the challenges we currently face, Stein's confidence and optimism about the future of analytical psychology are contagious. I salute him for his Alpine brilliance. He is far from naïve about the risk of succumbing to the superficiality of our times. Yet, his anxiety and doubt appear to have quieted after attending a meeting in Zürich with several Jungian colleagues to discuss the future of Jungian culture and practice. Stein recounts that he came home from this meeting feeling unsettled and somewhat dispirited. Writing from his home in Goldiwil, he recalls:

> I went to sleep, and had a dream in which Jung himself appeared. It's not frequent that Jung comes into my dreams. Obviously, he is a symbolic figure for me. It was a simple dream, and in it, Jung said to me: 'Don't worry. Analytical psychology has a long and rich future.'[38]

Stein awoke from the dream greatly relieved and has held this message close to his heart ever since. It sustains him whenever he feels overwhelmed by the rising tide of challenges and the encroachment of the spirit of the times. However, Jung's message does not lead Stein to complacency; rather, it fortifies his integrity and resolve to persevere.

After stressing the equality of the Four Pillars, Stein offers a simple yet profound prescription for readers who wish to practice active imagination:

1 let it happen;
2 receive whatever comes; and
3 if it moves, follow it.

Stein explains:

> These are the basic rules of active imagination: Let go and empty the mind; receive whatever comes; if it moves follow it; and then interact genuinely with it. If you follow these basic rules, you're sure to have success practicing active imagination.[39]

I love this prescription and have applied it in my own practice. Yet, when clients report no dreams and have no active imagination exercises to speak of, that is not a problem, as the analytical relationship itself serves as a space for interactive dialogue and expansion. Stein writes:

> This is what makes the critical difference. It is the quality of relationship, not the therapist's theoretical persuasion, that is the most important factor. To that

response, Jungian psychoanalysts would add: It's the relationship *plus* the co-operation of the unconscious and the self in the process that makes a critical difference between success and failure in analysis.[40]

It must be acknowledged that the objective consensus on the centrality of the analytic relationship is perhaps the most crucial variable in all analytic work. Neither dream work nor active imagination would be possible without the well-sealed vessel—the *vas bene clausum*—provided by the analyst to contain and hold the client's experiences during analysis. In this respect, Freud was correct, and Jung concurred. The transference/countertransference dynamic constitutes the alpha and omega of psychoanalysis. As Stein elaborates in this chapter, individuation is not possible outside the analytic relationship. That said, individuation also occurs outside analysis, in those who follow the call of their inner voice to pursue their vocation in the world.

One often-overlooked aspect of the relationship between Freud and Jung—an area Stein thoughtfully addresses—is a particular type of transference he describes as "man-to-man." Stein recounts that Jung once confessed in a letter to Freud that he had experienced a kind of:

> "religious crush" on him that had homosexual overtones, which scared him because of a childhood incident of sexual abuse by an admired older man.... Jung's was the kind of love a young man feels when he becomes enamored of an admired teacher. But as Jung soon realized, there was even more to it than that. For him, Freud was a numinous figure, almost godlike, therefore the term "religious crush." Later in his life, Jung would speak of this type of projection as an "archetypal transference."[41]

In his typically masterful way, Stein goes on to discuss the complexities of the transference/countertransference and the ways in which this dynamic evolved within the theoretical construct developed between Freud and Jung. This discussion is an invaluable resource for anyone seeking a synopsis of this history, as well as insight into the four stages of analysis Stein distilled from his reading of Jung.

What I wish to focus on now, however, are the less-than-ideal and more problematic situations that can arise in analysis. Stein writes:

> Perhaps an analyst's past problems are triggered by a particular client. This is certainly not useful or therapeutic. If this is the case, a decision needs to be made whether it's best for the analysis to be terminated. Sometimes the client has to decide, "This therapy is not helpful for me—it's actually harmful." If that's the experience, and the client has to trust his or her experience, he or she would have to stop working with that particular analyst.[42]

Stein proceeds to raise critical questions about the duration of therapy and when it may be appropriate to stop. He reports a termination moment shared by a "student," who described an illuminating dream she had experienced after nearly three years of analysis. There had been some uncertainty between her and her analyst at the time as to whether or not to continue with their work, and the night before a session, she had the following dream: *I am entering into the analytic space and everything was as usual, except that my chair has been removed from its usual place in the temenos. There is a backpack lying on the floor, packed to the full for a fulfilling journey ahead.*

The client shared with Stein that, in her dream, she looked at her analyst, who was standing, and he gestured for her to sit down in his chair—the only seat remaining in the room. Her own chair had vanished, signaling that it was time for her to incarnate her inner analyst. The dream then ended. Stein explains that it became clear to both the analyst and the dreamer that she was ready to be her own analyst, continuing the process of integration and transformation on her own journey through life and in service to her profession.

As he writes: "The maieutic analyst often spends a lot of time on dreams, because dreams are the womb of the future.... The value is in the birthing of the new."[43] This relativization of the emphasis placed on the Four Pillars will be further unpacked in the following chapters. Sometimes, deep reading requires the reader to discern elements that are not always explicitly stated. This became clear to me when reading Stein's 2022 essay, "The Marriage of Anima and Animus in the Mystery of Transformation," which I will review in Chapter 9. In my view, this essay is a masterpiece, as it updates Jung's psychology of the transference and his writings on the anima and animus, cutting through the political tensions surrounding gender identity and sexual orientation—issues Jung was oblivious to a century ago.

In closing, I want to note my appreciation for the metaphor of the backpack in the client dream Stein shared. As a former backpacker who undertook vision quests in my youth to the High Sierras—places like Desolation Wilderness in the Lake Tahoe region of California—and Mount Shasta with my wife during and after our analytic training, this image resonates deeply. What a marvelous dream to signal the client's termination.

By meaningful coincidence, my third analyst once told me that she, too, had gone on a backpacking and camping trip to Mount Shasta after she was certified! This felt affirming. So, in addition to dream work and active imagination, I would add to Stein's discussions on the fourth pillar the practices of poetic reverie and extended journeys into nature. I will revisit all Four Pillars later, as this chapter lays the structural foundation for what follows and, in my experience, evokes an active imagination image that holds meaning both inside and outside of analysis.

Notes

1 CW4, 339.
2 CW8, 162.
3 CW4, 318.
4 CW4, 323.
5 CW4, 391.
6 CW4, 404.

7   CW4, 398.
8   CW4, 311.
9   CW8, 162.
10 CW4, 361–362.
11 CW4, 320.
12 CW8, 253.
13 CW8, 250.
14 CW8, 253.
15 CW4, 341.
16 CW4, 344.
17 CW3, 68.
18 CW6, 168.
19 CW4, 357–358.
20 CW4, 397.
21 CW4, 402–403.
22 CW4, 317, 319.
23 CW4, 319.
24 CW4, 320.
25 CW4, 324.
26 CW4, 324.
27 CW4, 361–362.
28 CW4, 324.
29 CW4, 325.
30 CW4, 330.
31 CW4, 335.
32 Herrmann, S. "The Hypothesis of Psychic Antibodies: The Fight of the Kingsnake and the Rattlesnake." *Jung Journal: Culture & Psyche* 14, no. 4 (2020): 1–15.
33 CW4, 337.
34 CW4, 337.
35 Herrmann, S. *Spiritual Democracy: The Wisdom of Early American Visionaries for the Journey Forward.* Berkeley, CA: North Atlantic Press, 2014.
36 CW4, 372.
37 CW4, 415.
38 CW4, 338.
39 CW4, 420–425.
40 CW4, 361.
41 CW4, 368.
42 CW4, 375.
43 CW4, 381.

Chapter 3

Collected Writings Volume 1

Individuation

As Stein notes in his opening comments to Volume 1 of the *Collected Writings*, titled *Individuation*, from the time of Jung's break with Freud in 1913 until his death in 1961, the theme of individuation resounded like a leitmotif throughout all of his works, serving as the psychological bedrock and backbone.[1] In this first of the nine volumes of the *Collected Writings* now in print, Stein presents a distillation, synthesis, and aerial view of the Jungian tradition's most profound insights on individuation, which he defines as "the process of becoming the personality one innately is *potentially* from the beginning of life."[2] As previously mentioned, Stein advances Jung's theories into the 21st century, updating key hypotheses (e.g., the anima/animus and marriage archetypes) in line with contemporary cultural shifts, while also reevaluating Jung's libido theory in relation to the ego, persona, and Self. Stein postulates three major stages in the individuation process: (1) containment/nurturance, (2) adapting/adjusting, and (3) centering/integrating. However, his most significant theoretical contributions emerge in his discussion of midlife, old age, and what he refers to as the "Beyond." On this third stage, he writes:

> The therapist is not consciously or unconsciously related to as a nurturing mother or guiding father. Instead, the therapist is typically seen (truly or not) as a wisdom figure, as someone who has achieved individuality and wholeness and relates personally to the Self. This projection is cast upon the therapist because this is the unconscious content that the patient needs and must find a model for somewhere in the world at this stage of life. That job lands at the feet of the therapist.... A wisdom figure is someone who is seen to have arrived at an inner center and lives out of the resource found there.[3]

Stein's metaphor of the analyst as a model for the analysand—holding the projection of a wisdom figure and bearing the responsibility of carrying it—evokes the religious function of the psyche present in the analytic space. Stein has a great deal to say about this spiritual function in his works, particularly in relation to the figure of wisdom within the patient. For Jung, this inner wisdom figure took the form of Philemon, the wise old man with kingfisher wings and four keys, whom he saw flying across the sky in a dream. Jung engaged with Philemon by painting him and

DOI: 10.4324/9781003664024-4

conversing with him in his garden, much like one might relate to a guru in Indian traditions. Each individual has the potential to establish a personal connection with an archetype of wisdom. For some, this figure may manifest as Sophia, Athena, or Parvati. The analyst's task is to hold the idealizing transference for as long as necessary, allowing the analysand to awaken the archetype within. If this projection is successfully sustained in the transference, the patient may develop a religious attitude toward dream symbols containing wisdom, engaging with them through active imagination. Ideally, as a wisdom figure, the analyst serves as a representative of the deeper wisdom emerging from the unconscious.

Importantly, in Stein's view, individuation is not mere imitation. While some degree of imitation is expected—much like in any apprenticeship—true individuation moves beyond it. Beethoven, for instance, could not have become Beethoven without first imitating the styles of Bach, Handel, and Mozart. In the context of analysis, the analysand must transition toward an approximation of the "analyst within," integrating the imprint of wisdom into their own personality. As Stein writes: "It is precisely this inclination to imitate rather than individuate that led Jung to be so negative about the prospect of institutes and training programs set up in his name and teaching Analytical Psychology." Stein reports that Jung was "jaundiced" in his view of those who formed a "mere persona by identifying with the ideas and methods while neglecting the inner work demanded by the individuation imperative." Moreover, "Jung was clearly allergic to imitators."[4] Herein lies the central issue: excessive imitation fosters dependency at the expense of the Self.

One of the reasons Stein values the fourth pillar, active imagination, so highly is that he recognizes it as Jung's method for introducing the God function, which is so essential for awakening wisdom within the unconscious. As he explains:

> The main method for creating the transcendent function is active imagination, described by Jung in this text ["The Transcendent Function"] for the first time. What active imagination does is to raise the unconscious images and fantasies that operate in the background of the ego-complex to the level of consciousness. They can then be reflected in the mirror and observed. The images generated through active imagination are more coherent and useful for creating the transcendent function, Jung found, than are dreams.[5]

In *Transformation: Emergence of the Self*, Stein illustrates this concept with the case of an 80-year-old female analysand named Sarah. Sarah's active imagination produced an impressive array of imagery centered on various goddess figures, particularly Quan Yin, whom she experienced as a nurturing, compassionate divinity and her primary wisdom figure.[6] However, the archetype of wisdom can also be evoked much earlier in life, often through projection onto an older figure. In my case, the wise old woman was projected onto my first Jungian analyst when I was 20 and she was 79! She had trained in Zürich and had been analyzed by Jolande Jacobi. Stein's case study exemplifies patients' processes of projecting and introjecting wisdom figures at different life stages, particularly in old age. Thus, his work provides profound insight into the awakening of the Self within. In "Numinous Experience in the Alchemy of Individuation," he further explores this process, writing:

> Numinous experience creates a convincing link to the transcendent, and this may well lead to the feeling that character flaws like addictions or behavioral disorders are trivial by comparison with the grand visions recorded in the mystical state. The pathological symptom can be interpreted as an incitement to go on the spiritual quest, or even as a paradoxical doorway into transcendence, and this can denote meaning to the malady itself. Perhaps some degree of pathology is needed, in fact, in order for a person to feel strongly enough motivated to set out on the spiritual quest to begin with.[7]

Working with the Hephaistos Archetype within Analysis

The ultimate aim of Jungian psychoanalysis is to assist the analysand in awakening the Self and transforming consciousness, particularly in the second half of life. This process requires a lengthy analysis of the shadow, persona, and personal complexes, along with their archetypal cores. Among the numerous symbols embedded in the Western psyche is the archetypal image of Hephaistos. Stein's retelling of the Greek myth of Hephaistos, the crippled god associated with those in the "trades"— blacksmiths, metallurgists, architects, and other craftsmen—is particularly delightful.[8] In the myth, Hephaistos is cast down from Olympus by his mother, Hera, who, repulsed by his birth defects, rejects him with emotions of disgust and hatred. However, after being thrown into the Mediterranean, Hephaistos is rescued and raised in a cave by two loving nymphs, Thetis and Eurynome, who provide him with maternal care and affection. This myth illustrates the bipolarity of the mother complex and its archetypal core: on one side lies the abusive and rejecting mother and on the other side lies her compassionate and loving surrogates. I particularly appreciate Stein's section, "Hephaistos Within," in which he skillfully draws readers into the mythic dimension of his imagination, seemingly with the intention of addressing our own mother wounds. He asks: "What man among us does not share some of Hephaestus's wounds and dilemmas?" To illustrate this archetype in clinical practice, he recounts the case of a man he saw in analysis for several years—a patient named Jack—who suffered from a severe matriarchal wound and negative mother complex. From an early age, Jack had felt a deep urge to create art—an impulse shared by many young children. However, in Jack's case, this artistic inclination was not merely a childhood pastime, but a potential vocational calling. The therapeutic work required some age regression to help Jack reconnect with his childhood reveries. Stein recalls:

> The precise memories recovered that finally explained his inhibition around art supplies was that when he was around eight years old he drew a map of a certain

geographical territory in freehand. He held this up to his mother showing her proudly what he had done. Then the hammer fell. His mother, who was a school-teacher by training, sternly corrected him by showing that what he should have done was trace the territory of the map on a piece of transparent paper laid over the map in a book.[9]

This was no small matter. It was a profound injury to his creative calling—one leaving lasting mental and emotional scars—that he was called to work through in his analysis with Stein. As the analytic process unfolded, memories began to resurface revealing the child within—the boy who, even before the age of five, had known with certainty that his true passion was drawing and painting. Through Stein's careful exploration of his childhood complexes and his ability to penetrate to the archetypal core of Jack's vocation, a transformation began to take place. Gradually, Jack reclaimed his artistic expression and resumed painting.

In this essay, Stein offers a compassionate response to the Hephaistos wound in all readers who have suffered from similar psychological injuries. Jack's mother wound—embedded in his psyche during the latency state (around age eight)—functioned as an internal prohibition against his artistic freedom and individuation. As a result, his ability to consciously pursue his artistic calling in early adulthood and midlife was severely blocked. Over time, a neurosis developed around this wound, disconnecting Jack from his inner voice—his true calling to art. The shift in Stein's storytelling—from the myth of Hephaistos to a theoretical interlude and the case of Jack—reveals the Hermetic dimension of his analytic awareness: a wisdom figure at work within his psyche. This sagacious presence is evident in Stein's clinical observations, particularly in what he shares about the countertransference:

> From my experience as a psychotherapist and Jungian analyst, I can testify that this kind of Hephaistean wound is extremely common. In fact, it is highly unusual that I do not find such features in a person who comes for analysis. The image of Hephaistos, with his lameness, his story of rejection from the mother and father, his feelings of shame and at being found imperfect in some regard or another, vividly portrays features that reflect the experience of many people and their individuation process. In Hephaistos we see, initially, the marginalized creative rebel, angry and resentful.[10]

There is a certain element of pathos in patients when they become momentarily consumed by rage or anger toward their mother, their father, or an envious sibling who may have obstructed their creativity. Spite, fury, and outrage toward family members are significant emotions to work through in any psychotherapy process. If left unresolved, the ego can become overly assimilated by mother, father, or sibling complexes, leading to pathology—especially if the protest and sense of impotence persist without a creative breakthrough to initiate transformation. Regression to a developmental stage in which such a trauma occurred can serve a crucial purpose in analysis. This is where interpretation and amplification become particularly valuable. If a symbolic panacea can be found in the psyche, the patient may be guided toward an acceptance of their tragic fate, allowing for transformation. The result of this breakthrough can be extraordinary—especially when Sophia, the archetype of wisdom, steps in to nurture the patient's vocation with her healing balm of joy.

Among the four stages of anima development in a man or a woman, the highest is represented by wisdom. When properly engaged, it can serve as a powerful catalyst for transformation. However, this requires an analyst who is able to skillfully navigate the countertransference, working with myths and storytelling—an approach Stein models masterfully in his analysis of Greek myths such as Hephaistos, and his writings on the shamanic and maieutic processes underpinning individuation.

Jack had to confront his anger toward his mother before he could therapeutically resolve the obstruction to his creativity. In turn, Stein had to metabolize some of these affects within the shamanic countertransference and provide an antidote. The "medicine" in this case was Jack's freedom to create. Reading Stein's analysis of this Greek myth alongside the case study, I am struck by how skillfully he renders his clinical example as a potentially therapeutic experience for readers, as well. Through his storytelling, he invites us to participate in his generative powers as a culture healer. This area of analytic research—working with adults through the lens of myth, as Stein suggests—merits further exploration. Hephaistos wounds, he notes, are extremely common among those in analysis. Frequently, these wounds relate to an unlived vocation, and working through them can help to liberate the analysand from neurosis. As Stein states: "it is highly unusual that I do not find such features in a person who comes for analysis. The image of Hephaistos vividly portrays features that reflect the experience of many people and their individuation process."

Four Vectors of Analytic Space

Stein's books are bread for the soul and spirit, offering guidance for readers to reclaim their creativity and overcome obstacles to growth and wisdom. Another of Stein's patients, a man in his late 50s, suffered from a severe neurosis linked to a Hephaistean mother wound in the realm of vocalization and speech. In particular, he experienced a form of paralysis whenever he felt a need to speak up in his meetings at work. This impasse with diction stemmed from the harsh, critical tone of his mother's voice, which had been both destructive and abusive. Her vicious outbursts silenced him from an early age, and this inhibition persisted into adulthood. "Astonishingly," Stein remarks, "he was a poet by avocation."[11] A poet! What is a poet without a connection to their inner voice? The very essence of poetry is the ability to give voice to one's inner calling, just as the analyst-in-training must arouse their authentic voice and develop their own authentic analytical style.

Stein's discussion of the "transformative field" of Jungian psychotherapy is also of particular interest. What exactly is a transformative field, and how can one know when it has been activated in the analytical relationship? Stein suggests that all analytical relationships are potentially transformative. However, the transformational field is more than just a theoretical space—it is an intersubjective field in which *mutual* transformation occurs between the analyst and analysand. It exists in the liminal zone between public and private, professional and personal, internal and external. Stein describes it as a space that possesses "magical properties reflective of the reality of the psyche, in that synchronicity and parapsychological phenomena are often constellated in this space."

As a student of classical mythology, Stein refers to this as a "Hermetic space."[12] A transformative field, he teaches, contains two psychic worlds—two individuals, each with a full and complex life. This field has both an inner and an outer dimension, as each individual within remains deeply connected to the external world. Stein outlines four vectors within Jung's conceptualization of the analytic space, based on his deep reading of Jung's essay, "The Psychology of the Transference": (1) conscious-to-conscious between both partners, (2) conscious-to-unconscious within each individual, (3) unconscious-to-conscious between both partners, and (4) unconscious to unconscious between both partners. The fourth vector, writes Stein, represents a transmarginal space (i.e., a space of mutual engagement in which projective and introjective identifications occur unconsciously). He elaborates:

> Of the four vectors, the fourth is the most fascinating, for it is this one that represents the underground connection and implies the field of mutuality that defies the usual boundaries of time and space, inner and outer, mine and yours. Out of this ground emerges an individuation dynamic that will define the quality of the interactive field in each analytic relationship.[13]

This fourth vector touches upon what Jung, in his later formulations on the psyche, referred to as the "psychoid." As Stein explains:

> The psyche's boundaries bleed into liminal spaces in the psyche that show what Jung called 'transgressivity.' At the boundary of the psyche there is a psychoid area, psyche-like but not limited to subjectivity; it is both outside and inside the psyche.[14]

This transgressive area was activated in a formative experience in Stein's childhood, when, as we have seen, his father taught him to tell time on Resurrection Sunday in 1948. The moment was layered with meaning: between the clock's hands pointing to the hour and minute was Stein's anticipation of his father's Sunday sermon, which would celebrate the Resurrection—an event existing in eternal time. The memory of this moment remained with Stein and later shaped his understanding of transference after his move to Zürich. When I speak about the nuclear symbol in what follows, I will deliberately repeat the occurrence of this event in Stein's life because I'm talking about a source of great psychophysical energy that emanates from the Self, from the infra-red to ultra-violet spectrums of consciousness. Energies that are dormant in the psyche and are *evoked by figures of significance in the outside world are rendered symmetrical in dream-awareness.* For Stein, the most powerful of all of his nuclear symbols of childhood was the archetype of

Christ's transfiguration, which later shaped his theories. I call this energy-source nuclear because the analogy is with fire, explosive force, or great inner light; they are explosive symbols of psychic energy. The energy force in the Self is non-dual, positive and negative, instinctive and spiritual, loving and violent, aggressive and peaceful. My preference is to look at the nuclear symbol in an integral way, for its source of power is really the same in psyche and soma. It is a cosmic energy-source of all being, consciousness, and psychophysical energy. Nuclear energy is created in the universe and psyche simultaneously; once vocational symbols are tapped into, they can open a reader up to the inner and outer Cosmos. This is what happened to Stein on Easter morning at 4 or 5.

In the unconscious-to-unconscious connection between analytic partners lies the potential for discovery of a wisdom figure. For the young boy Murray, this figure was the Risen Christ who appeared to Mary Magdalene and the disciples. I can still recall my own childhood experience of Easter—my mother hiding eggs for us on Easter morning when I was four years old, my delight in finding them, and my joy in receiving a chocolate Easter Bunny in my basket. By re-entering this symbolic field—one in which a metamorphosis of consciousness may unfold between eternity and time—meaningful synchronicities may emerge, offering insights into the deep commonalities shared by the analytic pair.

In the case of the man who was a poet by vocation, Stein was able to access the developmental ground of wisdom within his psyche through his own mythopoetic reveries. His background in literature, having studied in the English Department at Yale, made this process intuitive. Speaking to the poet within his patient came naturally to him. The poet holds a primary place in the analytic field due to its archetypal lineage—from the shamanic healer to the modern analyst—within the history of human consciousness. Both Freud and Jung, in their own unique ways, identified with the poet Goethe during their formative years, just as Stein was captivated by the poetry of Rilke before writing *Transformation: Emergence of the Self.* (At one point, he even visited the poet's gravesite in Raron, Switzerland, as an act of homage.) Later in life, Stein became enchanted by Dante. In 2021, on the 700th anniversary of Dante's death, Stein delivered a lecture at a conference in Ravenna, Italy, interpreting the *Divine Comedy* as a story of individuation. The poet is the language-maker—the speaker of divine truth in both society and analysis. This truth is made particularly evident in Stein's 1989 meditations on the teachings of Jesus, particularly as recorded in the Gospel of John. Psychoanalysis has long been described as a "talking cure"—a term first coined by one of Freud's early female patients. Thus, Stein's discussion with Jack about his Hephaistean mother wound served as a form of amplification—precisely the intervention Jack needed to overcome his creative block.

The Story of the Rainmaker

In "The Ethics of Individuation, the Individuation of Ethics," Stein recounts the story of the Rainmaker, first told by Richard Wilhelm in a lecture at the Psychology

Club of Zürich in the 1920s. Jung later reported the story in one of his "Visions Seminars." As the story goes, there was a severe drought in the village where Wilhelm was living in Qingdao, on the North Coast of China. The land was parched, everything was drying up, and famine was spreading across the region. Catholics and Protestants alike prayed for rain, to no avail. Facing great hardship and suffering, the Chinese villagers sent for a Rainmaker.

An old wise man was summoned from another part of the country, arriving with an empty mind. Upon reaching the village, he retreated into a small house, where he remained in complete silence and solitude for three days. On the fourth day, dark clouds gathered and a great snowfall covered the village. When Wilhelm asked the Rainmaker how he had called in the rain and snow, the old man explained that he had arrived in Tao—in harmony and peace. However, upon entering the village, he was thrown off balance by the collective disharmony of its people. The atmosphere disturbed him, causing him to fall out of Tao. So, he secluded himself for three days, waiting in complete stillness until he could restore his inner equilibrium. Once he had realigned himself with the Tao, the natural order was restored and the rain and snow followed.

On the fourth day, the snowfall brought nourishment and relief to the village. Reflecting on this miracle worker, Stein writes:

> The idea behind Wilhelm's story and this aspect of Confucian philosophy is that the individual (especially the extraordinary individual) has the capacity to affect society and the cosmos (for good or ill) because the individual, society, and the cosmos are intimately connected parts of a single unified overarching reality.[15]

Stein then launches into a lengthy discussion on the subject of conscience, one of his key theoretical contributions to Jung's psychology of individuation.[16] He raises an essential question for the future of psychology—one that deeply preoccupied both Jung and Erich Neumann: How does the Self shape the development of personality as a whole? Stein extends this inquiry by exploring what he calls the "individuation of ethics," representing his own synthesis of Jungian thought. He suggests that, as consciousness evolves within a given cultural or historical field, moral values and laws also undergo transformation. Ethics, he argues, can individuate in an analogous way to individuals—provided the right conditions are met for such development.

For instance, Stein reflects on the issue of guidance by a "higher law," based on an archetypal image of justice aimed at restoring natural balance to the psyche. He cautions that integrating the complexes, persona, shadow, and anima/ animus during the individuation process may lead to the dangerous condition of possession by archetypal forces. In other words, one may become seized by an inner voice promising "a way forward" on a "higher road" toward some "higher destiny," claiming absolute certainty, as if it were a preordained calling—one to which the individual had been chosen. Yet being "chosen" can carry negative consequences, as Stein understands from his readings of the Old Testament. Most commonly, it may lead to scapegoating or persecution at the hands of envious or hostile rivals. At first, an individual undergoing individuation may feel as though they are being guided by a divine power—be that a god or a goddess—offering a solution to an otherwise insoluble conflict through the *vox Dei*, or voice of God. Jung explored this phenomenon in his 1932 essay "The Development of the Personality," and Neumann examined it in *Depth Psychology and a New Ethic*. However, as Stein points out, an elevated sense of individual conscience can lead to ego inflation unless it is relativized by justice, modesty, and higher wisdom. As he writes: "The elaboration of the archetype of Justice, an expression of the self, continues as human individuals and cultures evolve, change, and enter into new and unfamiliar areas."[17]

Guidance from the Self can lead an individual to feel special—singled out by fate for a higher destiny. Yet, such feelings of exceptionality can seduce the ego into a false sense of supremacy and an unquestioned certainty of success. The extraordinary personality, after all, remains an ordinary human being, complete with a shadow that is often overlooked. One might believe that a "higher power" is directing them—an irrational, numinous presence from above that appears to know the only path forward for the chosen individual. This sense of certainty can feel absolute. However, Stein warns that such conviction, arising from deep affective experiences, can induce inflation and create a mana-personality in the name of a "higher vision" or divine mandate.[18] This state can be intoxicating. By contrast, Stein describes what true transformation looks like in a non-inflated person—someone like the Chinese sage, the Rainmaker, who took no credit for the effects he produced. In his shamanistic withdrawal into solitude, the Rainmaker sought not personal power but a healing solution for others. His aim was:

> The integration of (not identification with) a transcendent archetypal image following upon separation from all prior distorting inflating identifications. It is by this means that the rainmaker brings himself into order and harmony with Tao. He separates (goes into a hut at the edge of the village), and there he connects inwardly to the archetype of unity and order (Tao), not however by identifying himself with it and getting inflated with the numinous power. He brings himself into alignment with the Tao.[19]

Being in proper alignment with the Tao means remaining connected to the veracity of the Self—not identifying with the archetype of the sage but maintaining a proper relationship to it. This requires active dialogue with the archetype and disidentification from external wisdom figures. Only through this balanced engagement can the sage within be activated—what Stein describes as the fifth stage of evolution in an individual's development beyond the mana-personality, representing the quintessence of individuation. That is, the problem of inflation is resolved by returning to a proper relation with the Tao. According to Stein, only by realigning with the Tao can the ethics of individuation and the individuation of ethics advance in tandem—both guided by the archetype of justice.

> When individuation passes beyond the boundaries of social and collective norms, the archetypal factor of conscience is constellated. This may, however, not make a mark on consciousness. If the voice of conscience (the so-called *vox Dei*) is repressed or simply remains unconscious for some defensive reason, it affects a person unconsciously — dreams, compulsive symptoms, etc.—and can also touch upon psychoid levels and thereby engender psychosomatic and other synchronistic phenomena.... In any event, restitution must be made in order for Justice to be satisfied, otherwise psychosomatic and other synchronistic phenomena remain strong candidates for bringing Justice to bear on the conscience of the guilty individual.[20]

Justice, as an expression of the Self, operates at the psychophysical level of experience. It can be activated through meditation, artistic creation, or active imagination—practices that often give rise to synchronicities, which help to restore order, harmony, and faith in the surrounding world. Like the Rainmaker, those undergoing individuation let things happen rather than attempting to impose control. By placing themselves in Tao, they provide a service, simply by "doing nothing."[21]

Notes on Betrayal and the Meaning of the Risen Christ

I now turn to Stein's masterful essay, "Betrayal: A Way to Wisdom?"—a commanding and deeply evocative work. Originally delivered as a lecture and later published in 2011, this essay carries a profound impact. Why is it so powerful? Because Stein addresses a fundamental psychological reality that is part and parcel of the human journey of individuation: an archetypal law that cannot be ignored, without consequence. After all, individuation is not merely a psychological process, but a transformative voyage that reaches into the very foundations of existence—into the psychoid realm of the Self, where psyche and world are unified.

Within this transpsychic domain—where dualities such as loyalty and betrayal, success and failure dissolve—betrayal emerges as an unavoidable necessity. Just as Jesus was betrayed by Judas, so too must we all experience betrayal in our own development. The crucifixion of the ego is a precondition for resurrection. This is the final stage of the Risen Christ, represented in the 20th image of the *Rosarium philosophorum*, which Stein explores in subsequent chapters.

In its deepest sense, betrayal is not merely an unfortunate occurrence, but an archetypal necessity embedded within individuation. Who among us has not been betrayed? The very ideals and attachments we most cherish are often destined to turn into ashes. Everything is vanity. In this vein, Stein warns of the perils of transference, precisely because of the trust we invest in transference objects:

"Transference objects, be they gods or humans, are dangerous to keep around." Betrayal manifests in families, social groups, personal analyses, and Jungian training programs alike. In fact, the Self may actively orchestrate betrayals and scapegoating to propel us toward greater consciousness. As Stein insightfully observes: "Power corrupts integrity, as does money, and so does desire in all of its forms and manifestations."[22]

We must all undertake a personal inventory of our shadows—our excessive pride and capacity for evil. This task is universal. According to Stein, the key when one feels betrayed is to forge a "new consciousness into a state of wisdom, through the treacherous doorway of betrayal." He further asserts: "If we take betrayal to its ultimate point—its archetypal apex—we will inevitably have to turn to the greatest betrayal of all, the betrayal of a blameless man by God Himself."[23] Stein's reflections on the biblical narrative of Jesus' betrayal are both unsettling and illuminating. His paradoxical model of the Self challenges us to accept betrayal when it occurs—not with resentment, but with a willingness to embrace our fate. Rather than resisting disloyalty, we are called to acknowledge its role in individuation. Evil, after all, is forever at our door: "This is the beginning of wisdom."[24] Stein also observes a curious omission in Jung's writings: "Jung rarely writes about the resurrection and the ascension. Easter is not his favorite holiday. Good Friday is more convincing."[25] But why?[26] For Stein, Easter holds greater significance.

In Stein's reading of the Bible, the Risen Christ represents the pivotal moment of transformation. Unlike Jung, who scarcely commented on the Resurrection—regarding it as a metaphysical event beyond the scope of empirical depth psychology—Stein consciously transgresses into transcendental territory. As a theologian, he steps over a boundary that Jung claimed to have crossed only once, in his disputation with Martin Buber. I have investigated this topic extensively due to my own vocational interests in both depth psychology and religion, which parallel Stein's.

At our San Francisco Jung Institute, for instance, one of the analysts who wrote most extensively on this neglected area of research was Joseph L. Henderson, whom Stein often cites. Long before encountering Stein's 1988 biblical lectures and his 2022 piece on the *Rosarium philosophorum*, I had read everything Henderson had written on the archetype of resurrection (though admittedly, his contributions on the subject were limited). Reading Stein's commentaries on the *Risen Christ* woodcut from Gerhard Dorn's 1555 manuscript were a revelatory experience.

In his biblical lectures, Stein writes: "The risen Christ is a key element of the symbol presented in all four Gospels. Especially in the fourth Gospel."[27] Moreover, in his meditation on the 20th image of the *Rosarium philosophorum*, he offers an insightful commentary on the final stage of the alchemical process of transformation and its relevance to Jungian analysis. Resurrection, he suggests, is an unconscious-to-unconscious communication that resists articulation in purely theoretical terms. It can only be experienced as a transcendental mystery within the analytic relationship in Jungian psychoanalysis. This dynamic corresponds to the fourth vector, which Stein describes as the gateway to the psychoid realm.

Henderson, in *The Wisdom of the Serpent*, also recognized the transformative nature of resurrection. In his final chapter, "Myths of Resurrection," he observed: "Finally, we have the mysterious power of the feminine in connection with resurrection."[28] Far from being purely metaphysical, the archetype of resurrection has played a significant role in the development of radical empiricism. The experience of William James exemplifies this: during his deep depression in 1870, the future father of American psychology found himself compulsively repeating the phrase "I am the resurrection and the life" to stave off his fear of insanity. Only after enduring this existential crisis was he granted a religious experience that transformed him. Such coincidences are far from trivial or accidental.

Henderson, whose book opens with a quote by James, did not initially consider this aspect of resurrection when the book was first published in 1963. However, in the book's appendix, he reflected: "Poets more than prose writers express clearly and poignantly the mythological theme of death and its archetypal corollary, rebirth, or of the quest for the certainty of an after-life, namely, resurrection."[29]

Among 19th-century American poets who wrote about resurrection, none surpasses Emily Dickinson in depth and visionary scope.[30] Her understanding of the archetype aligns more with the tribal wisdom of the earth's primal peoples, echoing the shamanic origins of culture and the Great Mother religions. Stein, in his *Collected Writings*, expands upon the significance of this archetype for the postmodern era. While Henderson identified a fundamental tension with the resurrection motif, stating, "His resurrection occurs once and for all,"[31] Stein demonstrates that Christ's rising from the dead holds universal significance—particularly for analysands with the psychological aptitude to experience resurrection during the final stages of Jungian analysis.

Butterfly Tales

No post-Jungian writing on synchronicity has, to my mind, spoken more succinctly than Stein in his "Butterfly Tales" on the theme of spiritual transcendence, or the transfiguration of the soul after death through resurrection. Stein's tales, which explore the intersection of eternity and time, have a mysteriously transformative effect on our typical daylight consciousness within Jungian psychoanalysis. They are spun in the dim light of lunar conscience. Analytic writing does not always compel us to consider questions of life after death, yet Stein does—just as Jung did in the late chapters of *Memories, Dreams, Reflections*. In "Moments of Meaning: Synchronicity and Individuation," originally published in 2012, Stein recounts a butterfly tale that is rich in suspense and profound in both psychological and metaphysical significance. The narrative unfolds like a novel of destiny, portraying a triumph over life's inevitable encounters with death, despair, and existential grief, including the sorrow of losing loved ones. This particular tale follows his account of an acausal experience at Saint Peter's Square in 1998, following the publication of *Transformation: Emergence of the Self*. I will explore this butterfly encounter in Chapter 7.

However, in another butterfly story, Stein describes that his wife, Jan (confirming Henderson's original intuition regarding the "mysterious power of the feminine in connection with resurrection") spotted not just one, but a "million butterflies" on a tree outside their bedroom window. This occurred not long after the sudden passing of their dear friend, the former analyst Kaspar Kiepenhauer. "It must be Kaspar," Stein whispered to Jan over the telephone after she called to tell him about the unexpected swarm. He continued: "I just got word that he died last night. You remember that he stayed in that bedroom for a week when he was attending the Congress in Chicago. He must have wanted to give us a splendid farewell." Several months later, Stein and his wife met Kaspar's widow at the Weinplatz in Zürich, just in front of their apartment—the very place where they had last seen Kaspar before he passed over into the beyond. As the three of them stood there, reminiscing, a small white butterfly stubbornly circled their heads, darting from one person to the next, as if delivering a message.[32]

Was Kasper somehow behind these butterflies? Many unanswered questions linger for readers to ponder. This tale also reveals something essential about Stein's personality and vocation—he is unafraid to express his belief in the afterlife. For Stein, a man of faith, belief in life after death is not merely intellectual—it is experientially *known*: Resurrection is not just a theological concept but a reality he perceives in both time and the eternal beyond. Synchronicities surrounding death serve as personal verification of his empirical hypothesis—one he both posits and trusts. To him, the Risen Christ is not a mere possibility but a proven reality, validated through repeated moments of transcendence and meaning. He does not require statistical verification from the miracles of Catholic saints to affirm his spiritual experiences, nor does he strive to emulate them. Rather, one senses that Stein exists on a different plane of awareness, with his feet planted firmly on his own ground. He is not a mere spinner of yarns, but a dedicated researcher of synchronicity, a skilled storyteller, and a builder of theory.

On the Paradox of Failure and Success

I now turn to Stein's lecture: "On the Role of Failure in the Individuation Process." Because of the therapeutic effect of alleviating deeply ingrained "failure complexes," this lecture is pivotal. We all suffer from them—no one is exempt from the experience of failure.

Reading two versions of this essay side by side—the first in *Outside Inside and All Around: And Other Essays in Jungian Psychology*, and the second in Volume 1 of the *Collected Writings*—I gained a deeper appreciation for the analyst-editor at work in the Oberland. Stein uses himself as an example, teaching through a humble act of self-examination, offering not just insight, but healing. This self-reflective approach marks the Hermetic attitude of the analyst—one who invites us into liminal space to engage with life's greatest struggle: the tension of opposites. Why does failure so often emerge at crucial moments in our lives, sometimes at the very height of what our egos perceive as success? And why is failure central to Jungian psychoanalysis?

Of the two versions of this essay, I prefer the one published in Volume 1 of the *Collected Writings*, because it has been edited with greater insight and infused with humor and a sense of detachment. Here, Stein embodies the sage who can laugh at himself, modeling self-observation of both personal and cultural complexes with objectivity, without being emotionally ensnared by them or consumed by a fear of failure. Is this not precisely what we, as analysts, strive to model for our patients—more detachment and objective cognition? This is the analytic attitude of humility par excellence when exploring a theme as vital as this. Stein writes:

> I have to confess that I have a difficult time getting into this Odyssey theme, "the crucible of failure." Partly this was due to a resistance I felt to this painful subject, perhaps it is even due to a "failure complex." I examined myself and of course found that this is partly true. It was also due to the fear of failing at such an important topic for psychology and psychotherapy, a fear of speaking only banalities and half-baked superficialities that take up a generously allotted time but do not bring much new insight.... Who wants to fail on the subject of failure? Not a pleasant prospect. But if one should succeed at talking about failure, would this not be a failure of another kind? Isn't it a paradox to succeed at speaking about failure and feel it's been a success?[33]

In the second version of this essay, Stein reflects on the "faltering steps" he took in the first. He suggests that the paradox and "equilibrium between the opposites success-and-failure in the individuation process" had, by the second version, expanded into a broader range of perception, accompanied by new insights that, as he puts it, "fell" into his "lap" synchronistically.[34] While he does not specify these synchronicities, one may have been his deepened engagement with the Italian poet Dante Alighieri, author of the *Divine Comedy*.

Stein's lifelong Christian calling emerges more fully in the second version, where his faith shines through with greater clarity, illuminating what he perceives as the hidden resolution of failure. In the first version, he appears less certain that the unconscious provides symbols offering guidance from within, helping to unlock life's most inscrutable mysteries. However, in the revised version, he adds: "Maybe this is the Christian element in my mind, which says that we cannot save ourselves, that we need another, grace from above, from outside."[35]

By "outside," Stein is referring to the grace of synchronicity. "Jung constructed a cosmology based on acausal orderedness," he writes. "This is as close as Jung would come to metaphysics."[36] I want to linger here on the edits Stein made for the second edition. In his later reflections, the cross is no longer a symbol of the transformation of failure into triumph within the Jesus parable, but a parabolic "crucible on which failure was transformed into triumph, a potent symbol of transformation."[37] This shift signifies that transformation is no longer the exclusive domain of individuals undergoing individuation in analysis. Rather, the cross serves as a crucible for the average reader, through which feelings or judgments of failure may be "transformed into a critical moment, even the pivot point, in the narrative of the self's incarnation in a person's life, i.e. individuation."[38] Here, we find evidence of Stein actively engaging in his own individuation of ethics, in service to not only the Jungian community but also the broader world.

Stein is potentially addressing multitudes here. Moreover, in the revised version, he introduces an added dimension to his reflections, noting that, when one is on their "knees," they may reflect more deeply on their psychic situation. He writes incisively: "Failure brings you to your knees, and when you are on your knees, you pray. The greater the failure the deeper the prayer."[39] A catastrophic event can bring anyone to their knees in prayer, as this act is archetypal, deeply embedded in the collective psyche across religious traditions and traceable to the earliest shamans. Recognizing that transformation follows certain "laws"—one of which is the inevitability of defeat or failure—is humbling, allowing for a shift in perspective.[40]

Notably, Stein references prayer a total of five times in the revised text. Why? What had changed in his awareness? In this later version, he appears to be reflecting on our collective failure as a species. Yet, he suggests that we may still influence the collective through publications, conferences, and media appearances. If we are humble enough, he proposes, "we may fall collectively to our knees and begin to pray."[41] This raises an intriguing question: What would a collective Jungian prayer look like?

Stein leaves us with a hopeful vision, though without the false assurance that we can reverse our collective fate. I find it refreshing to hear him incorporating prayer into his definition of active imagination, particularly given Jung's limited engagement with the concept. Nevertheless, Stein suggests that Jung's work on active imagination and synchronicity was, in essence, his own way of praying—scientifically.

Organizations and Individuation

In "Individuation in Organizational Life," which I referenced earlier in Chapter 1, Stein examines the fundamental tension between success and failure as intrinsic to transformation and transfiguration. He writes in no uncertain terms: "Organizations can be murder. Is there anyone who has not been badly mauled by one?" The essay instructs that our engagement with organizations begins with our families of origin. In fact, Stein insists that "our earliest infant experiences with mother is organizational life, a dyad. And families, we know, can be murder."[42] To navigate the pressures of collective life without losing our individual vision, Stein emphasizes the importance of remaining attuned to the "unique fingerprint, the still, small voice of a personal, nonrational conscience." Resisting the homogenizing force of organizational structures "requires a great effort of consciousness. And it is precisely this kernel of irreducible individuality that organizations often seek to murder."[43]

Rather than adopting a detached stance toward organizations, Stein argues that we should intensify our engagement with them. The more deeply we interact with the workplace, the more potential it holds for individuation. While Jung was understandably pessimistic about organizations, Stein suggests that contemporary individuals are engaged in an evolving process—one in which commitment to an organization can honor the Self. The discovery of a personal myth of wholeness, whether through family relationships, marriage, or workplace affairs, emerges through intentional acts of consciousness that ignite the drive toward individuation.

> Through an intense engagement with organizational life, one may find the opportunity to become twice-born, and the organization may also grow and change. The reward for this is what the alchemists called "philosophical gold," which Jung speaks of as the self. It is the *medicina catholica,* the magical transformer of lead into gold, the access to creative life.[44]

The transformative element here is what Jung termed a "symbolic attitude," or, as Stein describes it, a

> second birth if you will, in which the concrete tasks of life are taken up again but now in a more conscious way.... Without an archetypal connection, work is sheer labor. The archetypal connection transforms labor into meaningful work. One's role in organizational life similarly must be infused with archetypal energy in order to carry personal value and meaning.

He continues:

> The Protestant reformation affirmed the possibility of a vocation for all persons no matter what particular activity or work they engaged in. Vocation was not reserved only for the religious. What this said, psychologically, is that the archetypes are connected to many human activities besides the officially sacramental ones. Pluralism of vocation, rather than exclusivity and elitism, was at the center of the Protestant theological perception. This means that all human activities and roles are potentially meaningful if there is an archetypal connection, and all can be rendered symbolic for the performer of them if consciousness is brought to bear. [45]

As we have seen, 1994 was the year in which Stein experienced his spiritual vision of Christ. Around this time, he wrote: "It is helpful to practice some private daily rituals and to keep at hand some symbolic objects. Keeping a journal of dreams, reading a Scripture, praying, meditating, practicing active imagination are essential and generally available practices."[46] This quote was originally published in 1990 in *Psychological Perspectives*, though I first encountered it in Stein's fascinating 1995 book, *Psyche at Work: Workplace Applications of Jungian Analytical Psycho*logy. The essay was later republished under a different title in *Practicing Wholeness* (1996). In *Psyche and Work,* it appeared as "Organizational Life as Spiritual Practice," but in Volume 1 of the *Collective Writings*, it bears the title "Individuation in Organizational Life." Clearly, this essay holds great significance for Stein, as it underwent four consecutive iterations, with only minor revisions. Why so many reprintings?

In his latest version, "Individuation in Organizational Life," Stein explores the vital role played by the scapegoat in institutional healing. He writes, shockingly:

> The scapegoat in a group is usually regarded, from a detached distance, as an unfortunate and innocent victim of group process. This viewpoint is accurate precisely because the role has not been consciously adopted and symbolically understood. We do not yet fully understand the role of the scapegoat in organizational life, but it does seem to be the case that the scapegoat makes it possible for the rest of the group to feel freed from shadow contamination. The scapegoat carries shadow projections and, if successful in containing them, manages to dispose of them, temporarily at least. The scapegoat performs a cleansing function. To take on this role consciously and to do it well is perhaps the hardest part anyone can play in organizational life. It is a therapist function. It should be reserved for the wisest and most spiritually developed, though of course it is not... The scapegoat functions as a sort of lightning rod, and this person must be extremely tough, spiritually, to take the hits.[47]

Stein's insights in this work likely stem from both his theological education and his active imagination of Christ as the link between time and eternity. Could it have been this perspective that expanded his vision, allowing him to write in such a way that resonates beyond Jungian audiences? Perhaps he sees himself as a therapist for not only individuals, but also organizations. In psychological terms, this role aligns with that of the organizational consultant who helps institutions navigate transformation and complexity. Stein's paradoxical wisdom may offer organizations a new lens through which to view the role of the scapegoat as a sacred vocation. Addressing the Jesus connection, he writes:

> In our collective cultural history, the scapegoat archetype was played out consciously and with full symbolic understanding by Jesus Christ. The symbol of the cross is the lightning rod that takes full charge of the clash between the opposites good and evil. This symbol became the moral center of Western consciousness for two thousand years.[48]

Stein's education at Yale Divinity School trained him in the method of constructive theological criticism, which he has used throughout his career to build upon theological concepts, infusing them with his own wisdom to enrich theoretical discourse. However, in his many unique contributions to analytical psychology and Christianity, he has remained largely supportive of Jung. Rather than critiquing, he has built a bridge between depth psychology and religion, fostering dialogue between these disciplines.

When Stein, as a theologian, finds himself at odds with Jung on certain points, he occasionally corrects Jung's errors with measured restraint, never applying excessive force. His criticisms remain tempered by his deep admiration for Jung— admiration that, at times, approaches devotion of the kind accorded to spiritual teachers in India. Yet, while Jung is almost a guru to Stein, he never fully assumes that role. Stein may see Jung as a kind of missionary to Asia, South America, or Mexico, but he never projects the archetype of the messiah onto him. For example, when Jung describes Jesus as a so-called "perfect man" or as someone unconscious of his shadow side, Stein subtly but assuredly corrects this perspective. His writing conveys a sense of grace and confidence, never diminishing his gratitude to Jung for having led him to a deeper understanding of the Self. Still, for Stein, his first master is always Jesus, not Jung.

Who among us has not been moved by Jung's brilliance and ability to connect with his readers? His personality exerts a compelling influence. Similarly, Stein appeals to those seeking greater spiritual direction. He writes: "As told by scriptural texts, Jesus consciously accepted the role of suffering servant and scapegoat, carrying the sins of the world as projected upon him willingly as a mission from the Father."[49] It seems to me that Jesus holds a more central place in Stein's heart than Jung. This brings to mind something I recently heard from a bright, 79-year-old Catholic analysand. In an active imagination, a Native American chief asked this man where he placed his ultimate trust. When the analysand hesitated, the chief answered provocatively: "Jungian psychology has been helpful, but on your deathbed, who will be present: Jung or Jesus Christ?" For this lifelong Franciscan, the answer was clear. Yet for Stein, perhaps it is not so simple. Might he, in the end, find both Jesus and Jung beside him? Only the butterflies will tell.

Stein does not share Jung's occasional view that Jesus was unconscious of his shadow—such as when Jesus commanded Satan to "get behind me." On the contrary, Stein argues that the Gospels depict Jesus as fully aware of his fate, embracing betrayal, shame, and temporal failure as essential elements of his divine mission. For Stein, Jesus accepted his suffering not out of ignorance, but with profound intentionality—recognizing it as his destiny, his Father's will, and the path to a redeemed humanity. In Stein's view, Jesus not only foresaw Judas's betrayal but welcomed it with full consciousness, knowing it was part of the pattern leading to the cross. He did not repress or deny his shadow, but accepted it and transfigured suffering into love, compassion, healing, and resurrected Light. The cross, in this framework, functioned as the ultimate lightning rod, absorbing and transforming evil.

Astonishingly, Stein extends this idea beyond theology, encouraging individuals in organizational settings to consciously accept the role of scapegoat to bring greater awareness and transformation into the world:

> Individuals can, to some extent, bring this level of consciousness into their organizations, if they have reached it themselves. If they do, they may begin to play the role of the scapegoat, the bringer of new consciousness, through the conflict they provoke in the group. They may also find themselves playing the archetypal role of the wise old man or woman, who can see further than one generation and can look intuitively into the ageless depths.[50]

A pluralism of vocations has long been a hallmark of American intellectual life, as evidenced by the Puritans, Emerson, Whitman,[51] and James. Stein, writing in this tradition, speaks not only as a Swiss thinker but also as an American citizen. In "Helping Tradition to Individuate," he explores Jung's vision of the greenish-gold Christ on the cross at the foot of his bed in 1939, rendering it both translucent and metaphorically significant. For Jung, this was a deeply personal experience of the God within. Stein describes this moment as a revelation from the Self, remarking: "This vision was the response of the unconscious to Jung's shamanistic incubation of the problems of Christianity."[52]

As we have seen, Stein regards Jung as a shaman. Jung himself resisted this identification, yet during moments of transcendence, the healing energies of the shamanic archetype emerged unmistakably in his work. For those attuned to such manifestations, Jung's work radiates a healing light, akin to the energies embodied by the early Hebrew prophets. This theme first appeared in Stein's doctoral dissertation at the University of Chicago and reappears here, where he further refines and elevates his hypothesis on three forms of countertransference attitudes.

Ultimately, the Self calls each of us to individuate in our own unique way. The deepest vocation arises from within—from the sage, the analyst, or the shaman at the core of our being.

Individuation and the National Psyche

In "Individuation and the Politics of Nations," Stein poses two critical questions: (1) "Can the principle of individuation also be applied usefully to the scene of international politics and relations?" and (2) "Can nations and whole cultural communities also individuate?" These inquiries lead to a broader discussion of how Jungian analysts might contribute to the integration and wholeness of nations and societies. Here, Stein aligns himself with colleagues who have extended the concept of individuation into the realm of global politics, including the architects of cultural complex theory—analysts Samuel Kimbles, Thomas Singer, John Beebe, and Andrew Samuels.

In this seminal essay, Stein reflects on the tensions between North and South America, situating them within a larger meditation on humanity's destructive impact on the planet. He raises a pressing concern: the irreversible damage inflicted on the Earth. Yet, his vision remains cautiously optimistic: "Science is the key to gaining awareness to what is happening to the earth, and technology, which is the practical application of science, can be directed toward creating solutions rather than only furthering crises."[53] For Stein, vocation serves as a vehicle for creative solutions. Rather than viewing science and technology as inherently problematic or detrimental to progress, he expresses confidence in humanity's collective capacity to engage in the necessary shadow work required to counteract global crises. Through such efforts, he believes it is possible to mitigate both the environmental catastrophe and the destructive, evil forces within human nature, itself.

Bridging East and West

Stein's paper "Where East Meets West: In the House of Individuation," presented at the 20th Congress of the International Association for Analytical Psychology in Kyoto, Japan, was delivered in 2016 in memory of Hayao Kawai. It was later published as Chapter 12 in *Inside Outside and All Around*, though the edited version in Volume 1 of the *Collected Writings* appears, in my view, slightly more refined. In this essay, Stein integrates a vast body of knowledge into a vector of post-Jungian visioning, offering a deep and broad understanding of the aims of individuation in Jungian psychoanalysis.

Stein demonstrates how Eastern and Western spiritual traditions might be harmonized within the "house of individuation," fostering unity rather than division. Advancing the bridge-building efforts initiated by Jung and Richard Wilhelm, he argues that, once their differences and similarities are thoughtfully examined—through both wisdom and an open-hearted pursuit of inner peace—these traditions can be woven together in a meaningful way. Stein observes: "It would seem from all of this that East and West cannot very well meet on the ground of similarity in psychological development at the level of ego and persona."[54] But what about at the level of the Self? Stein suggests that Jung's experience of *unus mundus* in 1928, at the age of 53, was evidence of his arrival at a state of consciousness paralleling key experiences in Eastern traditions—*atman* in Vedanta,[55] the mandala in Tibetan Buddhism,[56] or the egoless awareness of "nothingness," in Zen.[57] What, then, is the practical consequence of reaching such a state? As Stein asks: "What difference in real life does it make to have reached this difficult summit of individuation?" This question was one that Jung himself explored in his "Foreword" to D. T. Suzuki's *Introduction to Zen Buddhism*.

Stein suggests that Jungians must continue the research Jung began, mapping the psyche's structure and inner dynamics through deep exploration of the unconscious. He raises the possibility of fundamental typological differences between Eastern and Western orientations, hypothesizing that the East may be more "introverted" and "sensate and intuitive," while the West appears more "extroverted" and "thinking and feeling."[58] However, he presents these distinctions not as definite claims but as hypotheses for future generations of Jungians to investigate, as the field widens on an international scale. Of particular theoretical interest is Stein's discussion of Jung's views on metaphysics. T. Izutzu, in his *Toward a Philosophy of Zen Buddhism*, describes an ultimate state of consciousness as "one's experiencing with his total being the epistemological-metaphysical state of Nothingness."[59] Stein emphasizes that this non-dual state is not limited to the Zendo—it is also attainable in analysis.

Anyone familiar with Jung's *Collected Works* knows that Jung was wary of the word "metaphysics." Yet, paradoxically, he wrote extensively about "nothingness." While empirical psychology and the transcendent function may attempt to exclude metaphysical considerations, the empirical method inevitably borders on metaphysics and cannot dismiss it entirely. My preference aligns with Stein's: rather than rejecting metaphysics altogether, he welcomes it as an essential dimension of psychological inquiry. In his characteristic style, he complements and extends Jung's work, identifying textual evidence that resolves some of Jung's more perplexing contradictions. While Jung occasionally drew a seemingly arbitrary boundary between psychology and religion, Stein effortlessly bridges the gap. A master of paradox himself, he does not challenge Jung's emphasis on extraordinary historical figures as the "great ones" of humanity, but makes Jungian psychology more democratically accessible to the multitudes, when writing about *satori*:

> Yet it is also an experience of wholeness that is shared across cultures, East and West, and today may not be limited to an elite class of the "great ones," thanks to Jungian analysis among other things. Individuation, as it advances, moves toward a place of possible convergence among all world cultures, including East and West, and surely this makes an important difference to the individuals experiencing it and to the surrounding world. It contributes to the formation of a possible world culture for the future, which would be based on an understanding of the individuation process.... In the house of individuation, East and West can sit down and bear witness to a common experience of the psyche, no matter how great the cultural differences may be. This is where East and West can meet.[60]

One of the reasons I view Stein as more democratically spiritual than Jung is the breadth of his experiences, including his time at the International School of Analytical Psychology Zurich (ISAPZURICH). His exposure to a diverse, global community has provided him with a broad empirical base for research—one that extends beyond that of Jung, whose patients were predominantly European or American. In this and other ways, I see Stein advancing beyond Jung.

For instance, in "Psychological Individuation and Spiritual Enlightenment," a lecture given in Xi'an, China in the spring of 2018, Stein examines the parallels between Jungian psychology and Zen Buddhism (*Chan* in Chinese), particularly in relation to enlightenment (*satori* in Japanese, *wu* in Chinese) and *samadhi*. The shared point of contact between Eastern and Western traditions is, he explains, "the transformation of consciousness" as "a point of contact between the two disciplines, a goal shared by both developmental pathways, by Eastern traditions of meditation and by Western analytical psychology, as different as their methods for attaining this may be."[61] I appreciate Stein's deep ecumenism here.

In the final essay of Volume 1 of the *Collected Writings*, Stein analyzes the 10 "Ox-Herding" pictures in Zen Buddhism, using them as a point of comparison between Eastern and Western spiritual paths. In doing so, he aligns the final stages of individuation with what he elsewhere refers to as the Risen Christ. This illuminating discussion is one I highly recommend to readers seeking to understand Stein's integration of Eastern and Western traditions.

Drawing on Erich Neumann's writings, Stein explores what he calls "the deepest roots of the human psyche"—aspects of the unconscious that can be "exposed to consciousness." He argues that making "the archetypal field that underlies all human consciousness" more consciously accessible is a shared goal of both Zen practice and Jungian analysis. The ultimate aim is to reach a state in which "gaining self-knowledge through separation from all identifications and entanglements with unconscious contents (cleansing the doors of perception) and bearing witness to the archetypal powers that underlie individual and cultural psychologies" becomes possible. However, as Stein acknowledges, such profound transcendence is "seldom reached" within Jungian analysis.[62]

Conclusion

Stein concludes Volume 1 by reaffirming that individuation is an ongoing, lifelong process.[63] His final essay underscores that liberation from projections is not a matter of achieving perfection, but rather an ideal of completeness, as integration of the shadow and the confrontation with evil are never-ending tasks. The state of consciousness Stein explores rank among the most significant possibilities within his theoretical framework and the practice of Jungian psychoanalysis. Moreover, they may signal the emergence of a shared communal goal that aligns with and integrates the Four Pillars of Jungian psychoanalysis.

Notes

1 CW1, 1.
2 CW1, 5.
3 CW1, 25.
4 CW1, 36.
5 CW1, 47, 48.
6 CW1, 49.
7 CW1, 52.
8 CW2, "Hephaistos: A Mythic Image for the Instinct of Creativity."
9 CW1, 121.
10 CW1, 123.
11 CW1, 125.
12 CW1, "Finding a Space for Individuation."
13 CW1, 144.
14 CW1, 143.
15 CW1, 150.
16 CW7, "Conscience."
17 CW1, 163.
18 CW1, 156–157.
19 CW1, 159.
20 CW1, 161.
21 CW1, 162, 163.
22 CW1, 180.
23 CW1, 181.
24 CW1, 191.

25 CW1, 186.
26 On February 19, 1954, Jung responded to a question posed by members of a seminar in Los Angeles, led by Dr. James Kirsch, on his book *Aion*. Several participants noted the absence of commentary in Jung's writings on the idea of the Resurrection—the ultimate event in the Christ narrative. In response, Kirsch wrote to Jung, prompting him to compose the piece "On Resurrection." In this brief work, Jung acknowledges that the historical validity of the Resurrection is doubtful, and he suggests that those who purportedly witnessed Christ's transfiguration may have been participating in a parapsychological phenomenon. Whether Jung fully grasped the significance of this for analytical theory and practice remains debatable. One might question why he did not interpret the event with the depth that Stein later would. Nevertheless, Jung asserted that "The better we understand the archetype, the more we participate in its life and the more we realize its eternity or timelessness.... The realization of the self also means a re-establishment of Man as the microcosm, i.e., man's cosmic relatedness. Such realizations are frequently accompanied by synchronistic events. (The prophetic experience of vocation belongs to this category.) ... Resurrection as a psychic event is certainly not concrete, it is just a psychic experience" (Jung, *Collected Works* 18, 1572–1574).
27 CW6, 164.
28 Henderson, J. and M. Oakes. *The Wisdom of the Serpent: The Myths of Death, Rebirth, and Resurrection*. Princeton, NJ: Princeton University Press, 1963, 203.
29 Henderson and Oakes, 235.
30 Herrmann, S. *Emily Dickinson: A Medicine Woman for Our Times*. Cheyenne, WY: Fisher King Press, 2018.
31 Jung, C.G. *Man and His Symbols*. Garden City, NY: Doubleday, 1964, 108.
32 CW1, 202.
33 CW1, 207.
34 CW1, 209.
35 CW1, 208.
36 CW6, 178.
37 CW1, 211.
38 CW1, 211.
39 CW1, 218.
40 CW1, 221.
41 CW1, 223.
42 CW1, 225.
43 CW1, 226.
44 CW1, 232, 233.
45 CW1, 240, 241.
46 CW1, 244.
47 CW1, 244.
48 CW1, 242.
49 CW1, 242.
50 CW1, 244.
51 Herrmann, S. *Walt Whitman: Shamanism, Spiritual Democracy, and the World Soul*. Durham, NC: Eloquent Books, 2010.
52 CW1, 261.
53 CW1, 275.
54 CW1, 287.
55 Herrmann, *Swami Vivekananda, and C.G. Jung: Yoga in the West*.
56 CW1, 292.

57 CW1, 298.
58 CW1, 280.
59 CW1, 298.
60 CW1, 300, 302.
61 CW1, 303, 304.
62 CW1, 315.
63 CW1, 321.

Chapter 4

Collected Writings Volume 3

Transformation[1]

Although many important books have emerged in the field of analytical psychology over the past six decades since Jung's death, few have spoken more directly to the needs of the soul than Stein's *Transformation: Emergence of the Self*. In this truly inspired work, Stein explores the nature of transformation, particularly as it unfolds during periods of deep structural change. His central thesis is that:

> transformation leads people to become more deeply and completely who they are essentially. Transformation is realization of potential. The transforming person is someone in whom the inherent self-imago emerges to the greatest possible extent that is possible in that individual's life. What that emergent self-imago is cannot be known until the process has reached its culmination.[2]

Since first encountering this passage in 1997, I have regarded it as one of the most lucid articulations of Jung's theory of transformation, as presented in *Wandlüngen und Symbole der Libido*. In just a few sentences, Stein encapsulates the essence of transformation as a process not limited to Jungians, but accessible to individuals in virtually all vocations. However, it remains a rare phenomenon, requiring disciplined habits and a strong and resilient ego. Notably, Stein's "Epilogue" to *Transformation: Emergence of the Self* was omitted from the *Collected Writings*.

To fully appreciate Stein's contribution to psychoanalytical thought on this theme, it is essential to examine the meaning of transformation within a Jungian framework—one that subsumes both developmental and archetypal perspectives. According to Stein, metamorphosis, or transformation, involves a passing over (*meta-*, *trans-*) from one form (*morph-*, *forma*) into another.[3] In the context of midlife and beyond, what undergoes this transition—from a state of unconsciousness into expanded consciousness—is the archetype of the Self: the innate image of wholeness within the psyche. This process is not merely theoretical, but an experience in which we partake, to greater or lesser degrees, through psychological and spiritual practice.

In this artfully argued *tour de force*, Stein extends Jung's theory of the Self by examining five case studies of individuals in Western culture who were seized by the archetype of transformation: Rainer Maria Rilke, William Mellon, Rembrandt,

DOI: 10.4324/9781003664024-5

Pablo Picasso, and Jung. Each of these figures underwent a spiritualization process that left an indelible mark on their lives and work. My comments here serve only as a brief review of this work. However, to fully grasp the depth of Stein's analysis, readers would benefit from reading the entire first half (153 pages) of Volume 3 of the *Collected Writings*.

Building on Jung's foundational idea that human life consists of two primary "developmental stages"—the first and second halves of life[4]—Stein postulates that there are actually *four* significant "eras" of transformation: (1) childhood and adolescence, (2) adulthood and midlife, (3) old age, and (4) death.[5] In line with his post-Jungian contemporaries, Stein acknowledges that important psychological developments take place during infancy and childhood. However, he argues that the most profound and spiritually significant transformations occur during adulthood, midlife, and beyond.[6] Accordingly, it is these later life stages that he explores in his attempt to uncover the deeper mysteries of human existence.

While Stein's primary focus is on midlife and old age, he does not suggest that archetypal images are absent from or insignificant in early life. On the contrary, he argues that such images may profoundly influence psychic structures in youth,[7] as evidenced by the formative experiences of Rilke and Jung. However, what he is most interested in exploring is "what actually happens to people inwardly when childhood, with its well-known 'stages' and its scars and complex formations, is completely outgrown, not only chronologically but psychologically."[8] He contends that such significant transformations of consciousness typically occur in midlife (early 30s to early 50s),[9] rather than childhood, adolescence, or early adulthood. Nonetheless, he acknowledges that childhood lays an "imaginal disc" on the fundamental structures of affect and feeling, which colors an individual's *oeuvre* and personal development.

Since my initial review of this book in 1998, I have found further confirmation of Stein's hypothesis in the case of a latency-age girl whose drawings beautifully illustrated this imaginal disc. The term "imaginal disc" (which Stein adopts from Adolf Portmann) must be understood, at least in part, within a biological context. To elucidate the process of transformation that is guided by this imaginal disc, Stein employs the familiar metaphor of the caterpillar's metamorphosis into a butterfly. As the caterpillar progresses from the pupa to the chrysalis stage, its potential fluttering structure—initially embedded as an imaginal disc—develops into a fully formed imago of the adult butterfly, capable of flight.[10] "In passing from one form to another," Stein explains, "the butterfly draws upon the latent structures that have been present all along but were undeveloped, hidden from view, or disguised by other features."[11] This transformation, akin to the instinctual drive toward individuation in humans, follows an intrinsic developmental trajectory, "obeying the guidelines inherent in this 'larger system' ['accompanied by a guiding image, a sort of vision'].... In analytical psychology, we refer to this master system as the Self." Stein further elaborates that the imago of transformation—a self-imago—is "programmed into the developmental agenda of the Self," representing the "fullest approximation of the Self a person will ever manifest."[12]

As the transformational process unfolds in adulthood and midlife, the imago of transformation may emerge with striking suddenness—what Stein describes as "lightning fast."[13] He illustrates this phenomenon in his study of Rilke's *Duino Elegies.*

> Transformative images are engaging and even arresting metaphors. To live through the transformational process they often engender is a special experience. From the moment these images appear, they take possession of one's consciousness and, at least temporarily, change it, sometimes dramatically.... Over time they become irreversible. This is because these images reflect psychological content that is emerging in a person's life and give it shape.[14]

According to Stein, out of the many formative images that shape a person's inner life, a central self-imago typically emerges, crystallizing and organizing the individual's identity. For the young Murray Stein, this image was the Risen Christ on Easter Sunday, which he experienced while playing with the hands of a clock, learning to tell time—a moment suspended in what he describes as eternal time. I referred to this process of evocation earlier in this book as the constellation of what I've called the nuclear symbol, a variable in my research that ties together Stein's concept of the transformative image during midlife and the emergence of the Self in early childhood, such as we saw in the case of Jack in Chapter 3. Stein will provide further evidence for this theory in his analysis of the poetry of Rilke momentarily. The extended period of midlife liminality, Stein argues, culminates in a rapid configuration and emergence of the newly formed imago, as seen in the life of Jung, himself. During the composition of *The Red Book*, he underwent a profound metamorphosis when, in an active imagination in December 1913 (at the age of 38), he "became the Crucified for a moment, and a miracle of inner healing took place."[15]

With Stein's theory of imaginal discs in mind, we may gain a new perspective on the transformative moment that shaped Rilke on the morning of January 20, 1912, while walking outside the Duino Castle near Trieste. As Stein recounts, Rilke was reading a letter from his lawyer concerning his impending divorce, when the future German national poet was suddenly stopped in his tracks by a mysterious voice that called out to him: "*Wer, wenn ich schriee, horte mich denn aus der Engel Ordnungen?*" ("Who would hear me if I cried out among the hierarchies of angles?").[16] This voice—later immortalized as the opening line of his *Duino Elegies*—was, according to Stein, the voice of Rilke's poetic calling, the Self speaking directly to him. It signaled the beginning of a sustained meditation on the role of poetry in the modern cosmos, a process that had been taking shape since his infancy. Stein describes that "Rilke's pupation began on January 20, 1912, and it continued until a second period of intense creativity shook the poet to his foundations in early 1922, when the self-imago suddenly became complete."[17] He continues:

> In January 1922, almost ten years after the first announcement in the wind at Duino castle, Rilke entered into a period of nearly sleepless poetic creation that

extended into February and left behind, as a monument to artistic enterprise and visionary exaltation, the completion of all ten *Duino Elegies,* as well as, remarkably, *The Sonnets to Orpheus,* a somewhat lesser companion work. After this intense labor, the butterfly was born and soared to meet the world.... Never before and never again afterwards would the poet be so thoroughly possessed by the Muse as when the text of the remaining Elegies poured from his pen. It was a furious culmination after ten years of waiting, a feverish burst into consciousness of images and thoughts and of a vision that had been waiting for release.[18]

In examining the psychological motivations behind Rilke's composition of the *Duino Elegies,* Stein identifies that "a mood of elegiac nostalgia and mourning dominates Rilke's entire artistic life." Born to "a mother who had recently experienced the death of her only child, a little girl, Rilke had a lifelong sensitivity to what he called the 'youthful dead.'"[19] Stein further elucidates the relationship between Rilke's self-imago as an Orpheus and the underlying affective structures that pervaded Rilke's childhood home, shaping his poetic vision. As he observes:

It is as though the elegy—not as a technical poetic form, but as a fundamental structure of feeling— were an imaginal disc carried in Rilke's unconscious from the moment of birth.... His entire poetic oeuvre is, in a sense, a monumental lament.[20]

Here, Stein ascertains that the feeling function was central to Rilke's transformation into the poet of Germany he was destined to become. His deep-seated feelings, Stein suggests, inevitably led him back to unsymbolized infantile memories, extending beyond his mother's grief over his sister's death into a broader mythopoetic "territory, the Land of the Laments."[21] He further postulates that: "Lament is the occasion, the necessary condition for transformation."[22]

To this therapeutic end, Stein asserts that Rilke provides a guiding example: "By the age of forty-seven, [Rilke] had assumed fully the self-imago of the Poet, an Orpheus, and he had become an archetypal lyric poet for the twentieth century."[23] Here, Stein is describing the transformative function of Rilke's narrative poem—not merely as an artistic expression but as a psychic energy converter through which an old form was radically reshaped into the imago of the poet Rilke was destined to become. In this context, the Land of the Laments served as both a functional metaphor and a symbolic link to Rilke's transpersonal origins in his Germanic cultural and linguistic heritage.

However, Stein emphasizes that such profound transformation does not occur within a vacuum. The central imago of transformation, he argues, must be evoked within the context of human relationships. As he writes: "Intimate relationships are perhaps the richest environments for psychological transformation throughout human life, including adulthood."[24]

To illustrate this further, Stein introduces the case of William Mellon, the American-born founder of a community hospital in Haiti. Mellon (related to Paul and Mary Mellon) experienced his own transformation in and through relationship, both with his wife and with the inner image of Albert Schweitzer, which he began to internalize after reading about the famous missionary in *Life* magazine. Stein writes:

> From the evidence, it is clear that Schweitzer became a compelling image for Mellon, one that changed his life permanently. One can only guess that, deep in the subterranean levels of Mellon's unconscious fantasy life, Schweitzer corresponded to a godlike figure, an archetypal image, whom he wished to emulate and with whom he identified.[25]

During midlife, an individual may become temporarily identified with another person as an image of their own potential transformation—what Stein refers to as a movement toward the Self's twin destinations. However, he cautions that remaining attached to such an idealized image for too long risks *imitatio Dei*—a misguided imitation of the divine rather than a true process of individuation. In Mellon's case, this might have meant becoming a mere replica of Schweitzer, rather than fully realizing his own unique identity. Fortunately, Mellon did not fall into this trap.

In his discussion of "The Transformative Image," Stein notes that Jung himself consciously attempted to disidentify from the figures of Christ and Aion, whom he had temporarily *become* during an active imagination experience—one he first presented in his 1925 "English Seminar."[26] According to Stein, Jung's psychological acts of reflection (*reflexio*) and separation from these religious images were crucial for the development of his analytical perspective. This process was further supported by his dialogues with Philemon, his inner teacher, who introduced him to the principle of "psychic objectivity"—recognition of the psyche as a reality distinct from literal identification with the archetypes. As Stein puts it:

> Jung strongly recommended letting oneself become affected by the images, even to the point of temporary identification with them.... He maintained a psychological distance from the archetypal images. It is this move that maintains identity as individual. Otherwise the archetypal images simply create replicas of themselves and individuality disappears. Jung's notion of individuation is based upon a twofold movement: temporary identification with the unconscious images in order to make them conscious, then disidentification and reflection upon them as an individual. The individual is affected by the contact but does not become totally controlled by the images.[27]

Stein observes that true healing cannot occur unless psychic energy is channeled through an archetype of transformation. He writes: "Jung was searching for a mechanism that could transfer and dispense energy from one channel to another."[28]

The nature of this mechanism—the very process Jung sought—is further clarified by Stein 15 pages later, when he revisits the theme of destiny. As previously noted, the instinct for individuation is not exclusive to humans but present across all forms of life. However, in Jungian psychoanalysis, this instinct takes on a uniquely human expression through transformative images and experiences, shaping the path of individuation in a deeply personal way:

> It is my argument, throughout this book, that a person's destiny which is made from qualities and markings that end up establishing themselves as the deepest etchings of character, mission, and meaning in life, the features that define a particular life as unique—is importantly, perhaps most essentially, constituted by a series of transformative images and experiences. What happens is that a person's integrity and potential as a unique human being become realized through these transformations.[29]

Stein elaborates that, when an individual taps into their innate potential at its source:

> [The] resultant self-imago then reflects and guides a person's destiny in the second half of life.... The formation of the self-imago is the precondition for full adult freedom to be oneself and to become the person one most deeply longs to be.... While the self-imago transcends character, it does not abolish it or change its fundamental features. It adds another dimension to the psyche that guides the disposition of surplus psychic energy.[30]

What distinguishes the deeply transforming individual from the average person— whose latent potential for higher awareness from the Self remains dormant—is the capacity to transcend the limitations of character, historical period, and culture through identification with "a self-imago of archetypal dimensions."[31] Such individuals carve out new channels in the collective psyche, creating transformative models that may be confidently followed by others. This, according to Stein, was Rembrandt's achievement. A more radical example, Picasso, did not merely redirect existing psychic channels but altered the very flow of the archetypal riverbed (of art). In Stein's view, Rembrandt "had astonishing natural talent. Quickly, he outstripped his masters, demonstrating the brilliant flair for dramatic gesture and expression that would characterize his work throughout his life."[32] In Rembrandt's self-portraits, Stein observes the union of artistic vocation with the transfigured light of sainthood: "Rembrandt depicted the process of psychological transformation as the emergence of an archetypal imago that combined the vocation of the artist with the spiritual illumination of a saint."[33] This transfiguration is most evident in his later works, in which the halo of the Risen Christ appears not above Jesus, but in the radiant light of Rembrandt's own face, eyes, and smile, marking a striking transformation from his earlier portraits.

While the archetype of the artist remained the same in both Rembrandt and Picasso, the character and style that emerged from their individuation processes profoundly differed. As Stein elaborates:

> While Rembrandt perhaps painted better than anyone before or after him, Picasso changed the course of painting itself, like some mighty Hercules redirecting the

flow of a major river from an ancient bed into an entirely new one. This is the very definition of transformation: to shift the flow of energy radically from one channel, one form or metaphor, into another. The total quantum of psychic energy poured by humankind into artistic expression—whether painting, drawing, sculpture, or ceramics—may not have changed as a result of Picasso's labors, but the forms that contain and express this energy were altered utterly. Picasso was a transformer on a vast collective level.... He changes styles of painting constantly, breaking old molds, inventing new ones, and ranging over the entire spectrum from classical and representational to abstract. But he does not remain committed to any one of them beyond an individual work. His self-imago as an artist now transcends style and technique.[34]

A careful examination of the stylistic changes in Stein's own editorial revisions reveals a striking evolution, suggesting his successful incarnation of the self-imago present in him as a latent potential from birth. This raises an intriguing question: Might Stein, through the publication of his *Collected Writings*, be actively shifting the flow of psychic energy from one channel of Jungian psychoanalysis to another—redefining its metaphors, frameworks, and modes of analysis?

Stein's work has played a pivotal role in advancing the field of Jungian psychanalysis into the 21st century, refining and expanding Jung's psychology of individuation. Notably, he appears to have moved beyond some of the divisions that Jung himself established between Eastern and Western psychological traditions. Furthermore, he has sought to reinterpret and integrate aspects of Christian theology, making them more transpersonal in orientation. At least, this is my view.

As we have seen, by 1985, Stein had already established himself as a leading global figure in analytical psychology. His first major contribution, *Jung's Treatment of Christianity*, marked the beginning of his dual role as a Protestant theologian and a Jungian analyst. I will undertake a deeper exploration of that work later on.

Man-Making in Postmodernity

Another important work to consider in Volume 3 of the *Collected Writings* is *Men Under Construction*. As briefly mentioned in the "Introduction" to this volume, this work originated as a series of lectures delivered at the C.G. Jung Institute of Chicago in 1988. It was later published in book form under the same title in 2020 and subsequently revised and reprinted in 2022 in the *Collected Writings*. It is from this later edition that I will provide selected quotes.

In this work, Stein explores five stages of transformation in a man's life (or the masculine principle in women): (1) mother, (2) father, (3) hero, (4) missionary, and (5) sage. In the "Introduction," he articulates the fundamental aim of this model:

The goal of the development I am going to propose, the *telos* of a man's inner development, is to achieve as much freedom from them [mother and father complexes] as possible, true freedom, in order to release the full panoply of potentials in the self.[35]

Stein's "mother" and "father" stages correspond to the first two phases of individuation, shaped by the archetypal dominants governing an individual's psychological development. While the specific archetypes may differ between men and women, Stein maintains that the underlying principles remain fundamentally the same. The first stage, associated with the mother complex/archetype, spans from birth to approximately age 12. During this phase, the child remains psychologically embedded in the maternal field, forming foundational attachments and early patterns of dependency. Subsequently, around the age of 12, the father complex/archetype assumes prominence, initiating the second stage of development. This transition marks the beginning of a period focused on identity formation, independence, and a move toward self-reliance. (Interestingly, Stein notes that it was at this age that his father taught him to drive in North Dakota.) The father stage extends for approximately 23 years, encompassing adolescence, young adulthood, and the early stages of professional life.

The third stage, beginning around the age of 35 and lasting until age 50, is what Stein terms the "hero" era. This phase is characterized by separation from the father, in pursuit of a deeper sense of self. The fourth stage, spanning the ages of 52–70, is known as the "missionary" stage. During this period, the ego-self axis becomes more fully developed and the Self emerges as the central organizing principle of the personality. This 18-year period is primarily concerned with the integration of wisdom, purpose, and legacy. Finally, the fifth and final stage is the "sage" era, representing the culmination of individuation. This stage, which is seldom reached by most individuals, is marked by a deep spiritual centering and a preoccupation with the "God problem," as the individual confronts questions of ultimate meaning.[36] At 81 years old, Stein himself is living within this phase.

Stein directs significant attention to the missionary stage (stage 4), which he describes as a period in which

> a man finds a mission in the world, which directs his vision onward beyond himself to embrace collective and cultural issues... As he moves into old age his missionary identity gives way to religious questions of ultimate meaning. His sense of identity shifts to 'sage' and he becomes a wisdom figure for others.[37]

By "mission," Stein means vocation—a deep calling that emerges when an individual recognizes that they are no longer the sole architect of their destiny. At this stage, they are guided by an inner voice from the Self, to which they must submit—bowing their head in symbolic initiation, as seen in rites across world cultures. To resist this calling, Stein asserts, is to risk remaining neurotic and unable to integrate the deeper wisdom of the unconscious. However, if the individual becomes an initiate, they will surrender to the guiding voice of the daimon, or *spiritus rector*. Stein elaborates on this guiding force:

> The *spiritus rector* is an uncanny guide. This is because it does not appear to be rational by usual standards. Its directives and messages imply a large unconscious plan or vision for life, a pre-set course of a life process that is not

culturally determined and therefore not predictable. By making choices on the basis of strong intuitions and a felt sense of Self, an unconscious life plan emerges and is revealed over time.[38]

What does Stein mean by life plan? At this stage, an individual moves beyond imitation of past masters. The anima, which plays a dominant role in the preceding hero stage, gradually recedes into the background—having fulfilled its function of opening new pathways to the Self. Meanwhile, the *spiritus rector* creates a sense of inner and outer spaciousness, in which all aspects of experience begin to converge toward a transcendent center—the nucleus of ultimate meaning. At this decisive point, an individual must step out of the master's shadow and embrace full individuation—no longer following external authorities but instead uncovering a deeply buried inner truth. This truth, like a hidden treasure, emerges from within as the Self reveals its deeper wisdom. As Stein explains: "Sometimes a vocational call for the remainder of a man's life will come about as a result of a strong encounter with the unconscious, that is, in a vision, a big dream or an impressive active imagination."[39]

At this stage, the voice of the *spiritus rector* becomes the dominant guiding force, demanding both inner discipline and obedience. This voice, rooted in the archetypal depths of the psyche, operates within what Stein calls the "Ground Plan" of an individual's life. For Stein, this vocational calling took a biblical and Judeo-Christian form following the publication of *In Midlife*. His work *Jung's Treatment of Christianity* emerged following four decades of reflection, deeply influenced by the mythopoetic cadence of the King James Bible, which he memorized in his youth. Reflecting on Jung's interpretation of Christ, Stein critically observes in *Transformation: Emergence of the Self*: "With regards to Jung's portrait of Jesus, Jung plainly errs in his judgment that it lacks a shadow."[40]

An individual in the missionary stage has awakened a guiding vision and is no longer dependent on external sources for direction.[41] Following this, the primary purpose of the fifth and final stage of the sage (age 70 and beyond) is "to come into contact with the Ultimate, the Ground of Being, to use the phrase of Paul Tillich, and to search for the question of life's meaning."[42] During this stage, none of the earlier psychological structures—mother, father, hero, missionary, ego, persona, shadow, anima/animus, or mana-personality—runs the show. Though temporary regressions to earlier stages may occur—often as a result of defensiveness or resistance—it is as if supernatural aid intervenes, guiding the ego toward its final destination: the Self. Now, the Self lifts the veil, revealing life's deeper mysteries. At this threshold, the distinction between psychology and metaphysics dissolves, and the individual enters the Ground of Being, where the psyche attains its highest spiritual realization.

Concerning the Transformation of God Images

The next work under review is a series of lectures delivered by Stein at the 2001 Annual Summer Conference at St. Hilda's College, Oxford University (later published by the Guild for Pastoral Psychology). In these densely packed lectures,

Stein explores the psychological implications of transformations in the God image—both in individuals undergoing analysis and in societies at large. As he explains: "A God image is a numinous symbol that claims for itself absolute and cosmic standing."[43] A numinous symbol, for instance, can be found in the Statue of Liberty. Standing at the threshold of the New World, *Lady Liberty* has long served as a welcoming figure, even for Stein's own family when they crossed from Canada into the United States during his early childhood. Raising her torch of religious freedom, she embodies a God image—expanding ego consciousness, facilitating a bridge between the eternal and time, and offering an intuition of absolute existence, cosmic significance, and infinite being at the center of the psyche.

In his lectures, Stein engages deeply with psychological and theological themes, particularly in relation to the Trinity in Catholic and Protestant thought. He also provides a clinical example of a God image that emerged in the dream of a female analysand in her 60s. Though she was not especially religious, in either traditional or non-traditional terms, she remained spiritually open to archetypal images of the collective unconscious—symbols whose numinous presence shaped her psyche's native terrain.

> She dreamt of an enormous snake, which appeared in her dream with the head of a woman and out of whose snake-body white orchids were growing. The snake confronted the dreamer with her gigantic face and she became frightened as it came near and stared at her with its dark penetrating eyes, which were firmly fixed upon her. The snake asked her who she was and she simply replied she was a psychotherapist. The snake then told her she was an architect of souls like Julius Cesar, and other historical figures she could not recall. The dreamer was dumbfounded. She looked astonished. Seeing this bewilderment, the Snake-woman told her that Caesar was an architect of souls in a previous lifetime. The dreamer then realized she was meeting a consciousness that had been around since the Universe began. At the end, the snake-woman's face lightened up, she smiled at her, and great streams of energy were exuding out of her body.[44]

The streams of energy described here function like streams of consciousness—emanations of numinosity from the Self. This represents a beautiful example of the emergence of a new God image. Stein acknowledges William James and Jung for pioneering new pathways to the Self in the early 20th century, opening the door for direct religious experience in a postmodern context. He further explores why God images change over time. As he explains, once a God image is integrated into consciousness, it often loses its numinous charge: "Its wildness becomes tamed."[45] Tamed numinosity differs significantly from its more primal, instinctually charged forms, as seen in the image of the snake-woman.

Stein then observes that, by 2001, history seemed to be entering a period of accelerated religious and psychological change, with the monotheistic God image undergoing rapid transformation on a global scale. This quickening, he suggests, increased "the probabilities of new God images appearing, and taking hold, on a collective plane," making the prospect of a new age of spirituality particularly high: "In times of deep cultural and social transformation, there is a strong likelihood that new God images will emerge in order to capture the new features of the Self, that are brought into play by the transformation process."[46]

Not long after Stein delivered these lectures, the terrible events of September 11, 2001 shook the world, unfolding in a manner that seemed strikingly synchronistic. The attack brought forth images of absolute evil, altering the consciousness of individuals across the globe. On television screens worldwide, individuals witnessed the Twin Towers consumed by fire, collapsing in a cascade of concrete, debris, and dust, claiming the lives of countless innocent people at Ground Zero in New York. Meanwhile, in the Middle East, radicalized Islamic groups celebrated the destruction, revealing what Stein might call the hidden shadow within monotheistic traditions. The attacks marked a global crisis—a psychic rupture in collective awareness. As the world reeled from the tragedy, anti-Muslim sentiment surged in the United States, revealing yet another shadow response to the unfolding trauma.

In time, Stein would offer his own answer to the problem of evil, arguing that God images do not change as a result of a mere individual dream or vision. Rather,

> There must be miracles, synchronistic events that match inner mental images and outer physical facts and events.... There has to be physical evidence.... Synchronicity ties the mental and the physical together... with synchronicity an inner event like a dream or vision becomes indelible.[47]

The horrific events of September 11 provided undeniable evidence for any doubting theologian that the God image encompasses both good and evil—a reality correctly predicted by Jung. However, the precise nature of the transforming Western God image remains difficult to discern, whether in Europe, Asia, the Middle East, or the United States. Whatever changes are unfolding, they may be shaped by a not-yet-perceptible organizing principle. The problem of evil that so preoccupied Jung will likely remain an enduring mystery. Yet, this subject has been one of Stein's central research interests, and he offers his own "Answer to Evil" later in this book.

Does a change in the God image reflect a transformation in God, itself, or merely humanity's perception of God? Stein approaches this question through both psychological and theological perspectives, remaining true to his dual vocation as both a Protestant and a Jungian analyst. He writes:

> Each human life is an incarnation of God in human consciousness.... When a person becomes aware, even partially, of the God factor within, of the self, then a God image becomes available, and the aspect of God reflected in this image enters consciousness.[48]

Whether God is equally good and evil remains a question that some theologians have called Jungians to address. Stein, however, resists splitting or taking sides, instead offering a perspective integrating both aspects of the divine:

> It matters to God that humans individuate, for in so doing they are contributing to the cosmic project of bringing God fully into consciousness. While this sounds highly metaphysical and theological, Jung does not mean it to be so. It is meant to be empirical, verifiable by experience, fully biographical in the lives of psychologically aware people. The data that holds evidence of this process lies in the stories of individuating people.[49]

Readers will recall that Stein's preferred image of transformation is the metamorphosis of a caterpillar into a butterfly, with the latter serving as a symbol of the Self or anima/animus. Caterpillars are not evil, but the destruction of their species by human activity certainly is. This is a scientific fact to lepidopterists, regardless of whether they happen to be Catholic, Protestant, or Anglican. To reach its final form, the caterpillar must undergo a complete liquification before entering the chrysalis stage. It then develops an imaginal disc, eventually emerging from its cocoon as an adult specimen of the *Lepidoptera* species. Stein uses this vivid biological transformation as an analogy for the emergence of new God images, which arise naturally (or supernaturally) through a double movement of de- and re-integration—both of which are necessary for individuation. A crucial phase in this process is disidentification from previous God images, leading to a temporary absence of guiding symbols. Stein advises:

> The ability to live without a God image is necessary in order to experience a new one offered by the Self, later to integrate it. People who are individuating often are void of guiding images and live in a state of psychic uncertainty. They are open to experimentation and new experience.[50]

We observed this morphic process in the emergence of the snake-woman in the dream discussed above.

Based on my reading, Jung never intended his work to serve as a "new dispensation" for the Age of Aquarius. The Self is neither exclusively Jungian nor bound to any particular tradition. Rather, it is ageless, eternal, and transtemporal. Stein, in turn, offers his own "personal theology," making a unique contribution to the intersection of analytical psychology and spirituality. He demonstrates (with Jung) that God and the God image are distinct notions—one empirical, the other metaphysical—yet both necessary. And he integrates Jung's metaphysical insights into analytical psychology primarily through the principle of synchronicity.

Stein argues that, to invite a new God image from the Self, one must first live without a God image altogether. Speculating on the future, he asks: "What sort of

God image will come into focus in the coming centuries? In the short term it is certainly impossible to make such predictions."[51]

Although we will revisit the problem of evil later, it is important to acknowledge that Jung was correct in asserting that the God image contains both good and evil. Dream analysis confirms this as a practical point. Moreover, Stein emphasizes: "Human must incarnate the newly revealed God image in their individual consciousness and patterns of behavior, otherwise the transformation of God will not come about."[52] This, he suggest, requires a deep vigilance against inflation and a recognition that no one is free from the shadow or evil thoughts. Everyone who witnessed the horror of September 11 was, in some way, psychologically affected. The key question is not whether evil exists, but rather, how can one metabolize and transform it into a panacea for higher consciousness—one that neither denies the reality of evil nor is paralyzed by it?

Dante's Divine Comedy: A Journey of Transformation

We now arrive at the final essay in Volume 3 of the *Collected Writings*, titled "Transformation." Originally written for a conference in Ravenna, Italy, in 2021, this essay was intended to commemorate the 700th anniversary of Dante Alighieri's death on September 13, 1321. Stein completed the final revisions in February 2021, while quarantining in Goldiwil during the COVID-19 pandemic. In this period of darkness and isolation, he turned to Dante's *Divine Comedy*, reading several English translations with increasing wonder and appreciation for the depth and beauty of its psychological insights. The trilogy—*Inferno, Purgatorio,* and *Paradiso*—revealed itself to him as a masterpiece of Catholic wisdom, astonishing him with its visionary scope.[53] Stein's essay, while echoing the eloquence of his analysis of Rilke's poetry, is even more vertically oriented, more totalizing, and more metaphysically expansive in its thematic and structural execution.

As a Jungian, Stein approaches the *Divine Comedy* not merely as a literary work, but as a record of psychological metamorphosis, chronicling the soul's ascent to the highest levels of metaphysical speculation—what he refers to as the trans-psyche. He recognizes Dante's spiritual transformation as an exemplar of what Jungians call active imagination, which Stein identifies as the fourth pillar of psychoanalysis. Stein regards the *Divine Comedy* as perhaps the greatest poem in Western literature, offering a Jungian perspective on the Self that transcends the horizontal plane of existence. He argues that, in the first half of life, individuals are naturally psychologically identified with time, place, practical tasks, persona, and social roles. However, in the second half and beyond, a different mode of consciousness is required—one that Dante's poem provides, catapulting the psyche toward a higher analytical or theological awareness. This verticality reaches its most profound, transpersonal expression in the final cantos of the *Paradiso*.

In this poem, Stein tells us, Dante's use of the term "trans-human" (*Transumanar*) signifies becoming one with God.[54] This trans-human experience unfolds only after Dante's arduous journey—first into Hell (*Dis*), then through Purgatory (where he is guided by Virgil), and finally into Paradise, where the appearance of Beatrice signals a new level of spiritual ascent. It is in this soulful region of divine love that Beatrice, for the first time, pronounces his name—Dante—marking a moment of profound psychological and spiritual recognition. As Dante progresses into Paradise, his final guide, St. Bernard, leads him through the final 13 cantos—verses that, according to Boccacio, were discovered only after Dante's death. In his reading of the text, Stein places special emphasis on the significance of the "trans-human." In particular, he celebrates Dante's beatific vision, in which the poet gazes into the three spheres of the Trinity, beholding the mystery of God within the Heavenly Rose mandala. Stein describes this as follows: "This sudden flash of visionary insight marks the final and supreme point of Dante's spiritual and psychological transformation—union with the *unus mundus*." Dante himself expressed this revelation in the closing lines of *Paradiso* as the "Love that moves the Sun and the other stars." Stein continues:

> The poet cannot describe what he saw in his vision. It is beyond his imagination and verbal capacities. My impression is that he gazed into the very bottom of the collective unconscious, into the Self, where All is made One. But even more importantly, he experiences union with the Self and becomes invested with Love, its fundamental energy. Individuation has here reached its ultimate goal and is now complete to the extent that this is humanly possible.[55]

Dante passed away on September 13, 1321, having just completed the final cantos of the *Paradiso*. Harold Bloom, quoted in Stein's text, reflected on Dante's mythic status: "Legend tells us that Dante was pointed out in the streets as the man who had somehow returned from a voyage to hell, as though he were a kind of shaman."[56] This characterization, Stein notes, closely parallels Jung's own descent into the spirit of the depths in *The Red Book*.

In his "Postlude," Stein asks whether psychotherapists may consider Dante's experience a real possibility for their patients. Moreover, he asks:

> Does numinous experience in active imagination over a period of time such as we find described in the *Divine Comedy* make a real difference in how people ultimately feel about life and themselves, in how they behave toward others, in how they formulate the meaning of life in the final analysis?[57]

This question echoes the revelatory experience of St. Thomas Aquinas, who, after encountering a vision of trans-human love, put down his pen and declared that his *Summa Theologica* was, by comparison, nothing more than straw.

While the number of patients in Jungian analysis who have undergone experiences comparable to those of great poets like Dante is unknown, such visionary journeys are no doubt exceedingly rare. Nevertheless, Stein asserts that, as an analyst, he has witnessed firsthand the lasting impact that engagement with dreams and active imagination can have over time. Many of his patients, like Dante, have passed through psychic hell and emerged with a heightened, more numinous awareness of the potential totality of the Self. He explains:

> We also know that this process in analysis does not entirely remove the effects of early traumas and the consequent complexes, although it does assist a person in outgrowing them and relativizing their effects on consciousness. The creation of an ego-self axis on the inner level shifts the locus of control from persona concerns about prestige and power to a type of selfhood that brings with it a considerable degree of loving acceptance of self and others.

Stein draws a direct connection between this psychological transformation and Dante's ultimate vision: "This would testify to the veracity of Dante's claim that one's being can be brought into harmony with the 'Love that moves the sun and the other stars.'"[58]

At the end of the essay, Stein contemplates whether personal and cultural complexes can be transformed and elevated to achieve "a transformed sense of self," transcending even the "most sublime archetypal images imaginable." He proposes that such an experience may culminate in an encounter with "nothingness"—not in a nihilistic sense, but rather as a sudden and total illumination, akin to being struck by lightning. This evokes the *satori* experiences in Zen Buddhism, as well as Dante's final ascent into the Heavenly Rose. At this level of trans-human awareness, consciousness undergoes such a profound transformation that it is ultimately governed by only two forces: the transcendent Self (God) and its energy (Eros/love). Stein compares this state of realization to that described in mystical traditions such as Kabbalah, Sufism, and Kundalini Yoga, and the seventh state of *samadhi*.[59]

Stein is in full agreement with Dante that love is the healing energy governing the cosmos—a sentiment that Jung never articulated with such clarity. The closest Jung came to expressing a similar idea appears in the final pages of *Memories, Dreams, Reflections*, in which he confessed:

> I falter before the task of finding language which might adequately express the incalculable paradoxes of love... In my medical experience as well as in my own life I have again and again been faced with the mystery of love and have never been able to explain what it is.[60]

Stein's vision of love aligns with his ecology of the soul, corresponding to a healing, shamanistic message echoing Jung's dream of the greenish-Gold Christ on the cross. This same greening message of love is beautifully captured in Marc Chagall's stained glass windows in the Grossmünster church in Zürich. When my wife and I first visited Zürich in 2008, we saw these windows firsthand—finding them simply stunning.

As we have seen, Stein's ancestral roots trace back to 16th-century Swiss soil—an influence that may have contributed to his decision to relocate to Switzerland at the age of 60. Two decades later, as he penned his Dante essay, his God image appears to have become more theologically well-defined, acquiring an increasingly transpersonal significance.

If God moves the sun and the stars by energy known as love, then Stein's interpretation of Dante undoubtedly hits the mark—not only for Jungian and non-Jungian readers, but also for Christian and non-Christian audiences alike. The transformative power of the *Divine Comedy* is so immense that it played a crucial role in shaping the cultural and national consciousness that ultimately gave rise to Italy as an independent nation. Dante's spiritual and political vision created the vertical imagery and psychic energy needed for cultural transformation during the height of the Holy Roman Empire. During this period, the papacy's shift to Avignon resulted in a decline of moral authority, leading to decadent leadership under an aged Pope. Meanwhile, Meister Eckhart was accused of heresy, only to be later exonerated. Yet, unlike in Italy, where Dante's vision laid the foundation for spiritual renewal, Eckhart's teachings did not provide Germany with a similar path to psychological or theological transformation. This, Stein suggests, was highly unfortunate for the history of Christianity. Had these two visionaries of the Church—the supernal poet Dante and Eckhart, the inspired preacher of God's Word—worked in tandem, they might have laid the foundation for a more spiritually unified Europe, under the aegis of transformation. It is precisely this process of the highest spiritual metamorphosis, granted to humanity, that Stein has spent his lifetime studying and promoting—both in service to the Jungian movement and for the spiritual benefit of the world. Yet, our field has not yet fully recognized or embraced the currents of the Holy Spirit that move through his vision.

Notes

1 Reworked from Herrmann, S.B. "Murray Stein: The Transformative Image." *The San Francisco Jung Institute Library Journal* 17, no. 1 (1998): 17–39. https://doi.org/10.1525/jung.1.1998.17.1.17 © 1998 C.G. Jung Institute of San Francisco, reprinted by permission of Informa UK Limited, trading as Taylor & Francis Ltd, https://www.tandfonline.com on behalf of C.G. Jung Institute of San Francisco.
2 CW3, 4, 6.
3 CW3, 11.
4 CW3, 12.
5 CW3, 14, 15.
6 CW3, 13.
7 CW3, 58.
8 CW3, 14.
9 CW3, 14.
10 CW3, 14–15.
11 CW3, 20.
12 CW3, 27.
13 CW3, 28.
14 CW3, 49, 50.
15 CW3, 57.
16 CW3, 33.
17 CW3, 34.

18 CW3, 36.
19 CW3, 37.
20 CW3, 37.
21 CW3, 39.
22 CW3, 37.
23 CW3, 44.
24 CW3, 83.
25 CW3, 55.
26 CW3, 53–57.
27 CW3, 57.
28 CW3, 61.
29 CW3, 76.
30 CW3, 116, 117.
31 CW3, 118.
32 CW3, 119.
33 CW3, 130.
34 CW3, 133.
35 CW3, 159.
36 CW3, 161.
37 CW3, 162.
38 CW3, 210.
39 CW3, 212.
40 CW3, 69.
41 CW3, 215.
42 CW3, 217.
43 CW3, 226.
44 CW3, 230–231.
45 CW3, 237.
46 CW3, 238–239.
47 CW3, 241.
48 CW3, 250.
49 CW3, 251.
50 CW3, 251.
51 CW3, 252.
52 CW3, 253.
53 CW3, 267.
54 CW3, 289.
55 CW3, 291.
56 CW3, 292.
57 CW3, 292.
58 CW3, 293.
59 CW3, 294.
60 *MDR*, 353.

Chapter 5

Collected Writings Volume 4

The Practice of Jungian Psychoanalysis

Volume 4 of the *Collected Writings*, titled *The Practice of Jungian Psychoanalysis*, includes Stein's essay, "The Aims and Goals of Jungian Analysis," originally published in the first edition of *Jungian Analysis*, a book he edited in 1982 and revised in a second edition in 1995. In its latest iteration, the essay has been further refined to reflect Stein's evolving perspective. For instance, when he discusses the goal of curing souls in analysis and assisting individuals in achieving wholeness, he mentions that, during "shop talk," analysts sometimes neglect deeply transformative experiences. As previously observed, transformation remains central to his theoretical contributions to the field of analytical psychology.

Stein situates shop talk within a broader cultural neurosis, noting that psychotherapists, social workers, psychiatrists, and professionals across various fields—including medicine, law, clergy, education, and finance—often become so immersed in their immediate tasks that they lose sight of their ultimate purpose and mission. He characterizes this pernicious condition as the "virus of superficiality," which defines postmodernity. Crucially, Stein argues that all professions, despite their apparent differences, ultimately serve the same organizing principle: the Self. In other words, our primary purposes converge toward similar aims, goals, and destinations. Each of us serves what may be understood as a "god," or a "foundational value or an idea." This applies as much to the diverse fields of psychotherapy as it does to clergy and jurisprudence. Regardless of our profession, we are all in service to an archetypal image—one that holds the potential for profound transformation. The task, then, is to uncover and engage with its secret springs of action.

Stein invites readers to reflect on two fundamental questions: "Can we spell out the Jungian psychoanalyst's overall goal and final purpose of conducting analysis? Which 'god' is being served in this practice of care of the soul?"[1] At the heart of these inquiries lies a deeper question about what transforms the conscious ego into its most authentic shape. Indeed, what is the agent of this "deep change?"[2]

According to Stein, the key variable is Self-experience, which dissolves the rigidities of ego consciousness and allows for an expanded identity to emerge. He asserts: "What actually creates the therapeutic effect in Jungian analysis is the increasing amplitude of a person's experience of the Self." Here, amplitude corresponds to a wider breadth of experience of the numinous. Such Self-experiences

DOI: 10.4324/9781003664024-6

are often accompanied by synchronistic events—chance events that, when properly attended to (often in analysis), may foster a transcendent "sense of meaning, future direction, and destiny."[3] However, Stein cautions that, for personality change to be lasting, such transformative experiences must be grounded in an archetypal framework. Otherwise, the shifts may remain superficial. Thus, to facilitate enduring transformation in the analytical setting, careful attention must be given to both the patient's dreams and the analyst's countertransference attitudes.

Power, Shamanism, and Maieutics as Countertransference Attitudes

Stein examines three countertransference attitudes in psychotherapists, identifying them as: "power-oriented, shamanic, and maieutic. Each one produces its own characteristic images and anxieties and shows a distinctive archetypally based patterning."[4] Most analysts are familiar with the power-oriented countertransference attitude, which arises when "the analyst is struggling to get control over his own chaotic unconscious."[5] Stein describes the second attitude, associated with the shaman, as follows:

> This type of countertransference, it might be imagined, occurs only with analysts who have excessively permeable ego-boundaries and a sort of elastic sense of personal identity.... As a shamanic healer, however, the analyst not only becomes infected by the analysand's illness but also finds a way to cure it. As the illness is taken in and suffered, the analyst begins searching for a cure: analyzing the inner psychological constellation created by this illness; scrutinizing dreams, associations, and other unconscious material relevant to the suffering; looking for symbols that emerge from the unconscious and represent the healing factor at work; active imagination. The unconscious responds to the healer's suffering, and the analyst applies the curative symbols to the wound, thereby healing the wound.[6]

Here again, Stein stresses the importance of the fourth pillar—the curative factor in the analytic process that sounds to the deeps. He also introduces reverie as a form of active imagination. Having undergone their own analytic "initiation" during training, the analyst sees the goal of analysis as an "amplification" of the patient's dream images and active imaginations. This amplification serves to transmit the *medicina*[7]—the transformative substance generated in the transference/countertransference. Stein describes that, in the shamanic mode of countertransference, the analyst, like a shaman, channels a mysterious psychological process that produces a kind of inner *linctus*—a healing essence to be passed to the patient. But how is this medicine harvested for therapeutic use? "The healing influence of the analyst's personality, which is constellated in response to the internalized illness of analysand, creates a curative effect within the analysand, because the analyst's self-healing process triggers a parallel healing process in the analysand's personality."[8] Ultimately, Stein suggests that the analyst's ongoing personality development—their lifelong process of individuation—can manifest as a birthing process within the patient, positioning the analyst as a kind of guide or midwife in the patient's psychological rebirth.

Therefore, the central aim of the third countertransference attitude, the maieutic approach, is fundamentally receptive, with the analyst serving as a witness and midwife to the analysand's birthing of a new personality. Stein refers to this process as the emergence of an "innate, autochthonous Self," with the word autochthonous referring to something indigenous, aboriginal, original, and ancient. Following the analyst's exploration of the ancestral deposits of the psyche, the analysand, too, may become receptive through "mutual reverie," attuning to unconscious motivations and ultimately:

> becoming self-maieutic to the unfolding drama of the Self's revelation.... Often the analyst is captivated by a vision of the analysand's wholeness and futurity (the "child"), of the still largely unconscious Selfhood that must be brought to light and integrated. The analyst sees beyond the source to the hidden core of a symptoms meaning. A divinity is perceived, a call is heard for its recognition.[9]

Importantly, in a long-term analysis, the analyst will witnesses not one, but multiple pregnancies and births—all of which will unfold through a proliferation of calling dreams revolving around a central nucleus of energy and meaning. As Stein explains: "Unlike childbirth, the emergence of the Self is not a one-time event, numinous as a glimpse of it in a dream in the animated field of analysis may be."

To illustrate, Stein presents the case of a middle-aged woman who reported an initial dream in which a large animal emerged from the ocean and transformed into a wise old woman standing on the shore. The figure then invited the dreamer on a long walk, during which they discussed the trajectory of the woman's life. Reflecting on this moment, Stein comments,

> It was as though I were speaking for the old woman myself.... The Self visited us that day, and we received it in the space between us. It was a birthing.... I felt that I had been privileged to witness a mystery.[10]

Here, the simultaneous interplay of active imagination and reverie facilitated the process of psychological birth.

Reverie is akin to dreaming while awake. This state of conscious dreaming enables the analyst to perceive beyond the symptoms generated by a complex, uncovering their underlying meanings within the broader context of the patient's life pattern. As Stein writes:

> Dreams function as X-rays, and the job of the maieut is to read them for information concerning the development of the process underway. Each dream

interpretation is also, though, one of the many mini-births necessary to bring the Self up into the full light of day.... The analyst is primarily focused on gathering aspects of the unconscious Self—the complexes and archetypal images—and on glimpsing their internal unity and structure. This requires hearing and seeing through the play of words on the surface of conscious communication and taking sonar-like soundings of the depths beneath.[11]

The many mini-births that may occur throughout the analytic process anticipate a more resplendent emergence of the Self—an event that can only be described as transcendent. To facilitate this process, an analyst must remain attuned to all three countertransference attitudes, ensuring a balanced approach in assisting the patient's psychological birth. This requires "empathic holding and containment. Another maieutic function."[12]

Amor Fati: Analysis and the Search for Personal Destiny

First published by Chiron Publications in 1987 and later revised and republished in *Practicing Wholeness* (1996), the essay "*Amor Fati*: Analysis and the Search for Personal Destiny" begins with a central question: "Is it possible to come to love one's own history and develop a sense of personal destiny as a result of analysis?" Stein's response is clear: "To love one's fate (*amor fati*) is itself an embrace of the whole complexity of one's life, one's wholeness."[13]

Such love is out of the ordinary, requiring a complete acceptance of one's entire existence. It demands that an individual integrate all aspects of themselves, without denial or rejection. Stein continues:

There is a feeling of momentousness when this happens. Both partners in this relationship are deeply affected and both are changed and transformed. Both are touched by agape love and infused by the energy of the love union. The healing that comes about through this experience is due to a profound conjunction of personal and archetypal factors, which can fuse and create the experience of meaning and destiny.[14]

Stein elaborates: "when the activity of reconstruction in analysis reaches an archetypal level, it takes up the question of meaning and purpose. Personal history and narrative then become infiltrated with archetypal elements that take on the nature of a personal destiny."[15] In his analytical framework, "the product of reconstruction—the narrative—often occupies the center of clinical treatment, forming a kind of center pole that supports the whole analytic edifice."[16] Personal destiny is inseparable from fate, which one must ultimately learn to feel into and embrace. As Stein notes: "Gazing into psychic background has the sense of studying life's fate."[17] Such an inquiry fosters a deeper love for the twists and turns of our hardships as well as our triumphs.

Stein distinguishes fate from personal destiny as follows: the former is what happens to us against our will, while the latter involves an element of choice. Importantly, he notes, we must say "Yes" to our fate in order to transform it into our destiny. He illustrates this with a painful example of a 50-year-old woman who, in a moment of emotional catharsis, found herself overwhelmed by grief and outrage at her fate. Amidst her tears, she perceived something soothing whispering through her distress. She then told her analyst: "'When I was seven years old and my mother gave me that doll with my sister's dress on it, I knew I'd never have children and she would. This is my fate." Stein reflects:

> The therapist feels inclined to look away from such finality, but a chord of truth is struck. The sensitive therapist shudders at the thought of such limitation. Who has dictated this course? And are we not in the business of helping people to change, to grow, to become what they are not and want to be? If we look for archetypal patterns, however, we come upon limits, sometimes cruel destinies, sometimes inexplicable charm and good luck. It does not always seem fair.[18]

Stein helps us understand the significance of Jungian reconstruction in an analysand's life, particularly when fate is accepted in such a way that the analyst recognizes they cannot alter it. By relinquishing the hope of discovering a panacea for the patient and instead allowing for an archetypal "intervention," something spiritual may crystallize, shifting the analysand's attitude toward fate into a "single vision" tinged with honey.[19] By "single vision," Stein means a shared perceptual experience in the analytical process—built through mutual reverie, active imagination, and visioning—that reveals a vague visitor behind the veil of mystery. Such shared moments may emerge through acausal coincidences at critical junctures of stasis and transformation, as both analyst and analysand endure life's stinging arrows—experiences that wound yet cannot be changed.

According to Stein, the force that ultimately heals all wounds is the transformative experience of love. He concludes: "The final psychic product of the stage of reconstruction I'm describing here is *amor fati*: not only knowledge of one's history, but a full embrace and love of it, as that which has been archetypally meant to be."[20] Such radical acceptance of one's fate is a rare experience indeed.

Dreams and the Reconstruction of History in Analysis

The next paper under examination, "Dreams and the Reconstruction of History in Analysis," was first published by Chiron Publications in 1989 and later republished in the book *Practicing Wholeness* (1996). In this essay, Stein describes the case of a female analysand in her late 30s who, after a year of analytic work, had become bedridden with an unexplained illness, accompanied by a mysterious and anomalous paralysis.

> During her illness, she dreamt she was in a church. As she walked to the church door, a gigantic butterfly suddenly flew past and fluttered outwards into the fresh

open air. She stepped out herself and was suddenly in a winter landscape. The place was Russia. She was standing on a roadway that ran through a forest for hundreds of miles. Looking down the road she saw her parents on a horse-drawn sleigh approaching her and she was surprised to see her mother and father coming her way.

The dreamer's associations led her to recall that her father was a second-generation Russian-American immigrant. She had long been fascinated by the stories of her grandfather in Russia, leading her to read and reread the great Russian novels. "But why the giant butterfly?" Stein asked. Why this particular landscape? Why her own parents and not her grandparents, or great-grandparents? Such analytic questions invite the analyst into a state of reverie through deep listening to the emotional tones of childhood ascribed to dream images.

Stein's reflections on butterflies never cease to astonish. In this case, the butterfly, as an archetypal soul image, passed through the doorway of the church in his patient's dream, heralding her re-entry into the land of her ancestors. It functioned as a boundary-crossing agent, bridging the transitional and archetypal space between past and present. The church, a sacred site of ancestral descent, signified more than just a return to childhood. Rather, it signified a return to Childhood with a capital C, connoting a deeper, archetypal connection to the dreamer's genetic lineage and cultural heritage in Russia. In this respect, the dream implied a kind of second birth—a renewal through the act of returning to her point of origin. Yet, as Stein observes, this return was not merely retrospective, but teleological—directed toward the future. He writes:

> The dream, with its escaping butterfly and return to the world of the ancestors, charted the course of this unborn soul…. The implications of a return to 'deep childhood,' to the point of ancestry even beyond one's personal beginning, is futurity. Because the archetypes are engaged at this level, the psyche's progressive movement toward wholeness can be touched.[21]

The Problem of Envy and Sibling Rivalry

The next paper I will examine, "The Problem of Envy and Sibling Rivalry," was first published in the *Journal of Analytical Psychology* (1990) and later included in *Practicing Wholeness* (Chiron Publications, 1998).

As in fairy tales describing the simpleton who discovers the pot of gold, the hen that lays golden eggs, or the "treasure hard to attain," the very thing that is most overlooked or dismissed as insignificant often holds the greatest value for individuation. Likewise, Stein's "The Problem of Envy and Sibling Rivalry" offers pearls of wisdom readers would do well not to overlook. Stein defines envy as "the root of the most malignant and chronic forms of sibling rivalry, and in the long run envy hurts both the caster of it and the recipient equally. Both can be blocked from moving toward wholeness."[22] Within the family dynamic, a child may unknowingly attract the "evil eye of envy" from a parent, sibling, cousin, grandparent, or even family friend, simply by virtue of the special role assigned to them by fate. This privileged position—whether based on good looks, athletic ability, intellectual gifts, or some other grace—may provoke resentment, leading to abuse or rejection. Stein explains:

> A child will draw the attention of an evil eye in a particular setting, for example, because children symbolize the highest value there: they are the "treasure hard to attain." With this realization, we can understand that envy is fundamentally based on a person's frustrated desire for direct access to the fountainhead of value, which in Jungian psychology is known as the Self.[23]

In this work, Stein covers a broad range of clinical research on envy, drawing on Freud's concept of "penis envy" and Melanie Klein's developmental theories and seminal paper, "A Study of Envy and Gratitude"—a classic in the field. He then elaborates on the Jungian perspective, viewing envy as a

> psychic symptom rather than as an expression of primary destructiveness, death wish, or evil. The arousal of envy is a signal of something being wrong, but it grows out of an unconscious benign hunger for full selfhood. Once constellated, however, envy can become chronic, and it can ally itself with the shadow side of the self.[24]

He also engages with the works of the London Jungian Michael Rosenthal, Aniela Jaffé, Mary Williams, Judith Hubback, and the Ulanovs' extensive study of *Cinderella and Her Sisters*. Notably, Stein remarks: "Envy may not be the most royal of the roads to the Self, but it does seem to offer some possibility for arriving there nevertheless."[25] This positive view on envy is both refreshing and insightful.

Stein also addresses clinical challenges commonly encountered in analysis, such as "writers block," which he identifies as a possible symptom of unconscious envy. He further articulates the core mechanism of envy in sibling dynamics:

> The eruption of envy and sibling rivalry occurs when a sibling gains privileged access to the Self (usually via a parent's special love and attentions) and becomes so identified with it—as the favorite child, the golden boy, the chosen one—in the mind of the rival that jealousy and the usual amount of normal sibling rivalry turns into envy. The heir to the Self (whether imagined as breast or phallus) can become its owner in such a way, or to such an extent, that its blessings and nourishment and enjoyment can be withheld from others.[26]

Stein traces the motif of the hostile brother in the Bible, citing Cain and Abel, Joseph and his brothers, King David, and even Jesus. He even extends this theme to the Risen Christ, exploring the historical tension between Christianity and Judaism. Stein explains:

> [The] risen Christ, Jesus offers entry by adoption into the Father's family, and those who enter through this means occupy the same position of privilege that Christ enjoys. This leaves Israel in the position of making rival claims to the place of honor as the 'chosen,' and so Judaism and Christianity fall into a sort of collective sibling rivalry.[27]

His historical survey of this theme is impressive.

According to Stein, chosenness

> is perhaps the Bible's most crucial theme. God makes a covenant with his chosen ones. Everything else hinges on this painful decision. When the Father chooses a favorite for some irrational, inexplicable reason, he sets in motion a dynamic that in turn generates jealousy, sibling rivalry, and ultimately envy and murderous attacks, both upon the chosen and the unchosen.[28]

This dynamic is central to Jungian analysis, representing an archaic complex with deep, archetypal roots. As such, it embodies paradox: both envy and delight, jealousy and joy. The chosen one often feels happy, while the unchosen one struggles with envy and resentment—two polarities of a single archetype, shaped by divine or fated selection (from God or the Self). Within the analytic process, these tensions can be brought into focus and reconciled through the transformative power of love.

When the complex of the unchosen son or daughter of fate is constellated in a patient, feelings of rejection may be compensated by secondary defenses. Stein observes:

> This person may not explode with rage, as is so typical of borderline personalities, but rather contain and compensate for the anger and hatred by overeating, heavy drinking, smoking, or overworking. In work, there is little enjoyment of success, however, because the result is always seen as second-best. As one patient put it to me many times, 'I am often almost it, but never quite the *one*.'[29]

To me, this sentiment rings true. How often we hear this refrain in our consulting rooms.

For the analyst, clients struggling with envy present both risk and potential reward. Stein writes:

> In making this much envy conscious, there is at the one extreme the danger of suicide or homicide; at the other, there is the possibility of redeeming the Luciferian envy-ego and forging a home for it within the order of the chosen and the acceptable.[30]

This paradox is quite Jungian. Rather than rejecting envy as evil or condemning it as sinful, the analysand must learn to divinize it, metabolizing its energy in the analyst's presence. Often, the analyst must take the lead in this process, first dissolving the envy within the countertransference.

This insight is rarely acknowledged in the analytic literature. The challenge for an analyst who endures the attacks of envy in the countertransference is to "contain all of this hostility while waiting for the Self to show its hand from another direction."[31] Through analysis, "envy can be reduced to a dynamic in search for the Self." Moreover, "envy takes on a prospective function by showing the way to the Self."[32] This is the key! Envy, rather than being purely destructive, assumes a prospective role, compensating for the evil eye with what Freud called "*lieben und arbeit*" ("love and work"). Love and vocation serve as an antidote to envy, jealousy, destructiveness, and hatred, offering a path to healing. This is why amplification in analysis is so powerful: stories make us conscious of the roles we sometimes assume, without our choosing, affirming what we intuitively recognize as the fate we must embrace, rather than resist.

In his "Conclusion" to this essay, Stein asserts that the only genuine, non-defensive resolution to envy lies in "an improved ego-self relation.... The ego needs to feel that 'I am the embodiment, the incarnation, of the Self' in his particular space-time continuum that is my body and my life. In short, we need to feel loved."[33] Love, he argues, is the transformative force that helps to transform negative emotions such as envy at their most pernicious roots. Envy, as a universal instinctive reaction, will always persist. But in the most hopeful cases, its destructive effects may be greatly diminished. Stein concludes:

> Ultimately, the Self image for both sexes must mirror ego, and the ego must feel that it is embodying the Self. "I and the Father (or Mother) are one" is a statement of the resolution that must take place in everyone. In this sense, we need all to become Christlike. Each must feel the ego to be the proper place for the incarnation of the divine. All this, while not giving up the ego's independence, self-assertion, and energetic expansion into the inner and outer cosmos.[34]

For this essay, I feel immensely grateful.

In the Field of Sleep

I now turn to an example of midlife development (transformation may be too strong a term) that Stein encountered during a particularly difficult analytic case—one that may have contributed to his shift toward a broader, more transpersonal perspective, as later articulated in *Transformation: Emergence of the Self.* The case in question, that of a patient named William, was first published by Chiron Publications in 1995 and later included in *Practicing Wholeness.* Through his description of this case, Stein explores what he terms an "interactive field of analysis"—a dynamic force as compelling in strength and determination as Freud's erotic field (Eros). However,

Stein's discovery is of a different nature: he calls this field "the magnetic force" of sleep, or the realm of "Somnus."[35]

William's pull toward unconsciousness was so great that Stein himself struggled to remain awake during sessions, often feeling as though he were caught in the leaden grip of sleep. He writes:

> For me the struggle with Somnus began the moment William ambled into the office. Eventually, it became so severe that his physical presence alone was a cue for me to want to nod off. I never did actually fall asleep completely, but many times my head touched the waters, and I would pull myself up from them with a start. The fantasy that came to me occasionally was of being mesmerized by a snake or by a snake charmer. The air would get thick, my eyes heavy, my mind utterly blank, and only by the greatest effort of will was I able to hang on to the slightest shred of consciousness.... William was hypnotic.[36]

Reading about Stein's struggle to maintain his sanity in this case evokes a sense of unease: Is this what it means to be a Jungian analyst? Stein's experience of shamanic countertransference, or "psychic influence," coupled with the oppressive weight of William's mother complex, possesses an unsettling contagion. When I first reviewed this paper 26 years ago, I too felt its "virus," or "psychic infection."[37] At the time, I experienced a temporary "writer's paralysis" that lasted for days—a creative impasse that was only resolved through a "synchronistic" event, when an older, "fatherly" friend invited me to join him at his gym for a workout. His mentor-like guidance, offered in casual conversation, dissipated my paralyzing fears—particularly the anxiety of not being able to complete my review. This relief was most welcome.

Studying Stein closely, we may gain invaluable insight into our own countertransference responses and the three attitudes he identifies. As he describes, shamanic countertransference unfolds within the "psychic body," as "The virus must search out a suitable host cell (i.e., complex) in the analyst's psychic body to fix upon and to enter."[38] He continues:

> When William first met with me, he almost immediately infected me with this hypnotic, deadening force.... I hypothesize that the pathogenic virus entered my psyche via my mother complex, through a similarity in structure. (Although my own actual mother was quite different from his in many respects, she shared the trait of unconsciously undermining my separation from herself and my identifying with my father.) Through this complex, the virus could enter and, in it, reproduce itself.... Thus, the shamanic contact was made, and the circuit was closed.[39]

Stein demonstrates his perseverance with this case, recounting a pivotal dream from William's analysis:

> In the single most important dream of the analysis, William finds himself trapped on his grandmother's farm. He comes upon his father's truck, however,

and steals it to make an escape. He is on the way out, having overcome the greatest barriers, when he awakes.[40]

Ironically, before William's abrupt termination of therapy, he failed to return a copy of Erich Neumann's *The Origins and History of Consciousness,* which he had taken from Stein's shelf. With the aid of the patient's dream, Stein interpreted this "theft" metaphorically as the theft of his father-analyst's "truck." In a moment of wry recognition, he attributed this act of kleptomania to none other than the god Hermes, himself. This interpretation suggests that consciousness, itself, was the aim of William's individuation process—just as it is for all of us navigating our destinies in postmodernity. The goal, Stein suggests, is to cultivate as much consciousness as possible within a lifetime, even if this requires invoking the trickster god Hermes to catalyze the highest potential awareness of the Self, shadow, and all. While such a dream image may not reach the transpersonal depth of the imagery found in Rilke's poetry, Rembrandt's paintings, Picasso's art, Jung's visions, or the butterfly woman's dream motifs, which formed the empirical foundation of *Transformation: Emergence of the Self,* it nonetheless sheds light on what an initial experience of transformation may look like during the midlife passage. Moreover, it underscores why the third pillar of Jungian psychoanalysis—dream work—is indispensable to analytic understanding and theory. Ultimately, the father's truck symbolized the evolution of consciousness triggered by the father archetype, which was activated in William's transference to Stein.

Spiritual and Religious Aspects of Modern Analysis

This paper was originally included in a volume published by Routledge in 2004, edited by Joseph Cambray and Linda Carter, and it stands as one of Stein's most transparent essays regarding his position on the developmental and symbolic splits that have occurred in Jungian institutes over the years. Throughout his career, Stein has navigated these divides, holding the tension between opposing perspectives. Here, I will provide a brief synopsis of the essay's main ideas.

Turf wars among Jungians and post-Jungians are a well-known phenomenon, familiar to virtually all analysts. Every institute has its dysfunctions, carrying the potential to divide into factions over doctrinal disputes, training methodologies, and differing ideals of analytical practice. After providing a fair and balanced overview of the conflicts that have arisen within Jungian institutes since the field's inception, Stein offers a critique that subtly reveals his classical leanings.

At the heart of this essay, Stein examines what he terms the "disease of modernity"—a condition marked by disconnection from the ego-Self axis and the religious function of the psyche. He argues that religious creeds can never substitute for authentic spiritual experience, which alone has the power to effect genuine personality change at any stage of life. For this reason, Stein asserts, analysts after Jung are essentially agnostic. He writes: "there are no Christian analysts, Jewish analysts, Hindu analysts, or Muslim analysts—there are only analysts." In this view, the "'analytic space' therefore, is ideally empty (negative) until material enters from the individual analysand who walks into a session."[41] He continues:

> The practice of organized religion gets in the way of the religious function when it is used defensively, or is taken too concretely and applied by the ego's defensive operations.... Religious leaders are famous for traumatizing people into belief and discipleship.[42]

From my reading of this rare piece, it is evident that Stein envisions "personal destiny and meaning within a cosmological symbol system" as the foundation of a new mythos.[43] Yet, he argues, modernity lacked transcendence, and this is one of the primary causes of postmodern malaise. In postmodernity, not only is transcendence absent, but there is also an increasing search for transcendental experiences. This is why I see Stein's writings at the forefront of the post-Jungian movement, advancing an integrative model of the psyche bridging the developmental and relational schools of analysis and the symbolic and transpersonal traditions. His writings create openings for metaphysical experience, allowing psychology and theology to intersect. Unlike Jung, who explicitly framed his religious analysis in reference to the God image, rather than God, itself, Stein does not force an artificial boundary between these disciplines. Nevertheless, Stein writes:

> For many of the people who came to see him for psychological treatment, Jung stated more than once that the major problem was not medical but spiritual.... They were alienated from their own psychological roots, without inner mooring, adrift on the open seas of modernity without a compass.... He therefore enlisted dreams to study the religious function at work within the unconscious of modern scientific people, on the theory that dreams offer a sort of X-ray of what is going on under the surface of the unconscious.[44]

Jungian psychoanalysis thus evolved into a modern form of spiritual practice, conducted "in conjunction with the analysis of complexes, dreams, and the transference." Jung himself saw it as "a modern type of spiritual discipline, akin to the Spiritual Exercises of Ignatius Loyola or the meditation practices of some Eastern religious traditions. In the analytic experience, a person can discover and recover the religious function."[45]

Stein presents a comprehensive survey of key writings on the religious function by both early Jungians and post-Jungians. He examines the works of C.A. Meier, Gerhard Adler, Barbara Hannah, Esther Harding, Jolande Jacobi, Aniela Jaffe, James Kirsch, and Marie-Louise von Franz, while also acknowledging the contributions of the Guild for Pastoral Psychology in London—where Jung delivered his 1939 lecture "The Symbolic Life"—as well as Michael Fordham's pamphlet "Analytical Psychology and Religious Experience." Additionally, he references the works of Nathan Swartz-Salant, Donald Kalsched,[46] Ann Ulanov, Edward Edinger, Mario Jacoby, and Lionel Corbett.[47]

What interests me most, however, is Stein's role as a "linking figure" within the field. He argues that personal meaning and destiny were largely deemphasized in analytic developments after Jung, noting that "the critics attacked his [Jung's] reliance on dream interpretation and activation of the archetypal layers of the unconscious through active imagination and his relative neglect of the transference."[48]

Stein's essay is rich in historical analysis. While he acknowledges the importance of "the careful reconstruction of early psychological development and attachment between parent and infant"—an experience often re-experienced in the transference—he also highlights the criticism leveled by Michael Fordham and the London group. Their argument, as Stein paraphrases, was that "the symbolic approach... was not clinically sharp and grounded enough. It did not address the psychological difficulties of patients who sought help for their common neurotic conditions, most of which revolved around problems with relationships."[49] At this juncture, Stein responds directly to these critiques. I will quote him at length:

> To this, the symbolically oriented analysts answered that the so-called clinical approach failed to deliver on the most important issue of all, namely establishing the ego-Self connection and generating a sense of personal meaning. It lacked the religious element, just as modernity lacks it, and it therefore failed to connect the modern ego to the transcendent, to the Self. Without this connection, wholeness is impossible. A person could be in analysis for hundreds of hours, could understand all the reasons for his or her suffering based on early childhood traumas, could be made more relational and competent in ordinary human relationships, but would not be "cured" of the disease of the modern, namely the lack of connection to the religious function and to the symbols that bring the ego into a more conscious relationship with the Self.
>
> As the debates raged in congresses and publications, the two sides gradually began hearing one another, and changes took place on both parts. The Zürich people became less archetypal and symbolic, and the London people started to talk about the Self in a way that could justify capitalizing the word.[50]

This essay offers one of the most succinct overviews of the infighting in our field and the attempts to resolve these conflicts that I have ever encountered. Even as a graduate of the Zürich school, Stein's perspective is not biased. His commentary remains inclusive of the entire discipline. At the same time, he delivers a sharp critique of the state of Jungian institutions, arguing that the religious function has been undermined, and there has been pervasive disregard for the transpersonal dimension of analysis. Additionally, the institutional schisms have eroded the precious emphasis Jung originally placed on the numinous, inspired by Rudolph Otto's *The Idea of the Holy*.

Amidst this discussion, Stein offers a compelling definition of the religious function in Jungian analytical practice. Previously, we saw how individuation unfolds in poets, artists, and even a philanthropist-physician, just as it did in the life of Jung, himself. Indeed, individuation, Stein emphasizes, is not elitist, but democratic. He describes the religious function as a "mythopoetic instinct of sorts,"[51] and argues (following Jung) that what truly heals the psyche is a religious attitude. He writes:

> The hidden network of object relations, which includes the psychological and physical domains of our lives, shows its presence sometimes in astonishing ways. If we could see the full extent of it, we would see that we are each connected by threads in a great fabric whose extent and intimate design are beyond our comprehension, and we touch each other in strange ways and surprising places. The net result of such a synchronistic experience is a conviction that there are unseen factors at work behind the scenes, which we do not control or understand. If we pay attention to them, we are engaged in what Jung called the religious attitude.[52]

Faith of the Analyst

The next essay under review is "The Faith of the Analyst," which Stein opens with a fundamental observation: "Faith is a mystery. Some people have it and some don't. It may depend on childhood."[53] He notes that, in analytic practice, patients who experienced significant physical, emotional, or psychological struggles during childhood—often hovering between life and death—frequently exhibit an uncanny connection to mental states akin to mystical spirituality. He writes:

> [the] supernatural hovers above them, and entry into another world is an ever present possibility. Sometimes this frightens them, but if it does not it can turn into faith in their destiny as individuals. If they become Jungian psychoanalysts, they often show a gift for sustaining the pressures of taking a deep dive into the unconscious with their patients. Their faith, which is based on personal experience of the transcendent, sustains them through thick and thin.[54]

"But faith in what?"[55] Stein asks. He defines faith as "a kind of knowledge—of the unseen, of supernatural and ultimate Power(s) operating behind the scenes and responsible for there being something rather than nothing and for destiny both individual and collective."[56] He then cites a letter Jung wrote to the Dominican theologian Father Victor White, who was struggling with his faith: "I don't want to prescribe a way to people, because I know that my way has been prescribed to me by a hand far above my reach."[57] This, Stein suggests, is the hand of God, the Self, or divinity—an ineffable force that can never be fully named, yet whose presence is unmistakable during moments of great meaning. Stein then poses an even deeper question:

> What is destiny, fate? Do they really exist? To hold that each life has a destiny or fate is itself a statement of faith and must be answered on the same level. And why would one want to change it? In reflecting on this question, I have to confess that I don't think we can interfere with an individual's destiny if that is what

Jung meant by "a hand far above my reach." But we can come to accept it, even to love it (*amor fati*). For the analyst to take this position, however, requires an act of faith, namely that each individual's destiny is of value, even of ultimate value and meaning. Without this attitude engendered by faith, the analyst might be tempted to play God and try to help a person change their destiny.[58]

Would it be fair to say that, for many—if not most—Jungians, destiny is closely tied to meaningful chance, good fortune, or synchronicity? Stein answers affirmatively: "The cosmological-metaphysical vision Jung proposes in the synchronicity essay, which von Franz develops in her work, *Number and Time,* has its starting point in the common human experience of meaningful coincidence."[59] Synchronicity offers insights into the patterns of our destiny, guiding us toward our destination— our ultimate goal in the Self. Faith, as Stein describes, "implies contact with and knowledge about Divinity, a supernatural reality."[60] Further, to know divinity is to have experienced it—perhaps not just once, but repeatedly.

This is a crucial insight that should not be overlooked. Regarding Jung's personal faith, Stein observes: "he often expressed hostility and defiance if pressed to accept authoritative teachings about transcendent or metaphysical teachings about God. But he did *respect* the religious traditions, all of them."[61] Nevertheless, Stein also notes, "Jung has great difficulty with the word 'faith.'"[62] This is indeed true.

What, then, was Jung's stance on faith within analysis? Stein explains: "One could say that he looked at all of them [all faiths] from the outside with an unprejudiced gaze, and from this perspective all were of equal value—for psychology." Stein challenges readers to take Jung at his word, particularly regarding the importance of owning up to experiences of synchronicity. He asks: "do we go as far as Jung did in owning up to, trusting, and submitting to a 'hand far above [our] reach'? I mean this as a challenge."[63] How many of us can truly say that we have met this challenge?

In this thought-provoking paper, published in the *Journal of Analytical Psychology* in 2011, Stein reveals his own personal faith:

> Put in a few words and rather abstractly, my faith platform is that time and eternity intersect and assure the transcendent value of certain numinous experiences, which in turn offer a deep sense of meaning for life…. The element of numinosity in this moment is key. In my experiences, however, the Deity who is present in this moment is not always the biblical one, although for me the symbol of Christ remains central.[64]

How, then, can an analyst best support a patient grappling with questions of destiny, fate, or faith—questions that demand individual answers? Stein argues: "To hold that each life has a destiny or fate is itself a statement of faith and must be answered on the same level."[65] Faith in individuation goes hand in hand with faith in destiny. Thus, with the process of individuation comes experience, and "here the analyst must hold on to the faith in individuation as an archetypal process."[66]

Stein further explains that faith implies personal experience of something transcendent—a force "higher" than the ego, such as an unseen hand that sustains us through obstacles on our pilgrimage to the Self. He writes: "Faith here means a kind of knowledge... for destiny both individual and collective."[67] His perspective on Providence reflects a Protestant influence, shaped by his upbringing and education at Yale. He asserts:

> Faith is not trust in just anything, it is trust specifically in Christ. And the mystery of faith is resolved by John Calvin in his notion of predestination: the people of faith are blessed and given their capacity for faith by divine Providence. Faith itself is rooted in transcendence.[68]

As we have seen, for Stein, faith is inseparable from individuation, numinous experience, synchronicity, and destiny—all of which are rooted in transcendence and divine Providence. Jung, however, struggled with faith—a difficulty that Stein attributes to a broader and more encompassing "Christianity complex." For Jung, faith could not be accepted passively, Instead, it required direct experience—both personal and analytic—through rigorous exploration of dreams, visions, myths, religion, synchronicity, alchemy, relationships, and life itself. His father's own struggles with faith became, in many ways, Jung's heavy cross to bear.

> This nexus of emotionally charged material—the basis for what could be called Jung's "Christianity complex"—was made of images of pious church elders in black coats burying corpses of children, of threatening Jesuits in black dress, and of references to Lord Jesus, who, the child heard, liked to steal children from their homes when they slept. Then, there were the eight parson uncles, most of whom inspired fear in the boy, and a frightful dream of an underground phallus that his mother called the "man-eater."[69]

Stein coined the term "transformational moment" to describe a numinous, transcendent experience. He writes:

> The intuition of an intersection or interpretation of time and eternity, the finite and the infinite, the concrete and the symbolic is the essence of this experience. It has a feeling of timelessness, and it communicates a sense of meaning that can be trusted for the present and the future. The hand behind the timing and exact location of these intersections is hidden in the Great Mystery. It is the "hand far above my head," as Jung says.[70]

For Stein, faith in the Great Mystery is synonymous with faith in God, and what is encountered in the Great Mystery is nothing less than "infinite potential":

> The horizontal interpersonal relationship, with all of its transference and projections, illusions and disillusionments, love and hate and other dramas, is

intersected by a vertical line of infinite value and potential for meaning that extends beyond the two empirical humans in this joint venture. In this we can trust.[71]

Trust is another word for faith. For Jung, it meant faith in transformation—understood in the broadest possible sense. Stein explains that this trust was central to Jung's thinking after the writing of *The Red Book*: "If we look at how Jung came to his faith in transformation and personal Gnosis as described in *Liber Novus*, we see many encounters with the Dead and even with Death itself." From the "depths of the millennia," Jung's "phoenix" finally ascended from the ashes and dust. With this ascent, Stein concludes, Jung encountered "the experiential/existential ground of his faith in the individuation process."[72] Faith in transformation, then, requires surrender to a higher pattern of destiny—one that guides us, provided we place ourselves in its service.

The Symbolic Attitude: A Core Competency for Jungian Psychoanalysis

First published in a Routledge volume in 2022, "The Symbolic Attitude: A Core Competency for Jungian Psychoanalysis" includes some of Stein's most recent thinking. In the essay, Stein emphasizes that a symbolic attitude is fundamental to both the research and clinical application of Jungian psychoanalysis, particularly through the study of dreams. Moreover, this attitude is necessary for advancing individuation as a cultural goal for postmodern society, facilitated through analytic practice, teaching, and writing. The analytic relationship itself must be understood symbolically, particularly in the interpersonal dynamics of the transference. Individuation, Stein asserts, cannot be fully grasped without symbolic thinking—whether regarding instincts, archetypes, motivations, or moments of meaning. As a core competency, this attitude serves as the foundation for all Four Pillars of Jungian psychoanalysis, representing the single most important attribute of an analyst.

Stein's own engagement with the symbolic spans more than 50 years. Since writing his dissertation at the University of Chicago, the concept of vocation has been central to his thinking about analytical psychology, religion, and their intersection. He believes that "adequate training of Jungian psychoanalysts must not only include but directly focus upon and strongly emphasize the art and craft of working with symbols in analysis."[73]

As described in his earlier essay, "Spiritual and Religious Aspects of Modern Analysis," Jung's 1939 lecture, "The Symbolic Life," delivered at the Guild for Pastoral Psychology in London, was pivotal in shaping Jungian thought. Expanding on this, Stein writes:

> Symbols are the key to discovering and unlocking the treasure chests of the unconscious. They provide direction for movement forward in time in the individuation process, and they suggest meaning looking backward at one's personal

and collective history. The task of the analyst is to take careful note of them as they emerge in the therapeutic relationship, to lift them up and hold them in mind as the analysis proceeds, and to help the analysand to reflect on them and let them suggest the meanings they may convey to the conscious mind.[74]

This means that anyone who wishes to train and to acquire the skills necessary to perform the work of analysis competently must have acquired the skill to work with symbols as they occur in the analytic process.... The vocation of the analyst is similar to the religious vocation in the sense that one is drawn to this specific way of thinking about the meaning of images and experiences.[75]

In the next chapter, Stein examines 1939 as a watershed year in Jung's life—not only because of his London talk (a contribution Stein considers among the finest in Jung's *Collected Works*), but also due to an important vision of Christ that emerged that same year, as well as his seminal essay on "Rebirth" (a theme that recurs throughout Stein's writings). At 64 years old, on the eve of World War II, Jung stood at a significant turning point. Symbols of great vitality were converging, shaping the course of his unfolding future. One of the most profound shifts in Jung's inner trajectory at the time was his deepening engagement with the archetype of Christ, beginning what would become a 20-year preoccupation with Christianity—Stein's specialty. As Stein will explain, this shift in Jung's calling was directly linked to his numinous vision of the greenish-gold Christ on the cross, which remained with him for the rest of his life.

Notes

 1 CW4, 2.
 2 CW4, 17.
 3 CW4, 6.
 4 CW4, 27.
 5 CW4, 31.
 6 CW4, 36.
 7 CW4, 37.
 8 CW4, 38.
 9 CW4, 41.
10 CW4, 42, 43.
11 CW4, 43.
12 CW4, 46.
13 CW4, 51.
14 CW4, 51, 52.
15 CW4, 57.
16 CW4, 66.
17 CW4, 67.
18 CW4, 67, 68.
19 CW4, 71.
20 CW4, 73.
21 CW4, 98–100.
22 CW4, 115.
23 CW4, 116.
24 CW4, 120.

25 CW4, 122.
26 CW4, 123.
27 CW4, 129.
28 CW4, 128.
29 CW4, 129.
30 CW4, 132.
31 CW4, 133.
32 CW4, 133.
33 CW4, 136.
34 CW4, 137, 138.
35 CW4, 166.
36 CW4, 164.
37 CW4, 178.
38 CW4, 180.
39 CW4, 181.
40 CW4, 173.
41 CW4, 202.
42 CW4, 189.
43 CW4, 191.
44 CW4, 193.
45 CW4, 194.
46 CW4, 194–195.
47 CW198, 199.
48 CW4, 198.
49 CW4, 198.
50 CW4, 198, 199.
51 CW4, 185.
52 CW4, 209, 210.
53 CW4, 239.
54 CW4, 239.
55 CW4, 253.
56 CW4, 241.
57 CW4, 244.
58 CW4, 249.
59 CW4, 180.
60 CW4, 241.
61 CW4, 243.
62 CW4, 243.
63 CW4, 245.
64 CW4, 447.
65 CW4, 249.
66 CW4, 253.
67 CW4, 241.
68 CW4, 242.
69 CW5, 92.
70 CW4, 246.
71 CW4, 248.
72 CW4, 255.
73 CW4, 299.
74 CW4, 299, 300.
75 CW4, 313.

Chapter 6

Collected Writings Volume 5

Analytical Psychology and Christianity

Jung's Treatment of Christianity: Jung as a Shamanic Healer and His Incubation of a New God Image

When I was first invited to review Stein's 1985 book, *Jung's Treatment of Christianity: The Psychotherapy of a Religious Tradition*, in 1998, my analysis was necessarily brief, as the primary focus of my essay was *Transformation: Emergence of the Self*. However, while writing this book, I found myself pulled into deeper reflection on Stein's central thesis, particularly as applied to the field of Jungian psychoanalysis. Nearly 40 years ago, Stein observed:

> Jung's relationship to Christianity has remained largely unexamined to date. No one has ventured a full-scale study of how his life and thought are to be related to Christian tradition or of how his writings on Christianity are to be related to his personal and psychological thought.[1]

This statement remains thought-provoking, given the enduring relevance of Jung's ideas. My own undergraduate thesis at the University of California, Santa Cruz, submitted in 1982 as part of my Bachelor of Arts in Depth Psychology and Religion, explored a specific aspect of Jung's engagement with Christianity, particularly with respect to Meister Eckhart. That research has only recently been published in a significantly expanded and revised form.[2]

Building on the model he first introduced in his book *In Midlife*, Stein compellingly argues: "Repeatedly he [Jung] made the request, most especially of the clergy and the theologians, that he be regarded not as a philosopher or a metaphysician but rather as an empirical scientist."[3] This characterization of Jung has always resonated with me. However, just a few pages later, he makes a somewhat surprising assertion: "Jung's identity as an empirical scientist was a disguise for another secret identity, that of the philosopher-theologian or even prophet."[4] It is important to remember that Stein wrote his manuscript four decades ago, and his ideas have remained remarkably consistent over time.

Stein argues that Jung emerged from his midlife crisis by gradually shedding his persona as an empirical scientist—a process triggered by his confrontation with

DOI: 10.4324/9781003664024-7

internal images of the philosopher-theologian, prophet, and ultimately "shamanic healer." This blurring of boundaries between various masks led to an expansion of Jung's personality, allowing him to integrate multiple aspects of himself into a greater unity of character. This transformation involved numerous transmutations, many of which were initiated by dreams and visions containing Christian symbolism. One of the most striking of these was Jung's 1939 vision of a greenish-gold Christ on the cross—a vision that led Jung to reflect on Christianity's potential for healing its own "illness," namely "the goal of its development toward wholeness."[5] According to Stein, this meaning was constellated through Jung's "'shamanic' suffering of his Christian heritage."[6] In Stein's view, Jung fully embraced the wounded healer archetype in his most controversial work, "Answer to Job." Regarding the distinctive style of this work, Stein observes:

> This is the approach of the shamanic healer who allows himself to become infected with the illness of the patient. This type of healer takes the disease in, creates a medicine to cure it, and then returns the medicine to the patient by means of influence.[7]

Over time, Jung's shamanic role evolved, though his early persona as a natural scientist remained his primary identity throughout most of his adult life. This foundational aspect of his character was affirmed in a revelatory dream from his student years at the University of Basel, as recorded in *Memories, Dreams, Reflections*. However, the healer-therapist does not formulate a cure solely through reason or solar conscience. Instead, the cure is generated by something mysterious and irrational within the psyche—an aspect closer to lunar conscience (characterized by the feminine mysteries and the reflected light of the moon). Such medicines arise naturally from the psyche, through the transcendent function. Christ, as a physician, healer, and miracle worker, embodied the wisdom and power of the shaman—an archetype accessible to anyone who responds to its call. Yet, as Stein emphasizes, this does not mean one needs to become a Christian or shaman. As he provocatively states: "As the old God-image of Christianity dies and decays, a new one is incubating."[8] What, then, is the nature of the God image emerging at this time? While many Jungian have explored this question, few have surpassed the depth of Stein's original insights. In his view: "The image of God as quaternity in conjunction with the concept of human wholeness would function in this transformed religious tradition as the master symbol."[9]

Building on his analysis of four significant dreams and visions recounted in *Memories, Dreams, Reflections*, Stein explores transformations in Jung's images of Christ. Among these is Jung's dream of fetching the Holy Grail while bedridden in India in 1938, followed by his 1939 vision of a greenish-gold Christ on the cross, which occurred while he was meditating on the spiritual exercises of St. Ignatius of Loyola. According to Stein, these experiences marked the emergence of something mysteriously post-Christian, alchemical, and deeply transformative within Jung's psyche: a new God image. Clearly, this God image catalyzed a fundamental shift in

Jung, changing him from a strictly medical man into an analyst-shaman, or culture healer. Stein interprets the first dream as follows:

> The beginning of Jung's intensive exploration of the religious meaning of European alchemy dated from the dream he had in 1938, which had presented him with the theme of the quest for the Holy Grail. This dream, the last major turning point in Jung's vocational life, had launched him on the path that he would travel during the last two decades. His purpose became no less than the therapeutic transformation of Christianity and Western culture.[10]

Notably, Stein refers here to the "last point in Jung's vocational life." By this, he intends to illustrate that Jung's life was guided by a symbolic attitude, shaped by vocational dreams emerging at key waystations on his path to the Self. The dream of fetching the Holy Grail marked a pivotal transition in Jung's calling, shifting him from a psychiatrist to a cultural shaman tasked with healing the wounded Fisher King of post-Christian culture. As Stein observes elsewhere, a process of incubation had already begun during Jung's crafting of *The Red Book*. However, in 1938 and 1939, the shamanic archetype was becoming manifest, summoning Jung to find a cure for what was ailing the West. This trajectory later crystallized in Jung's vision of a greenish-gold Christ on the cross—a revelation that emerged as an outgrowth of his travels to India. Stein further notes that Jung "regarded himself as a Parsifal to the ailing Christian dominant and a bringer of the Holy Grail back to Christendom."[11]

As Stein highlights throughout his *Collected Writings*, Jung dedicated the final two decades of his life to exploring the Christ symbol—in his analytic practice, his teaching, and his writing. In Stein's view, the Grail represents Christianity's "child"—a nascent form of spiritual renewal. Jung's ultimate calling was to deliver this child, like a maieutic midwife, to contemporary civilization and culture. Stein likens this to the "age of the Holy Ghost, in which the spirit of God comes to function as the *spiritus rector* of everyday life for the conscious individual through the transcendent function." In such an age, an individual (whether or not they are in analysis) may "experience his or her own religious symbols and create a personal theology."[12] However, it is important to note that Stein's use of the term "theology" here is his own, not Jung's. Though Jung wrote of his personal myth in *Memories, Dreams, Reflections*, he never professed to be constructing a new theology. In fact, he consistently avoided theological assertions, maintaining a firm commitment to empirical inquiry over metaphysical speculation.

As a Jungian and theologian, Stein sees his vocation as one of synthesis, revision, and correction. He seeks to address the critical gap of metaphysical considerations left by the natural sciences, which has excluded something essential from the lexicon of Jungian psychoanalysis—particularly in relation to the "child" that Jung symbolically delivered to the modern world. Additionally, Stein points to the need for a more nuanced approach to Jung's biography, critiquing the "hagiographical overtones" of the accounts of early disciples such as Lawrence van der Post, Barbara Hannah, and, to some extent, Marie-Louise von Franz.

While Stein himself generally avoids such idealization, he does not shy away from exposing lesser-known, and sometimes unflattering, aspects of Jung's personality. He writes:

> Nor did his life especially exemplify any of the great Christian virtues such as humility, long-suffering, patience, generosity, forbearance, or charity. He was not a saint. In fact, many accounts of his behavior and attitudes indicate shortness of temper, irascibility, bluntness to the point of brutality, impunity and skepticism, and intolerance of differing opinions.[13]

Here, Stein engages in an analytic assessment of Jung's humanness, acknowledging that, despite his profound psychological insights, he was not always able to transcend his own complexes—though he did achieve a form of liberation from them. This paradox, Stein suggests, is one that persists in postmodernity, confronting even those who consider themselves enlightened.

Stein offers a more balanced biographical perspective on Jung than the accounts of first-generation Jungians, who tended to idealize their subject. And he does so intentionally, suggesting that the era of striving for perfection is over. In the wake of Jung, the path forward is one of wholeness. In this regard, the developmental school has played an important role in advancing Jungian psychology, both refining its theories and addressing its shortcomings. Stein himself harbors no illusions of Jung's totality. Instead, he seeks to humanize Jung, avoiding the problem of over-identification. However, despite his somewhat critical stance, I sense Stein's deep love for Jung—perhaps akin to the love he felt for Jesus in his youth.

One unresolved issue in Jung's early writings, which I will explore further in my review of Volume 7 of the *Collected Writings*, titled *The Problem of Evil*, is the precise meaning of the Self. This concept, and its implications for Christianity, has understandably perplexed many of Jung's readers, and perhaps theologians most of all. Stein often addresses theologically minded readers in his works on the Christ symbol, aiming to clarify Jung's actual meaning—a crucial task for psychotherapy, given the general lack of religious education. Unlike Jung, Stein is unafraid to tread on theological ground, exploring ideas Jung himself avoided. For instance, he writes:

> The one-world theology that would flow from this [new] doctrine of God would lead to a definition of God as inclusive of all aspects of reality, mundane and transcendent. God would become synonymous with reality and include all dimensions of what we crudely discriminate as good and evil, spiritual and physical, constructive and destructive, strong and weak, entropic and negentropic, active and passive. In this theology, God would be excluded from nothing and nothing would be excluded from God.[14]

Stein even notes an emerging development within Christianity that he describes as a "Hinduistic spirit of ecumenical tolerance for every conceivable image of God and for every possible expression of the self."[15] This formulation provides a clear articulation of Jung's vision of religious pluralism.

In his 1989 lectures, "A Psychological Reading of the Bible," Stein further refines Jung's interpretations of Jesus, particularly in the Synoptic Gospels. Here, he offers critical corrections to what he views as Jung's misreadings of Christ's life and teachings. With keen insight, he asserts:

> Often those with a healing occupation will themselves become seriously ill patients and in finding healing within themselves, they are able to offer it to others. The suffering servant [Jesus] is such a figure. "By his stripes we are healed," is the telling sign. Because he takes on the sickness of the people who need healing, he can eventually produce, from his own willing and conscious suffering, the medicine that will heal the others. Thus, the suffering servant must be looked upon as a spiritual healer who has obtained the power to heal by virtue of his acceptance of suffering—and by the consequent constellation of spiritual "medicine."[16]

This interpretation closely resembles what Stein claimed for Jung only four years earlier in his dissertation. Here, however, Jesus emerges as a shamanic healer who not only provided a cure for his own time but also continues to do so even today, as the Christian myth remains very much alive (as is evident in the faith of more than 1.4 billion Catholics and 840 million Protestants worldwide). In *Jung's Treatment*, Stein observes: "Jung never completely clarified the nature and full meaning of his writings on Christianity."[17] Thus, Stein's first and only major book on the subject was a welcome addition to the growing post-Jungian literature. At this early stage, however, his own views remained somewhat veiled, as he was still in the process of finding his authentic voice in relation to Jung. This would shift during his biblical lectures just a few years later, in which he would resurrect aspects of Christianity that Jung left unspoken.

Throughout his analytic, teaching, and writing career, Stein has remained deeply engaged with Jung's repudiation of the traditional portrayal of Christ as the "perfect" man—one entirely without sin or evil—seeking to revise this misperception within a psychological framework. In his view, the Jesus of the Synoptic Gospels was not a flawless divine figure but rather the "Son of Man"—a humble, human being. He mingled freely with commoners, ate and drank affectionately with publicans and prostitutes, performed his first miracle by turning "water into wine for the added merriment of a wedding party," defied "rigid religious rules regarding the Sabbath," and even displayed "anger at the point of being intemperate." This, Stein argues, is hardly a portrait of a perfect human being. As he puts it: "He breathes, he sweats, he cries. This is not the image of abstract and inhuman perfection."[18]

Throughout his extensive scholarship, Stein has observed that Jung was guided by "a largely unconscious *spiritus rector*. This guidance... was supplied by his strong urge to heal Christianity, which led him unerringly to the very heart of the tradition's ailments and demanded that he offer his psychotherapeutic help."[19]

Further emphasizing this point, he writes: "Jung's stance toward Christianity was fundamentally that of a psychotherapist, and so the goal of all his efforts with this 'patient,' Christianity, was its psychotherapeutic transformation."[20]

Like Jung, Stein has been called to advance the psychotherapeutic transformation of Christianity, across cultures and denominations. Also resembling Jung, he is a culture healer. However, I propose that Stein's works have, in many ways, performed therapy on Jung's psychology of Christianity, making it more theologically grounded and practically applicable. Undertaking this near-Herculean task, Stein has creatively reshaped Jung's writings on God and evil, rendering them more accessible for both theologians and therapists alike.

My hypothesis as to why this is the case is as follows: Stein's first encounter with Jung at Yale was, as we have seen, through *Memories, Dreams, Reflections*. Prior to the publication of that book (1957), Jung had insisted—almost invariably, with one exception—that he was not writing about the Absolute. However, *Memories, Dreams, Reflections* marked a significant shift in his focus. No longer constrained by the demands of empirical psychology, Jung turned to narrating his personal myth—his subjective account of individuation. In this task, he no longer needed to omit God from psychology. He could let go of the mask of the natural scientist and speak freely as a mythmaker for modernity. This perspective left a lasting impression on Stein, shaping his approach to analytical psychology and allowing him to acknowledge and analyze Jung's plural personas. Stein recognized that these various identities—Jung's different masks of the Self—were expressions of the evolving nature of the Self as it spoke through him.

Jung's "Green Christ": A Transformational Symbol for the Future of Christianity

As we have seen, Jung's vision of the luminous greenish-gold Christ at the foot of his bed in 1939—one year after his dream of fetching the Holy Grail—was no doubt a milestone on his path to wholeness. Stein, in his 1987 essay "Jung's 'Green Christ': A Transformational Symbol for the Future of Christianity," described it as a "response of the unconscious to Jung's shamanistic incubation of the problems of Christianity."[21] By incubation, Stein meant that Jung's psyche had, by this time, produced the necessary conditions for something to gestate and grow into a symbolic medicine—a cure for what was ailing Christendom. In Stein's view, Jung functioned as a shaman, seeking to heal the Christian West from its estrangement from instinct, its repression of the feminine face of divinity, its neglect of the dark side of the Self, and its avoidance of the reality of evil. Jung's vision pointed toward a reintegration of the transformative power of the numinous, bestowing grace and a psychological path to spiritual liberation. He elaborates:

> As Christianity opens the pages on its third millennium, it becomes increasingly evident that its symbolic core has begun to undergo a profound process of transformation.... As a therapist who is deeply affected by the suffering of a patient

may take that suffering inward for purposes of finding a healing remedy, so Jung took the suffering of one-sidedness in Christianity into himself and found suggestions for solutions in the responses that his psyche produced.[22]

Furthermore, he writes: "The numinous spirit within the unconscious is symbolized in Jung's Green Christ."[23]

Stein appears deeply fascinated with Jung's vision, returning to it time and again for the medicine it offers.

Jung as a Theologian

In his 1990 essay, "C.G. Jung, Psychologist and Theologian," Stein explores Jung's twin vocations in psychology and theology, presenting them as fundamentally "non-dual." Here again, Stein articulates his perspective on Jung's new God image for postmodernity: "As his autobiography attests, the terms 'psyche' and 'God' were for all practical and existential purposes interchangeable for him. The experience of the psyche's wholeness, i.e., the Self, was for Jung equivalent to an experience of God."[24] This idea echoes Stein's earlier statement about a one-world theology in which "God would be excluded from nothing and nothing would be excluded from God."[25]

Theologians have sometimes objected to Jung's forays into theology, and perhaps with good reason. As Stein argues, the two Jungs—the scientist and the theologian—were at times divided over the issue of evil. In some of Jung's works, the God image appears dualistic, while in other works it appears non-dual. In Stein's words: "On one side, the Good God lives and rules in heaven; on the other side, the Evil Power, i.e., Satan, lives and rules in hell. A vast gulf divides these two realms, but they ultimately belong to One Cosmos."[26]

In this essay, Stein provides an overview of early Jungian perspectives on the challenges posed by a God concept that, on the one hand, relativizes good and evil and, on the other hand, unites them into a singular Oneness. Stein is one of the few Jungians who has carefully examined this issue, offering valuable insights for both theologians and psychoanalysts seeking to understand Jung's true conception of God.

In this vein, we might ask: What did the greenish-gold Christ on the cross represent, if it was Jung's shamanic solution to the inherent one-sidedness of Christianity? As previously noted, Stein addresses this question by distinguishing between two aspects of Jung: Jung the psychologist and Jung theologian. He asserts that these two facets of Jung's character coexisted "side by side" in "relative harmony," with no "inner conflict in Jung's personality or in his vocation between two competing voices… There is no gap between psychology and theology."[27] According to Stein, this unification was achieved by 1939.

In his numerous writings on evil, Stein clarifies some of the misunderstandings surrounding Jung's contributions to Christian thought. Notably, he asserts that Jung was never lenient in his treatment of evil. "And yet," he observes, "he did not want to argue that evil is an independent force, self-standing and totally autonomous. This would lead to severe dualism, which is precisely what he wanted to argue against. His vision stood strongly in favor of unity." Stein elaborates:

> Evil must be considered a part of the whole, therefore, and remain in relationship with the good.... As a category of thought, evil is not an embedded aspect of nature, psychical or metaphysical; it is a product of the mind.[28]

He further contends that "it is evident that he [Jung] genuinely intended to enter the domain of objectivity, albeit through the door of subjectivity... William James's work *The Varieties of Religious Experience* is not dissimilar."[29]

Having studied James extensively at the University of Chicago, Stein expands on Jung's perspective: "For Jung, the conscious subject's orientation to the archetypal Powers of the psyche is the same as the orientation to God, and the experience of the ultimate archetypal Power of the psyche, the Self, equals the experience of God."[30]

Stein's definition of evil, as outlined above, should not be unduly exasperating to theologians, even if they do not see eye to eye with Jung, particularly regarding his sometimes-paradoxical statements. The equivalence of the Self and God should not present an issue, given that in Vedic philosophy and mythology, the Self (*atman*) and God (*Brahman*) are understood as one. The question I raise regarding Stein's hypothesis of the two Jungs (the theologian and the psychiatrist) is that Jung never defined his science as theology. In this book, I argue that the non-duality of these vocations, as Stein presents them, may reflect more of Stein's own twin callings, rather than Jung's. One page later, Stein clarifies his stance, referring to Jung's theologizing as "psychology-based natural theology."[31]

In his 1995 essay, "On C.G. Jung's Psychology of Religion," Stein further underscores the compatibility between Jung's views on religious experience and those of William James:

> Jung strongly resonated with James's empirical, pragmatic, and phenomenological approach. While not necessarily agreeing with all of his philosophical positions, Jung appreciated that James did not discount or distort the psychological value of religious experience.... Just as William James collected individual experiences of diverse kinds and then compared them, looking for commonalities in structure and meaning, Jung accumulated a great diversity of images, ever watchful for patterns of symbolic significance.[32]

Stein further affirms Jung's psychology-based natural theology when he writes:

> Jung thus stands in opposition to the view that religious experience is essentially defensive, regressive, or pathological.... Again, Jung is much closer here to that of such thinkers as William James than to those who see religious experience as nothing more than regression, defense, or pathology.[33]

Here, Stein establishes a much-needed connection between Jung's views on the Self and those of James, who introduced the notion of a fourfold structure of the Self and the concepts of pluralism and radical empiricism. This perspective aligns with my own appreciation of James's influence on Jung, countering the often lop-sided, Eurocentric portrayal of his intellectual lineage. Stein offers his own inter-pretation of what the Self signifies when he writes:

> Thus, God images, which exist as psychological phenomena, may in some fashion correspond to 'God' as an objective or ontological reality beyond the psyche. This is a point that has not been taken up widely enough in the field of analytical psychology, in my opinion; too frequently Jungian authors have landed in the mire of reductionism... in their discussions of religious work.[34]

In expanding Jung's thoughts on the Self and Christianity, Stein's theological advance pushes us to the transformative edge—an area where Jung himself, in his resistance to metaphysics, did not fully mature.

I could not agree more with Stein on this point: "This human project of con-sciousness creation is, in Jung's view, the ultimate meaning of human life in the universe."[35] In Stein's view, Dante, in his journey through the *Divine Comedy*, gazed into the deepest realms of the collective unconscious—into the Self—where all was made one. More significantly, he not only experienced union with the Self but he also became infused with love, its fundamental energy. In Dante, individua-tion reached its ultimate goal, at least to the extent that is humanly possible.[36]

Jung never articulated it in quite these terms. Yet, the integration of good and evil through Jungian psychoanalysis ultimately deepens our capacity to love. After all, the realization of the Self in the universe is, at its core, a call to love—to align with what the higher Self asks of us, both within and without. As Stein affirms, "Religious images all have their point of origin in the Self and refer to the Self."[37] As Jungians, we continue to regard Jung as our ancestral shaman—the unparal-leled pioneer of our psychological field. Freud, despite his foundational contribu-tions, could not surpass him in this regard. Stein recognizes this. Seldom opposing Jung, Stein transmits Jung's teachings in an accessible and grounded manner. His approach fosters a broad communion, transcending sectarian divides in psychology and theology and embracing all perspectives within a framework of non-duality, free from exclusion or discrimination.

The Future of Christianity

The final chapter of Volume 5 of the *Collected Writings* is aptly titled "The Future of Christianity." And what is Christianity's future? This question is ultimately unanswerable. We simply do not know, and it is doubtful that Jung believed he provided a definitive answer in either *Aion* or "Answer to Job." Stein, in turn, offers a partial answer in the concluding paragraphs of this chapter, published in the same year as his book, *Transformation: Emergence of the Self* (1998). Here, Stein's discussion becomes axiomatic while engaging with Jung's well-known claim in "Answer to Job"—namely, that Christianity's resolution to the problem of Christ as the "only" God-man will, in the postmodern era, evolve into a far more democratic dispensation of the indwelling of the Holy Ghost. According to Jung, this shift will bring about the "Christification of many."[38] This idea, however, might be easily misunderstood. Importantly, it does not imply that all will become Christian or even post-Christian. Rather, because the Christ archetype functions as a central symbol of the Self within the world soul, we are all, as Stein puts it, already (potentially) Christ-like.

For some, the term "Christification" may be problematic due to its lack of specificity regarding the Paraclete and the "fourth" figure that emerges from it: the Self. Stein clarifies that Christ and the alchemical Mercurius represent two opposing poles of the psyche: "above" (Christ) and "below" (Mercurius), or spirit and instinct. He further emphasizes that, despite Jung's occasional suggestions in *Aion*, Christ and the Antichrist are not reconcilable: "Christ and Mercurius are not opposites in the sense that Christ and anti-Christ are irreconcilable opposites."[39] He concludes with an intriguing proposition: "The potential dialogue between Mercurius and Christ would be, if realized, enormously fertilizing and rich culturally."[40]

As we will later see, Stein engages in this dialogue most profoundly in his meditations on Jung's vision of the greenish-gold Christ on the cross. Within this discussion, he also explores a related figure in Islamic and Sufi literature—Khidr, the Green Man or Verdant One, as referenced in the 18th surah of the Koran. Stein revisits this theme multiple times, offering necessary clarifications on the interrelationship between Mercurius and Christ. I applaud Stein for his assertion that Christ and Antichrist are forever irreconcilable, since to suggest otherwise might mislead patients into believing that they must integrate them in some imaginary union.

Jung on Christianity Again

In "Introduction to *Jung on Christianity*," Stein further examines Jung's personal theology in relation to important Protestant and Catholic theologians, particularly Karl Barth and Victor White. For those unfamiliar with these figures, Stein's essay is highly recommended, and he also expands on their significance in later essays. Here, I want to highlight a particularly striking passage that stood out to me. In it, Stein poses a rhetorical question: "Does not individuation—a person's lifelong journey toward wholeness and consciousness—imply that the Self which guides its trajectory is purely good?" Of course, any reader even mildly acquainted with Jung's writings on Christianity will anticipate the answer. But then, Stein delivers one of his most memorable tributes to Jung, capturing his uncompromising stance in a single German word, "*Nein!*" ("No!"). He describes:

> At this point, Jung, the master and creator of analytical psychology vigorously shook his head and thundered, "Nein!" Evil is as real as good, God is darkness and light, and the doctrine of evil as *privatio boni* is a convenient rationalization

of the ego-dominated theological tradition…. Analytical psychology… is permanently open to revision and challenge. It is unlike theological doctrine, which claims immutable veracity and finality. It is not dogmatic.[41]

To me, Jung's emphatic *"Nein!"* resonates deeply.

Notes

1 CW5, 2.
2 Herrmann, S. *Meister Eckhart and C.G. Jung: On the Vocation of the Self.* Bloomington, IN: iUniverse Publishing, 2024.
3 CW5, 5.
4 CW5, 11.
5 CW5, 193.
6 CW5, 193.
7 CW5, 213.
8 CW5, 237.
9 CW5, 243.
10 CW5, 132.
11 CW5, 245.
12 CW5, 246, 247.
13 CW5, 248, 249.
14 CW5, 243.
15 CW5, 250.
16 CW6, 125–126.
17 CW5, 22.
18 CW3, 68, 69.
19 CW5, 23.
20 CW5, 23.
21 CW1, 261.
22 CW5, 251–253.
23 CW5, 260.
24 CW5, 264.
25 CW5, 243.
26 CW6, 196.
27 CW5, 275.
28 CW6, 130.
29 CW5, 277.
30 CW5, 278.
31 CW5, 279.
32 CW5, 285, 286.
33 CW5, 287.
34 CW5, 288.
35 CW5, 290.
36 CW3, 291.
37 CW5, 298.
38 CW5, 301.
39 CW5, 305.
40 CW5, 308.
41 CW5, 325.

Chapter 7

Collected Writings Volume 6
Analytical Psychology and Religion

Volume 6 of Stein's *Collected Writings*, titled *Analytical Psychology and Religion*, reflects Stein's expertise as both a theologian and a Jungian analyst. Part One, "On Reading the Bible Psychologically," establishes the fundamental interpretative approach that informs the entire work. Although the lectures compiled in this part were originally delivered in February 1989 at the Jung Center in Evanston, and later the Catholic Seminary in Mundelein, Illinois, they are clearly influenced by Stein's reading of Jung's works, as well as those of other major thinkers. However, the predominant voice throughout the text is that of the Self, as expressed through Stein's reflections. In his "Acknowledgments," Stein pays tribute to his intellectual mentors, including C.G. Jung, Erich Neumann, Marie-Louise von Franz, Rivkah Kluger, and Joseph Henderson, along with his professors at Yale, especially Paul Schubert, Professor of the New Testament. Lastly, he credits his parents, Walter and Jeanette Stein, for their influence on this work.

Stein describes the Bible as a "sacred text," emphasizing that "it has been protected zealously by generations of believers and defended by brilliant theologians and by ordinary men and women of faith."[1] He elaborates:

A psychological interpretation of the Bible resembles the psychological interpretation of a dream…. The symbols of dream and vision are grounded in history, and the history is illuminated by the dreams and visions…. Through the narrative we can sense the presence of the *spiritus rector* that guided the visionary experiences, the history and the edited presentation. And this *spiritus rector* gives this collective narrative its unique stamp.[2]

In Stein's view, God possesses a heightened awareness of dualities—perhaps even more so than Jung attributed to the divine:

It would be totally contradictory to my thesis that Yahweh is an archetype that wants to be incarnated in human form and to also say that he did not want humans to know good from evil. For it is precisely, as the serpent says, by knowing good from evil that Adam and Eve will become like God. So, we would have to conclude that God put the tree in the garden knowing full well that Adam and

DOI: 10.4324/9781003664024-8

Eve would disobey him and would eat of it, because he wanted him to do so.... God intended it. He planted the trees there.... God also knew the difference between good and evil in a similar way. Moral intelligence is especially valued in this story.[3]

Stein's vision of divine purpose is so uniquely his own, shaped by his distinct postulates. At times, I find his reading of the Bible more compelling than Jung's, particularly because Jung's persistent need to engage in polemics with theologians over the problem of good and evil sometimes distracted from his broader aims as a psychologist of trans-dualism.

When preparing these lectures, Stein was apparently in a semi-conscious, dreamlike state. For him, the Bible itself functions as a dream, though this perspective may predominantly reflect his personal reveries on unitary awareness and the continuity of thought that exists in the delicate relationship between the Bible's metaphysical teachings and Jungian psychoanalysis. "Sometimes we think that 'conscience' represents the voice of God," Stein observes, "but who is to say?" He continues in a classically Jungian manner, "it is not the voice of the Adversary, the doubting thought within God himself?"[4] Here, we see Stein ruminating on some of the same questions that Rivka Kluger explored in *Satan in the Old Testament*.

Early Jungians often approached Jung's "Answer to Job" with almost unquestioning acceptance, despite the fact that his perspective—deeply personal in nature—stood in opposition to traditional Catholic and Protestant theology. Stein, however, acknowledges the evolving nature of analytical psychology, stating in his concluding remarks: "Analytical psychology... is permanently open to revision and challenge. It is unlike theological doctrine, which claims immutable veracity and finality."

Stein offers an alternative reading that is at once classically Jungian and post-Jungian—developmental yet archetypal, symbolic yet relational. Departing from Jung in certain respects, he states: "Jesus dialogued with Satan, engaged in active imagination with his shadow—obedience confronting disobedience, submission to the Father's will standing up against rebellion and self-assertion."[5]

In these reflections, we hear Stein employing Jungian concepts to further illuminate aspects of Jung's thought—clarifying what Jung may have implied but neglected to state explicitly regarding the historical figure of Jesus and the role of the Paraclete. Through his nuanced interpretations, Stein provides deeper insight into the meaning of incarnation, particularly through his amplifications of the meaning of the Resurrection:

They see the risen Christ, they are reoriented, and finally they receive the gift of the Holy Spirit.... And what a spirit it is. It creates some kind of mystic states in them, and they can speak in strange languages. They can heal the sick.... In the Holy Spirit, we can see the release in this personality of the transcendent function, the *spiritus rector*, the guiding spirit of the Self that is not under ego control, but rather controls the ego and gives it purpose and mission in life. Of the three persons in the Holy Trinity—as this was later conceived in theology—it is the Holy Spirit who most nearly represents and speaks for the self. It is the reconciling, peace-bringing spirit.[6]

In his lecture "Faith and Individuation," Stein steps into the domain of his own authentic realization of the divine, offering his perspective on what this implies for the future of Christianity as a bridge between psychology and theology. He challenges Jung's formulation in *Memories, Dreams, Reflection*, arguing that the Holy Spirit cannot be equated with the entire Self (or reduced to the "psyche = God" equation). Instead, Stein suggests that the Holy Spirit represents something higher, more integrated, and more transcendent than the totality of the collective unconscious. Throughout his work, Stein's most enduring commitment has been to teaching the path to the Self through the transcendent function—a theme that remains central to his thought. This continuity is also evident in his exploration of the soul image, particularly in his invitation for us to consider the figures of the chthonic mother and wisdom, in dialogue with the spiritual father.

Envy and the Self

"Lecture Seven: Election and Adoption—Envy and the Self" is one of Stein's most original works and perhaps the most relevant of his efforts to integrate emotion with interpersonal relationships within the psychoanalytic matrix. He writes:

> Envy is an alarming signal of rupture in the ego-Self relation…. The stimulation of envy is a signal of an important need that is rooted in a legitimate hunger for full Selfhood…. Once constellated… envy can become chronic and come into alliance with the dark side of the Self.[7]

Here, Stein's exploration of envy aligns with his broader engagement with the role of the willing servant of the Self, as seen in his work on the healing archetype—the shamanic medicine person in organizational life—and Jesus' conscious acceptance of the role of scapegoat.

In Stein's interpretation, Jesus exhibited a heightened awareness of his divine mission, as well as the roles played by Satan and Judas in his path toward fulfilling his calling as the Messiah. Without Jesus' capacity to embrace and transmute even the evil wiles of his adversaries, Stein suggests, the redemptive narrative emerging from Bethlehem would not have been possible. Stein's early theological training at Yale Divinity School, particularly under professor Paul Schubert, provided him with a broader perspective than that of Jung, whose interpretation of the Jesus narrative was not informed by formal theological education. Stein observes that:

> Jesus takes the identity of king but also undercuts it, deconstructs it, and psychologizes it. It is with grim irony that he allows himself to be crowned and named King of the Jews. In taking this identity upon himself, he also destroys

it, grinds it to powder, and relativizes it. It is decisively subsumed under his identity as the suffering servant.[8]

Jesus was not merely an innocent victim of Roman society, Stein suggests. Not at all! While the scapegoat makes it possible for a community to free itself from its collective shadow—which may include toxic emotions of envy, hatred, and evil—by projecting these onto a chosen individual, this individual (the scapegoat) cannot effect real healing without a spiritual perspective on their assigned role. When the scapegoat successfully contains and temporarily dispels the shadow projections placed upon them, they may serve a cleansing and purifying function for the collective. In Stein's interpretation, Jesus embodies this archetype by emptying the Self and accepting his destiny as an uncrowned king. The crown of thorns suffices for such a fate. From the outset, his divine calling was to be crowned as the spiritual King of the World—a role he embraced through kenosis, or self-emptying.

Stein further presents Jesus as a therapist of sorts, anticipating elements of analytical psychology in a shamanistic sense. Through his symbolic "marriage to the cross," he acted as a lightning rod for human suffering, demonstrating extraordinary spiritual resilience in enduring betrayal, particularly from Judas. He did not resist but willingly accepted his suffering, including the lance that pierced him.

Stein's portrayal of Jesus resonates with me more profoundly than that of Jung, as it presents a figure who is less divided within himself, more conscious of his shadow, and more attuned to the complexities of evil. Unlike Jung's Jesus, who appears less savvy to the wiles of the serpent, Stein's Jesus is not a passive victim of Satan or the Adversary. Rather, he acknowledges and integrates the presence of these figures in the divine drama. This portrayal renders him more human, humble, and closely aligned with the feminine wisdom. In Stein's reading, Jesus possesses an acute awareness of humanity's need for healing—a need met through love, serving as a protective force against the virus of our times and the pervasive evils of the world.

Stein's Gospel, According to John

We now turn to Stein's Mundelein lectures on "The Gospel According to John," delivered to a Catholic seminary. Comparing these lectures—intended for a private group of Roman Catholic seminarians—with his earlier biblical lectures—presented to a predominantly Jungian audience—is particularly illuminating. The seminary, chartered by the Illinois General Assembly in 1844, provided a distinct context for Stein's theological reflections.

In his lectures, after analyzing the opening verses of the Gospel of John describing Jesus as the "Word" (Logos) of God, Stein clarifies for his audience of seminarians and future preachers what Jungians truly mean by the transcendent function.

As previously discussed, this concept is symbolized in Scripture by the indwelling of the Holy Spirit. Here, Stein offers a lucid exposition of Jung's notion of the Self, bridging psychological and theological perspectives:

> The transcendent function, according to Jung's theoretical formulation, is a psychic structure that allows for a certain amount of detachment of the ego from egoistic claims and identifications. It allows even for some detachment from one's pet ideas and compulsions, one's so-called rational attitudes. It creates an open space in consciousness to receive the words and viewpoints of other voices (inner and outer) and, if need be, for giving up one's own preferences for the larger good of a relationship or commitment... Jesus, dramatically demonstrating the possibility for a constellation of the transcendent function within the human psyche, reveals a state of development beyond that of legalism, heroism, and even mature kingship and rulership... Unfortunately, the Christ stage of individuation may be so advanced, developmentally speaking, that few individuals can actually attain it in their lifetimes.[9]

What I find most compelling about Stein's reading of the fourth Gospel is his keen awareness of his audience and his avoidance of dogmatism as a Jungian. Rather than imposing a rigid Jungian framework, he invites Catholic priests, future parishioners, and analytic candidates into a more nuanced exploration—one serving the broader good of relationships, commitments, and the possibility of a transcendent function capable of shaping a global society or "one-world theology."

Stein's work is inclusive, welcoming all. Moreover, his upbringing as a pastor's son appears to have provided him with a counterbalancing perspective to some of Jung's more critical assessments of the biblical God image. Unlike Jung, Stein admits that the Christ stage of individuation is so spiritually and developmentally advanced that few individuals attain it within their lifetimes. Such modesty mirrors Jung's approach in his seminars on Eastern religions, though Jung was often less restrained in his psychological-theological critiques of the Judeo-Christian tradition. For Stein, Jesus is not only good enough, but embodies the nurturing qualities of a "good mother."[10] His own childhood experience of Jesus as a maternal figure profoundly shaped his faith, reinforcing his conviction in Dante's cosmic vision of divine truth. Furthermore, Stein's Jesus is more attuned to wisdom than Jung's portrayals suggest. He is human and down to earth—evident in his act of humility when he "touches the feet of each of his disciples, washing them and wiping them... The fourth Gospel holds the tension of opposites Logos and Eros. They are united in the figure of the Gospels protagonist."[11]

Additionally, I find Stein's portrayal of Jesus to be more transcendent: "Love is stronger than death: this is the gospel message.... The risen Christ is a key element of the symbol presented in all four Gospels. Especially in the fourth Gospel."[12]

Unlike Jung, who largely omitted the Risen Christ from his writings—viewing this figure as a metaphysical phenomenon beyond experiential scope—Stein fully embraces the trans-psychological dimensions of the Self that are central to the Jesus narrative. He writes:

> What Jesus promises is that his followers will not experience the spiritual death. Their spirits, if they follow the Way, will not die. This is to say that on the spiritual plane of reality, there is no death once one reaches it, and Jesus is the way to reach it.... Jesus offered a glimpse into eternity. His words and life and especially his death and resurrection brought into consciousness what had been a dim realization before, that the individual can have contact with eternity and participate in it.[13]

What does it mean to "see" the Risen Christ? Stein explores this question in his extended commentary on the *Rosarium philosophorum*, a series of 20 alchemical images portraying the complete process of individuation. Jung, in his essay "The Psychology of the Transference," does not include the final image of the Risen Christ in his analysis. However, Stein highlights its significance, emphasizing its profound psychological and spiritual implications.

In his lecture titled "The Way," Stein addressed his Catholic audience with a statement that must have astonished them—as it did me:

> There must be some predisposition to respond to the symbol of Christ before one has ever actually seen it or been exposed to it. There are some who just "see," no matter their background or heritage. Psychologically we would suppose that the archetype represented by Christ is already half constellated in their psyches. They are already spiritual people potentially and only need a concrete figure on which to project the symbol of the Self. Their souls are Christ-like before they ever know Christ.... The Christ within matches up with the Christ without.[14]

I trust this kind of analytic writing. Here, Stein is at his finest, with his language reflecting a vision for a psychology of the future. His concluding words assert that love may subsume the all. By this, he suggests that love exists wherever the human shadow and evil are absent, particularly in contrast to the Antichrist: "Through the image of Christ, human consciousness discovers Love as belonging to its own essential nature and perhaps the essential nature of all that is."[15]

In my view, Stein's biblical lectures should be required reading in all Jungian institutions to foster ongoing discussion on Holy Scripture—examining it psychologically and theologically, in parallel. I have yet to encounter another Jungian writer who speaks to me in such a direct way, almost as if through a spiritual transmission. I only discovered these lectures in the summer of 2024, yet of all the works I have read on Jung and Christianity, none comes close to the kernels of truth contained within them.

Synchronicity and Providence

In his 1999 essay "Synchronicity and Divine Providence: A Dialogue Between Jungian Psychology and Christian Theology," Stein opens with an account of a private yet fortuitous meeting of the Basel Psychology Club on November 1, 1958. During this gathering, Jung spoke about the improbable connection between synchronicity and the theological doctrine of predestination.

"The theory of predestination," Jung asserted, "has nothing of course to do with synchronicity. Synchronicity is a scientific concept and the predestination theory is a dogma."[16] He then proceeded to ridicule the Protestant theologian Karl Barth's stance on the subject. As Stein notes, "Jung enjoyed making fun of theologians, as they in turn took some pleasure in ridiculing him."[17] Indeed, having faced ridicule throughout his career, Jung was accustomed to intellectual sparring. Despite lacking in formal theological education, his natural theology was remarkably advanced (informed by his Protestant upbringing, alongside some early instruction from Meister Eckhart), and he was both modest and eager to deepen his understanding—as evidenced by his early collaboration with Victor White.

Stein's essay is well worth reading, offering a classically Jungian perspective on the interplay between synchronicity and human destiny. Perhaps its most compelling section, I feel, contains his reflections on evil:

> The principle of evil within the cosmos is the tendency within it to move from being to non-being... evil is the tendency within the system to break down and corrupt both matter and energy, to move the whole system of being toward non-being, to extinguish both matter and energy in a black hole. And this tendency toward non-being is included within the cosmic expression of the Self as an inherent element within its structure and dynamic movement.... Synchronicity is a kind of God principal, the transcendent unifier of all that exists.[18]

Every major crisis in human history has presented the collectivity with the inescapable realities of life, including the inevitability of death. Both physical and symbolic death are deeply interconnected, forming what Stein aptly describes as the "unity of being" and "non-being." Jungians, in turn, owe a nod to Freud for popularizing the term *thanatos*, named after the Greek god of death.

To fully accept and live in the spacious domain of rebirth, one must recognize resurrection from the tomb of death as an integral aspect of psychoanalysis. More than any other Jungian I have read, Stein presents this stage of individuation—though rarely achieved—as a possibility worth serious consideration. My own understanding of this has been shaped, in part, by my experience of deep listening to Bach's *Mass in B Minor*. Resurrection, as an archetypal reality within the objective psyche, is not merely a symbolic approximation of death or a ritualized enactment of consciousness evolving toward its highest potential. Rather, it is a lived spiritual experience—an existential reality. Jung's concept of "symbolic death" represents a universal confrontation that Stein further situates within the dynamics of the transference. Crucifixion, in whatever form it manifests (as delivered by the three fates), demands a response from the fourth figure—the Self—which preserves the integrity of our totality. We do not choose crucifixion experiences; they are *imposed upon* us. As Jung observed, they often arrive violently, through the blows of fate, leading to a temporary death of the ego on the cross of our gravest suffering.

As Stein clarifies, "evil is not an embedded aspect of nature, psychical or metaphysical; it is a product of the mind." Within theology, the problem of evil is among the most vexing. William James grappled with it in his reading of the book of Job before Jung, but Jung confronted the issue with unparalleled depth, elevating it to a higher octave on the scale of affect and thought. He wrestled with it mightily. What is distinctive in Stein's psychological theology of evil is his argument—following both John Calvin and Jung—that evil operates within the framework of Providence. This perspective is most evident in his biblical lectures, where he suggests that Judas, too, had a divine vocation to fulfill—one he ultimately answered.

At the core of Stein's analysis lies one of his favorite subjects: the role played by meaningful chance in theology. He argues:

> Synchronicity breaks the tyranny of causal determination on which the notion of fate depends in the modern scientific world-view. Hence fate is removed from any sort of absolute domination of the cosmos. What about chance events? Can they bespeak fate?[19]

At such a high level of intellectual engagement, readers may benefit from a concrete example of Stein's argument. One such example is provided by Stein's story of wandering into the Grossmünster church in Zürich, where he read his mother's surname Reiman on a list of Anabaptist ancestors. This was a chance "moment of meaning," filled with numinous significance, which deepened his connection to Jung through a new realization of his Swiss heritage. Yet, even as an infant, he had felt an emotional pull toward his maternal grandmother, who was also of Swiss descent. What forces were at play in these experiences—predestination or Providence? Fate or destiny? Both? For Stein, the answer is Providence, and the distinction lies in choice: Providence allows for human agency, whereas predestination offers none, as the choice has already been made by God. This tension can be seen in the destinies of both Jesus and Judas.

In 2003, Stein relocated to Switzerland because it felt right to both him and his wife. It was a joint decision. His theological perspective, situated at the intersection of Christian doctrine and natural science, aligns with human experiences of the numinous. This personal theology, in concert with a transcendent order, finds resonance in the mathematical structures of the cosmos, as explored in von Franz's *Number and Time*. Ultimately, the experience of Oneness is central to questions of fate. When a moment of divine providence presents itself, we must choose to say "Yes"—for consciousness remains the deciding factor.

Soulful Reality

In the next essay in Volume 6 of the *Collected Writings*, "The Reality of the Soul," Stein revisits the theme of synchronicity while offering insight into his personal life as a writer, analyst, husband, and friend. He begins by defining his central focus: living in responsible relationship with a unified whole—the *unus mundus*—especially during moments of "transcendence." He writes:

> There are certain special moments in life—I call them 'openings to transcendence'—when we confront a symbol and see reality as the unconscious regards it all the time. At this level, the psyche knows no difference between spirit and matter. They are the same.[20]

Readers may recall the story of Kaspar Kiepenhauer (see Chapter 3), who passed away suddenly, only to seemingly reappear in the form of a butterfly swarm outside Stein's bedroom window. A lover of books and symbols might recognize this as an authentic religious experience—one in which Stein's faith in Christ's Resurrection shattered the limitations of his ego, opening his soul to transcendence and the reality of transfiguration. Patients in analysis sometimes recount similar experiences surrounding the death of a loved one or near death experiences. Yet, the following story is even more improbable than the first.

This butterfly tale unfolds within the context of Stein's relationship with a close friend of a similar age who had recently passed away—a Roman Catholic nun he had known for a decade. She had possessed an unwavering belief in God and the afterlife, while Stein, by his own admission, is a Protestant rationalist with a deeply ingrained habit of skepticism. Yet, despite his half-skeptical Protestant disposition, he never doubted the sincerity of her Catholic faith or the certainty with which she held her beliefs.

Shortly before her death, Stein came across a newspaper column announcing that Pope John Paul II had confirmed the sainthood of Edith Stein, the Carmelite nun. As an admirer of Edith Stein's work, he was eager to attend the canonization and turned to his friend Irene, knowing she could obtain tickets for him. Indeed, Irene secured two tickets—one for him and one for his wife—and he thanked her profusely. Tragically, Irene was soon diagnosed with pancreatic cancer, and only just before the Rome event, she departed this life. Stein recalls feeling disappointed, as he was in the midst of completing his book *Transformation: Emergence of the Self*, which I briefly reviewed in Chapter 4. What made the timing especially poignant was that he had hoped to give Irene a signed copy. The central metaphor of the book? The metamorphosis of a caterpillar into a butterfly.

On the day of Irene's funeral, Stein and his wife, Jan, set out for the church but mistakenly arrived at the wrong location. Their car had been parked in a lovely garden behind the home where Irene had lived, and as they drove away in search of the church, Stein felt an inexplicable sensation that something had entered their car. Turning to Jan, he asked her to check the rear window. "It's a butterfly!" Jan exclaimed in surprise. Hoping to guide the butterfly back outside, she reached into the back of the car, expecting it to flutter away. Instead, it hopped onto her hand and remained there, unmoving. As the story unfolds, the situation becomes even wilder. The narrative itself seems to break free, and Stein's prose takes flight—his words mirroring the wonder of the experience:

> As we stood together under the street lamp, Irene the butterfly jumped to the ground and began dancing wildly at our feet. Round and round she went in a frenzy of motion. Suddenly, I remembered Irene's ardent wish to dance again in eternity, and I burst out, "Irene, I see you've made it! You're dancing!"[21]

Now, let us fast forward to Saint Peter's Square in Rome, where Stein and his wife sat in attendance as Pope John Paul II confirmed the Carmelite nun Edith Stein to sainthood. As the aging Pope delivered the final benediction in four languages, Stein followed along in Latin. When he reached the words *Ora e sempere* ("Now and forever"), an astonishing thing happened! Out of nowhere, a brown butterfly, tinged with flecks of blue, fluttered down from above the vast congregation of thousands and alighted softly on the opened page before him—precisely on the words "Now and forever." It remained there for several minutes.[22]

Stein was stunned. That a butterfly should appear at that exact moment, amidst a sea of faces, and settle upon those three hallowed words defied comprehension. His wife gasped, then whispered lovingly in his ear as the Pope solemnly continued with his prayer: "It's the same butterfly!" How could this be? The moment reminds me of Jung's famous encounter with the scarab beetle, catching it midair and showing it to his patient. Though in this instance, it was Stein, not a patient, who was left in astonishment. Surely enough, the butterfly's coloring was unmistakably identical to the one that had accompanied them in Chicago. As realization dawned, Murray whispered to his wife, "This is Irene." Then, as the Pope spoke his final word—"Amen"—the butterfly took flight.

To fully grasp and feel into the profound silence that this miraculous experience evoked in Stein's soul, one must read the entire essay. Immersing myself in the text, I too feel the depth of the moment shared between husband and wife—the sheer soulfulness of their encounter. For them, there was no doubt: it was Irene. That was their belief, their faith, their irrational knowing as Jungians. "As psychotherapists," Stein writes, "we must take up matters of the psyche with the utmost respect—especially if we are handling symbols."[23]

Introduction to Minding the Self: Jungian Meditations on Contemporary Spirituality

As discussed in a previous chapter, Stein conceptualizes five life stages within analytical psychology, extending from birth to old age. The fifth and final stage represents the quintessence of the individuation process in later life (age 70 and beyond)—a stage Stein designates as that of the "sage." *Introduction to Minding the Self: Jungian Meditations on Contemporary Spirituality* comprises a series of lectures originally delivered at the C.G. Jung Institute of Chicago in 1988—the same year of his biblical lectures—when Stein was 44 years old and in what he identifies as the fourth life stage of the "missionary."

In the opening chapter of the revised and published edition (2014), titled "Introduction to Minding the Self," Stein, writing now at the age of 71, explicitly positions himself not with Catholics but with his Protestant forbearers, Zwingli and Calvin. These church leaders "stripped the cathedrals of their statues and images and offered the Word instead—intellect, abstraction, meaning based on ideas and not influenced by painted images, physical rituals, colorful windows and sculpted forms," characteristic of medieval Roman churches throughout Europe.

By "Word," Stein does not mean traditional Protestantism, which he critiques as lacking in profundity, psychological depth, and the heights of true wisdom. He observes,

Today, the words of the Protestant churches are banal and the ideas largely outdated.... I asked myself: is there still a way that true symbols, which are powerfully convincing in the moment, can hold out and maintain a sense of spiritual reality and meaning even in modernity?[24]

In Stein's view,

Neither metaphors nor science seem to be sufficient for providing us with a reliable compass, and yet we cannot do without them. What is missing is the true symbol, which would balance them with a sense of transcendence and a guiding star.

Writing this lecture at a pivotal stage in his individuation process, Stein sought to articulate "an intuitive vision of reality based on numinous experience of true symbols."[25]

Indeed, this "Introduction" specifies Stein's personal spiritual path—one rooted in personal experience. We have already seen how a symbol such as a butterfly can take on a life of its own, becoming charged with numinosity and a sense of the miraculous, becoming utterly real. Such experiences, he suggests, may serve as portals to transcendence. Stein writes:

In modernity and now in post-modernity, we have to live both with and without symbols of transcendence. It is a subtle balancing act. We have to live with them because they come to us spontaneously and without special invitation, as visitations of the numinous.

He further clarifies:

What I am advocating is an individual path to spirituality that is grounded in personal experience and lived by reflecting upon them using a psychological perspective. This path exists outside of all religious organizations and structures.

I speak of this way of attending to the spiritual and material aspects of life as 'minding the self.'[26]

This approach, which Stein actively champions, represents a post-Jungian path. However, his advancement of Jung's psychology of individuation into postmodernity aligns with Jung's original vision, offering a way of living a Jungian life without attachment to or identification with organized religion.

Imago Dei as a Psychological Reality

In his 2016 essay "*Imago Dei: On the Psychological Plane,*" Stein explores what the incarnation of the Self might look like for post-Jungians, encouraging individuals to forge their own paths toward self-discovery and live authentically in pursuit of the Self. True transformation, he writes—and the ability to incarnate the sage (or wise old woman) archetype in later life—cannot occur if one remains overly attached to external figures such as Jesus, Krishna, Jung, or any other authority. For Jungians, the process of reading and teaching Jung can sometimes become routine. However, on occasion, new insights emerge—such as with the 2009 publication of *The Red Book*, which reinvigorated interest in Jungian thought. Yet what now? Where can we turn to find the living waters of life?

To answer this question, we might pose another: How and why did we become Jungians in the first place? Was it not to discover and embody the meaning of our own personal myths—our subjective truths of individuation, as Jung taught? The instinct or urge toward individuation requires an artist's array of paints on a palette, and a brush stroke that is singular and unique to our individual life. As Jung taught, our destiny is to live out our individual patterns fully, like a bird whose feathers and colors are distinct and true to its nature. To fulfill this destiny, we must remain faithful to our archetypal essence.

Stein invites readers to reflect the following:

> An individual's ego identity is not a given. It is a construction. The Self, however, is a given from the beginning of life, as the *imago Dei* that is implanted by the Divinity in human nature from inception and birth. Psychologically, there are three actors involved: the one we might call the implanter, which is the archetype per se and exists invisibly behind the scenes in the world soul, a kind of God figure, the Self; the implanted structure, which is the archetypal image, the individual lower-case self; and the Self is realized in consciousness in the course of individuation.[27]

It is the calling of the lower-case self to realize the upper-case Self in consciousness by living out the urge for individuation at the Ground of Being. The implanter—the archetype per se—exists invisibly behind the scenes, within the world soul, and can only become realized through transformative relationships, dream work, and active imagination.

In Stein's theory, this implanter is the Self, which embeds an image of God within human nature from the moment of conception. However, realization of the Self occurs gradually over the course of individuation, unfolding through the five stages of life. In old age, the sage looks back on this developmental trajectory, embodying the wisdom of the medicine man or woman. The Self, as the fundamental archetype, operates behind the masks of personality, and one might even describe the God image it implants as the nuclear image of our identity.

To make this latent divinity conscious, one must discover one's true calling or vocation. For Stein, the implanter is inextricably bound with futurity, serving a teleological function. However, the ego is actively involved, constructing the ego-Self axis that forms the sturdy spine of character. This process often unfolds over decades, though at times it is lightning quick. This brings us to the next essay.

Jungian Psychology and the Spirit of Protestantism

Throughout his work, Stein emphasizes Jung's deep familial and cultural roots in Protestantism. Jung was the son of Paul Jung, a Swiss Reformed pastor who preached in Basel, the city where Jung was raised. His maternal grandfather, Samuel Preiswerk (1799–1871), was also a Protestant pastor, as were six of his uncles. Jung was baptized and took communion in the Swiss Reformed church. He was also married in it and ultimately buried in the Protestant cemetery in the village of Küsnacht. Given this strong ancestral and cultural background, Stein argues that Jung's psychology of individuation—and by extension, our own—was strongly shaped by the spirit of Protestantism. Stein explores this theme most directly in his essay "Jungian Psychology and the Spirit of Protestantism," published in the 2017 in *Outside Inside and All Around: And Other Essays in Jungian Psychology*—now part of Volume 6 of the *Collected Writings*—when he was 74 years old.

In this essay, Stein writes from the maternal ground of his ancestral unconscious, just as Jung did. Indeed, a mirror symmetry is evident between these authors, reinforcing the continuity between their respective journeys. Often, this symmetry has manifested in meaningful synchronicities, such as those informing Stein's future vocation while at Yale, or his decision to establish roots in the Swiss countryside.

To fully grasp the historical underpinnings of Jungian thought, Stein suggests that every Jungian reader should be familiar with key moments in Swiss religious history. One of the deepest divisions within Switzerland's collective psyche took shape through the Reformation, beginning with the thoughts and deeds of Martin Luther (1483–1546), followed by Ulrich Zwingli (1484–1531) and the French theologian John Calvin (1509–1564).

After Luther's historic journey to Rome, where he beheld the inflated opulence of the Catholic Church at the height of the Renaissance—its economic and political excesses on full display in the Romanesque cathedrals—he returned to his native Germany incensed. Fueled by indignation, he used his influence as a preacher and writer to incite religious conflict, at times calling for violence against Catholics and, later, the persecution of Jews, including the destruction of synagogues. Ironically, Luther himself had spent six formative years (1505–1511) in the Augustinerkloster (St. Augustine's Monastery) in Erfurt—a German city associated with Meister Eckhart. Augustine, whose theology deeply shaped the medieval Christian tradition, had developed the theory of "just war," later promulgated by Bernard of Clairvaux and Thomas Aquinas to justify the Crusades.

Ulrich Zwingli (1440–1531), another key figure of the Reformation, argued that the wine and bread of communion should be understood symbolically, rather than literally. His stance contributed to theological divisions within Protestantism, and he was ultimately killed in battle during a conflict between Swiss Catholic and Protestant forces. Stein's 2017 essay engages with this historical and theological legacy, reflecting on his own years of service to the global Jungian community. He underscores how the Swiss Reformation shaped not only Jung's vocation in Basel, but also his own path in New Haven—and, more broadly, the trajectory of post-Jungian thought. Indeed, this Protestant heritage offers insight into the *spiritus rector* that continues to drive the work of Jungian analysts, scholars, and even readers. In this sense, anyone drawn to Jung's writings carries with them a Protestant ancestor.

Stein recounts that, as a student at Yale in 1964, he attended a Protestant worship service one Sunday morning at Battell Chapel, the largest chapel on campus. Built between 1874 and 1876—during the centennial of the American Revolution and roughly around the time of Jung's birth—Battell was originally established as a Trinitarian place of worship. The invited preacher that day was the Rev. Dr. Thayer Green, a Jungian analyst from New York and a former Protestant chaplain at a nearby college. Green's sermon explored the problem of evil and the dark side of God, drawing on Jung's "Answer to Job." At the time, Stein was coming of age at Yale, and although Green's sermon did not immediately transform his consciousness—he was, after all, only 21 and still an undergraduate—it planted a seed that would preoccupy him for the rest of his life: the problem of evil. As we will see, Stein would eventually devote an entire volume of his *Collected Writings* to this very topic. However, in 1964, his vocational path remained uncertain. He was torn between literature and theology, with psychology having not yet emerged as a vocational possibility. At that stage, he was still undecided as to his future academic path, and whether he should pursue graduate studies at Yale Divinity School. It was only in 1968, at a garden party, that a pivotal moment occurred: a young woman named Elizabeth O'Connor asked him if he had ever read Jung. Their conversation, which took place against the backdrop of a larger discussion of the Vietnam War, led her to recommend that Stein read Jung. Following her suggestion, Stein purchased *Memories, Dreams, Reflections*. As he wrote in an email to me dated September 27, 2024, *that* was the "big life-changer." It was not "Answer to Job" that awaked his sense of vocation, it was *Memories, Dreams, Reflections*. A book has the power to do that for a person. As an archetype, it can transform us.

Although Green's sermon did not directly awaken Stein's calling as a Jungian, Stein nevertheless admits that it was:

> one of the most exciting and memorable sermons I had ever heard in this Protestant church, which was justly famous for the liberal theology of its ministers—whose fiery social justice sermons stirred many to march for civil rights in America and to oppose the unjust war in Vietnam. To my quite uninformed mind at the time, Jung's thought and the theology of liberal Protestantism seemed to fit together hand-in-glove. Jung's ideas can be preached in church![28]

Years later, while pursuing his doctorate at the University of Chicago under the guidance of Professor Peter Homans, Stein came to discover that Jung's theological writing and his personal attitudes toward Christianity were not entirely compatible. Thus, he began to see a more complex relationship between Jungian psychology and Christianity. Stein reminds us that the Protestant Reformation of the 16th century was fundamentally a reaction against the authority of the Roman Catholic Church in regulating religious life. The Reformers sought to base their theology on Scripture, rather than established tradition, which, over time, had solidified into a rigid cultural and moral canon. Luther's opposition to priestly authority and papal power ultimately gave rise to a new vision: the inalienable rights of the individual to stand alone before God, without clerical mediation. While a community of believers could offer moral support, salvation and redemption were understood as matters of personal conviction, independent of institutional structures. At its core, Protestantism championed independent thought and the right to personal interpretation of Scripture—principles that profoundly shaped not only Western religious consciousness but also, as Stein suggests, the intellectual foundation of Jungian psychology.[29]

This historical perspective helps to illuminate both Jung's feuds with theologians and the perennial divisions within Jungian institutes. In his incisive analysis of the split between Freud and Jung, Stein suggests that Freud assumed the role of the Roman Pope, while Jung positioned himself as a militant Zürich reformer in the spirit of Ulrich Zwingli. To this day, Stein observes, "there is an uneasy relationship between the two 'churches,' psychoanalysis and analytical psychology."[30]

Stein further elucidates how the transformative experiences recorded in *The Red Book* constituted, for Jung, a psychological equivalent to Paul's conversion on the road to Damascus. Jung's subsequent vocation was a gift of grace—one that, as Stein describes, brought him to his knees in Küsnacht, when he found the voice of his calling.

While composing *The Red Book*, Jung developed a religious attitude, ultimately bowing his head to his calling as a doctor of souls. Stein writes: "This notion that the individual has a God-given vocation is not peculiar to Protestantism, but is certainly an important strand in the Protestant tradition." He adds that "John Calvin, the French-born Swiss Reformer was a prime example of the God-ordained

Protestant individual with a divinely inspired mission."[31] Expanding on this theme, Stein introduces the figure of Karl Barth (1886–1968) as "the most influential Protestant theologian of his era."[32] He also mentions the influence of Protestant theological thought on Jung, particularly through the contributions of Friedrich Schleiermacher (1768–1834) and Rudolf Otto.[33]

Stein presents this Protestant history as essential reading for Jungians, as it deepens our understanding of our intellectual and spiritual ancestry within the international psychoanalytic community—a community that has, on multiple occasions, fractured into opposing "churches." Rather than attempting to dissolve these differences, Stein seeks to heal the divisions by weaving them into a higher order of meaning, using the transcendent function. In doing so, he shows that we are all occupying the same trans-marginal field, doing the best we can to walk our own unique paths through life.

Stein then dives into a lengthy discussion of the central themes in Jung's "Answer to Job," focusing on the role of suffering in the individuation process. He writes: "The cross symbolizes the suffering, which is to be expected for individuating people when they take up the vocation of uniting the opposites within themselves."[34] Rather than viewing Jesus as a mere victim of violence, Stein sees him as a hero of individuation—one who achieved victory for the Self by consciously assuming the archetypal role of a divinely ordained scapegoat, bearing the burden of the world's suffering and evil. According to Stein, following the path of individuation leads to a form of "victory." With the conviction of an analyst, he assures us that this victory can only be achieved if we remain true to the symbolic life and our vocation—from God or the Self—at the highest level of moral service.

Stein concludes this inspired essay with an account of Jung's parting words to a group of analysts in New York City, after delivering his historic "Terry lectures" at Yale University in 1937. Jung's ultimate message, Stein describes, was:

> *Imitatio Christi*—that is to say, in Jung's post-creedal understanding: Follow your own personal myth as you discover it in your experience of the psyche, and never mind if it conforms to public opinion, to collective religious teachings received in your tradition, or to generally accepted cultural patterns. This journey will be your greatest treasure in life—possibly also your greatest burden and suffering—but it will carry you to your individuation's goal.[35]

I appreciate the personal tone in these sentences, with Stein speaking directly to his readers, urging them to follow their own personal myth. This mantra represents the core of his analytic faith. Protestantism, as he describes it, is not merely a historical movement but an enduring psychological attitude, present within us whether we recognize it or not. A Protestant, Stein argues, is defined "by a readiness to protest against external authority—especially if it is corrupt—and by a tendency to think independently."[36]

Knowledge of our Protestant intellectual ancestors—Luther, Zwingli, Calvin, Schleiermacher, Barth, Otto, Jung, and Stein—may offer essential insight into our history. Moreover, Stein offers a model for engaging with our "inner Protestant" through his method of deep reading the Bible as a dream. With this method, he advances the classical Jungian legacy with integrity and grace.

To conclude, I wish to quote a passage from Stein's essay "Analytical Psychology and Religion," which captures the essence of Jung's intellectual method:

> Just as William James collected individual experiences of diverse kinds and then compressed them—looking for commonalities in structure and meaning—so Jung accumulated a great diversity of mythological, religious, and folk images and motifs, always on the lookout for patterns of similarity and meaning.[37]

One of the many fine quotes that appear in this essay concerns the question of what Jungians mean by the God image—a subject that has been explored in depth across numerous books. What, then, does Stein have to say about the God image in his essay? He encourages us to remain mindful of the "mystery and the possibility of an objective and cosmic and spiritually grounded reality."[38] By grounded, he means rooted in our earthly existence, our egos, and the Self's lived experience.

Notes

1 CW6, 5.
2 CW6, 10, 11.
3 CW6, 35.
4 CW6, 37.
5 CW6, 39.
6 CW6, 55.
7 CW6, 95.
8 CW6, 128.
9 CW6, 145, 146.
10 CW6, 149.
11 CW6, 150.
12 CW6, 164.
13 CW6, 165.
14 CW6, 167, 168.
15 CW6, 172.
16 CW6, 173, 174.
17 CW6, 175.
18 CW6, 187.
19 CW6, 191.
20 CW6, 208.
21 CW6, 212.
22 CW6, 213.
23 CW6, 219.
24 CW6, 243–247.
25 CW6, 248.
26 CW6, 248.
27 CW6, 260.
28 CW6, 269–270.
29 CW6, 273.

30 CW6, 274.
31 CW6, 277.
32 CW6, 278.
33 In this chapter, Stein notes that his unique position at the International School of Ana-
    lytical Psychology Zurich (ISAPZURICH) has allowed him to observe the complexi-
    ties involved in the reception of Jungian ideas by individuals from diverse cultural and
    religious backgrounds. Among both students and faculty, discussions frequently arise
    regarding how Jungian psychoanalysis and theory can be adapted to align with the cul-
    tural perspectives of people from various countries, including the People's Republic of
    China, Taiwan, Japan, Korea, Russia, Brazil, Israel, Tunisia, Mexico, and others across
    a broad spectrum of world cultures. "In this milieu," Stein writes in a footnote to the
    text, "one quickly recognizes just how specifically shaped many of Jung's ideas and
    writings are by Northern European, Protestant cultural attitudes." (CW6, n 202). This
    remark appears as an addendum to the second paragraph. Following the footnote, Stein
    continues: "As a science and as a form of Jungian psychoanalysis, analytical psychol-
    ogy is thoroughly modern and neutral with respect to religious belief of any kind, but
    it's early history and, above all, the Swiss Reformed cultural background of its founder,
    C.G. Jung, are deeply rooted in the Protestant Christian tradition" (CW6, 186).
34 CW6, 283.
35 CW6, 293.
36 CW6, 273.
37 CW6, 298.
38 CW6, 301.

Chapter 8

Collected Writings Volume 7

The Problem of Evil

Bipolar Conscience and the Problem of Evil

The first half of Volume 7 of Stein's *Collected Writings* is a slightly modified form of *Solar Conscience / Lunar Conscience*, originally published by Chiron Publications in 1993. In this work, Stein extends the Jungian notion of "vocation," which itself can be understood as an extension of the Protestant tradition of the "call to conscience." By this, Stein is referring to the divine summons—the "voice of God"—that shaped Luther's destiny at the Diet of Worms, famously expressed in his declaration: "*Hier stehe Ich, Ich kann nicht anders, so helfe mir Gott*" ("Here I stand; I cannot do otherwise, so help me God").[1]

Stein integrates Jungian psychoanalysis to build upon this formula, drawing on a deep reading of Jung's alchemical studies and broader corpus. He postulates that conscience has two fundamental and opposing aspects: one rational, the other irrational; one Christian, the other Mercurial; one masculine, the other feminine; one solar, the other lunar. These "bipolar" aspects create a tension of opposites that must be endured for greater consciousness to emerge. Stein writes:

> Both Mercurius and Christ have a part to play within the workings of conscience, and the inevitable and frequent conflicts between these two figures produces tensions within conscience. Conscience may at one time insist on the sacrifice of ego values for a noble Christ-like spiritual value; at another time, it may insist with equal forcefulness on sacrifice of an ego's values for an instinctual mercurial value. This is the dilemma described by Paul.[2]

For Stein, conscience functions as an archetype—a *unio oppositorum*, or union of opposites—that never fully resolves but instead remains in a continuous struggle to create harmony through the individuation process.[3] What, then, are the bipolar functions of conscience? Stein explains: "The function of the solar aspect of conscience is to press the ego into the service of collective norms, ideals and values," whereas lunar conscience is "based more on the unknown factors of the collective unconscious than on a contemporary society's rules and customs. I conceive of it as representing 'mother right' rather than 'father right.'"[4]

DOI: 10.4324/9781003664024-9

When considering the transformational processes that occur at midlife and beyond, we inevitably move into the realm of lunar conscience. Here, the distinction between right and wrong no longer derives solely from societal norms but instead emerges from an instinctive-spiritual domain. This domain expresses itself principally through the symbols that arise in our dreams, fantasies, play, and active imaginations.

Before proceeding with my overview of Stein's attempt to address the problem of evil, I will trace the historical root of the term "mother right," one of Stein's key phrases in defining lunar conscience. Stein links the concept to the renowned German scholar of comparative mythology, J.J. Bachofen (1815–1887), who was born and died in Basel—the Swiss city where Jung spent his early years. At the time of Bachofen's death, Jung was a 12-year-old schoolboy. Bachofen's seminal work, *Das Mutterrecht* (*Mother Right*), was published in 1861, coinciding with the American Civil War and exactly 100 years before Jung's death.

Like Jung, Stein found great value in Bachofen's work, particularly his insights into Roman law and jurisprudence. Bachofen, a former judge on the Basel criminal court as well as a professor and anthropologist, viewed mother right as a foundational law of kinship, operating "in a world of violence as the divine principle of love, of union, of peace." Stein translates this concept into psychoanalytic terms, asserting that lunar conscience originates in the "relational matrix" of early interactions between "mother and infant."[5] He explains that

> lunar conscience does not place the highest value on conforming to collective authorities and standards, and in many cases it even turns against the grain of convention and repudiates the collective moral certainties of the day.... It is the conscience of the serpent.[6]

Moreover, Stein suggests:

> Lunar conscience would have all the archetypes live and prosper within the psychological realm, for the sake of the whole system, which is a supra-ordinate structure (the One). Its function is to regulate this wholeness so as to give each part its due.[7]

Early in his career, through extensive study of the works of Jung and Erich Neumann (particularly *Depth Psychology and a New Ethic*), as well as insights drawn from his psychoanalytic practice and dream research, Stein recognized a fundamental principle: true healing cannot occur unless psychic energy is channeled through an archetype of transformation. As we have seen, Stein refers to this central force of metamorphosis as the "transformative image." By this, he does not mean the vocational aptitudes that emerge in the first half of life through heroic inflations of solar conscience, but something far deeper—beyond the world of violence and evil: what Bachofen called the divine principle of love, union, and peace.

As a Protestant, Stein naturally understands this transformative impulse through the lens of his own ancestral heritage, identifying it as synonymous with the love of Christ. He associates the lunar impulse with the mother-infant Eros he personally experienced in his early bonding with his parents and his Swiss grandmother, as well as with his boyhood admiration of Jesus. When discussing the activating force of transformation, Stein refers to something lunar and mercurial that arises from the depths when solar conscience is temporarily eclipsed. This may occur when the professional persona—the heroic mask—is dissolved through grief or mourning, or when the ego is humbled and forced to bow low before the voice of God or the Self. In such a moment of surrender, enforced by a higher hand of Providence, the individual may enter a deep process of renewal and integration.

The relationship between Stein's work on conscience and the perennial problem of evil remains to be fully explored. In 2023, during his 80th year, he posited his own "Answer to Evil," offering a post-Jungian perspective on this enduring question. In this work, Stein poses a fundamental question: "What does conscience want?" His answer is deceptively straightforward: "The simple answer to the question of what conscience wants is that it wants the 'right thing.'"[8] But how can one discern whether one is following the right path rather than the wrong one? Stein explains, "Conscience comes in the form of an intuitive knowing. It is a kind of gnosis."[9] He elaborates: "As a universal human given, it is archetypal. And like all archetypal factors, conscience is a complexity and contains complexities."[10] The very word "con-science" means "knowing with."[11] Stein describes this concept as paradoxical, noting that "it gives voice to both the instinctual and spiritual sides of the self" as a "true psychological entity."[12]

In Greek mythology, lunar conscience is embodied by the Titaness Themis, who presides at the head of the Olympian table. Stein writes:

> While Themis opposes the dominance of one over many, she ultimately supports unity over multiplicity, wholeness over fragmentation, integration over repression. In this holding and binding activity, Themis reveals the fundamental operative principle of lunar conscience: the law of love.[13]

As the second wife of Zeus and "a Titaness, her roots lie in the archaic world of pre-Olympian times and extend outward to include a cosmic vision of the ultimate and final workings of the whole cosmos."[14] Stein further explains: "When Themis takes the lead in the dialogue between solar and lunar aspects of conscience, the issues always hinge on questions of the soul and fate."[15]

Stein's Clarifications of Jung's Thoughts on Evil

Stein begins his impressive "Introduction to *Jung on Evil*" by posing a series of questions that Jungians would do well to consider. As is his custom, he begins by quoting Jung: "We know nothing of man, far too little. His psyche should be studied, because we are the origin of all coming evil." From this foundation, Stein asserts and inquires:

> The problem of evil is perennial. How to think about it? How to define it? Theodicies abound throughout history that have sought to explain God's purposes. If God is good, what is the purpose of evil? On the other hand, mythological and theological dualisms explain it by asserting evil's equal metaphysical reality and speaking about the eternal conflict between good and evil. Humans have forever wrestled with questions like, who or what is responsible for evil?[16]

For readers unfamiliar with Jung's extensive and varied statements regarding the vexing persistence of evil, Stein's essays in the latter half of Volume 7 of his *Collected Writings* are essential reading. As a response to the enduring presence of evil, Stein observes:

> Evil has certainly been an active presence in recent history. Some people have argued that despite the technological progress of the last centuries, moral progress has not advanced, and that evil is a more urgent problem than ever before. The problem of evil, whether addressed specifically as such or not, is a dominant concern of our time.[17]

Jungian analysts confront the problem of evil in their daily work, just as Jung did during World War I, World War II, and the Cold War. Evil is an intrinsic force—one that every psychoanalyst must learn to metabolize via the various forms of countertransference that Stein describes elsewhere. With this in mind, Stein turns to a fundamental question: What is the *source* of evil, according to Jung—and according to Stein himself? His reply:

> Jung did not want to be soft on evil. And yet, he did not want to argue that evil is an independent force, self-sustaining and totally autonomous. This would lead to severe dualism, which is precisely what he wished to argue against. His vision stood strongly in favor of unity. Evil must be considered part of the whole, therefore, and remain in relationship with the good.[18]

If it is true that God created both good and evil to serve as a mirror for moral reflection—viewed, as it were, through the eyes of the serpent—then what, precisely, is evil? Stein's answer to this question offers a postmodern guide for the perplexed, cutting to the chase while waxing theologically:

> Evil is a necessary category of human thought. Human consciousness necessarily differentiates aspects of experience and cannot function without utilizing the categories of good and evil. As a category of thought, evil is not an embedded aspect of nature, psychic or physical or metaphysical; it is a product of the mind... The judgment about good and evil belongs to a certain level of conscious development.[19]

Evil, he explains, is not an inherent property of nature or the cosmos, but rather a necessary category of human thought. It is a product of the human mind—a judgment, rather than an objective reality. In this, Stein aligns with Jung, who felt that we, as humans, are the origin of all evil. Stein agrees with this, holding evil as an undeniable fact of the human psyche that cannot be denied—scientifically, psychologically, or theologically.

Jungian psychoanalysts have approached the study of evil empirically, examining its many manifestations in the form of dream symbols, thoughts, fantasies, and actions. Stein explains:

> Jung puts forward a theory that places the burden for making this judgment upon ego consciousness. To be ethical is to work.... Because Jung considered this to be perhaps the central human task, he ventured into the risky project of making such judgments about God. Is God good, evil, or both?[20]

Stein refers to Jung's engagement with these ideas as a "risky project," likely because his own introduction to Jung began with *Memories, Dreams, Reflections*. Jung's approach to the question of God got him into a load of trouble with theologians, who felt that he, as an empiricist, was treading on sacred theological ground. However, as a theologian, Stein defends Jung out of deep respect for his intellectual contributions. He writes: "It is an advantage to be able to say that evil is a judgment of consciousness, for if it were metaphysical, one could do nothing about it."[21] Following Jung and Neumann, Stein argues that we must actively engage with evil, recognizing its relationship to the good rather than dismissing it as a non-reality. To frame it as purely metaphysical, he warns, would be perilous.

Jungian psychoanalysts have a responsibility, therefore, to work with evil in human thoughts, actions, and emotions. That is an essential part of Jungian work, particularly with respect to countertransference responses during treatment. Jung provided the tools for this endeavor with his theory of complexes—personal, national, and trans-cultural—as well as his concept of the shadow, which, in *Aion*, he described as containing both relative and absolute evil. Stein builds upon Jung's foundation with his complementary theory of two types of conscience. He writes: "It is the rare individual who retains a personal sense of good and evil and continues to hear the voice of conscience [lunar and solar] in the midst of a collective state of archetypal inflation."[22]

As we have seen, solar conscience must be balanced with lunar conscience to maintain a personal sense of integrity, particularly during periods of what Jung called "psychic contagion." Such periods, driven by affect-toned contents of the collective psyche, can lead to mass inflation with general ideas or political propaganda.

Moreover, in his discussion of the Book of Revelation and Jung's astrological reflections in *Aion*, Stein clarifies Jung's perspective on the source of evil. He writes: "If we judge this movement to be evil and the work of Anti-Christ, the source is to be located in God's need to incarnate His own destructiveness."

Whether this is truly God's need or merely our own human need projected onto a God image remains an open question. Stein acknowledges this tension, observing:

> There is an obvious logical contradiction in Jung's wanting to say that evil is the product of conscious human judgment on the one hand but also that the persistent presence of evil in the world is due to God's will on the other.[23]

It is essential for readers to understand that, whenever Jung used the word "God" in his scientific writings, he was referring specifically to the God image, rather than the divinity, itself. Jung approached the concept empirically, studying how the God image manifested in dreams, active imaginations, fantasies, symbolic acts, and mythologies across cultures, and especially in the Bible (which, as Stein notes, became an increasing focus of his work from 1939 onward). However, in *Memories, Dreams, Reflections*, a different approach is evident. No longer writing as an empirical scientist, in this more personal work, Jung conveys himself as a man with a healing vision, constructing a narrative for the ages and the betterment of society. Despite Jung's occasional contradictions regarding evil, Stein reassures us that he remained committed to the unity of the Self and did not propose a metaphysical dualism in God. In fact, Jung refrained from making definitive theological claims about the divine, and his metaphysical explorations, as we have seen, were reserved for his scientific theories—most notably, those of synchronicity and numbers, which von Franz developed further.

Stein argues that contemporary psychotherapists must actively work to bring evil into responsible relationship with the good. He writes: "Jung would advocate a form of political activism that would bring psychological awareness to bear upon collective human affairs. This would be to carry psychotherapy out of the clinical setting into the world."[24] This, in essence, is the work that Stein himself has been engaged in for the past 50 years.

Stein's Formula for Violence

Understanding the "roots" of violence in dreams or symbols of the imagination can lead us beyond the confines of the consulting room and into the delicate fabric of today's troubled world—a world that, as Jung observed, hangs by a thin thread. Trauma is undoubtedly one of the most virulent causes of criminality, violence, vice, and evil within the human psyche, and psychoanalysts bear repeated witness to its insidious aftereffects, particularly in the moral splitting into good and bad conscience. Addressing this division remains one of the most pressing challenges of psychoanalytical work, and an increasingly complex task in our rapidly evolving world. To achieve it, psychoanalysts must provide an imaginative space for patients to integrate their solar and lunar conscience.

It is important for psychoanalysts to recognize that educating patients—be they children, adolescents, or adults—about conscience is an essential task. Equally important is the ability to discern when a conflict of conscience has driven a patient into crisis. If so, the crisis will require careful confrontation, compassion, therapeutic intervention, and ultimately integration.

Stein is known for taking on such difficult subjects. In his essay "A Formula for Violence," he gets to the core of the underlying mechanisms contributing to the deep moral and ideological divisions shaping world affairs. He begins by asking:

> What causes people to commit acts of violence? Violence stalks us like an ever-present shadow. It is critically important to understand the source of violence among human beings—for individuals, for societies, and for international relations. This is a perennial topic, but today it is especially essential to understand the shadow feature of human behavior if we are to make any headway at all in slowing down the rapid proliferation of violence. Violence is spreading through the world like a wildfire, and we ask: Why? Why is this shadow so active today? What causes these eruptions of violence on every side?[25]

One need only turn on the daily news to see that this is true. Jung was the first to provide us with the theoretical tools needed to understand the affective origins of violence within the human psyche, through his theory of complexes. While Freud adopted the term "complex" in his famous hypothesis of the Oedipus complex, the Jungian school added significant depth to the concept, through dream and relational analysis. As a result, Jungian psychoanalysis offers a rich framework for comprehending violence and its archetypal roots in the killing instinct. Stein provides a first-rate explanation of this, writing:

> Emotions are complex constellations of chemicals in neuronal responses that form a pattern. If they have a traumatic core, we call them *complexes*. When activated by an event, complexes develop into energetically charged fields that break into consciousness as strong feelings.... Violence is essentially a psychologically driven phenomenon. It results from the failure to metabolize or contain unbearable feelings.[26]

Stein's extensive knowledge of the Bible enables him to trace the archetypal origins of violence and evil to the story of Cain and Abel, in which God's favor toward Abel incited Cain's envious rage, resulting in murder. He even proposes a mathematical formula for calculating the "risk of violence," illustrated through a case example from recent history.

In his essay "Explorations of Shadow: An Interview with Len Cruz," Stein revisits the theme of envy, which he previously examined in his analysis of Cain and Abel. In his interview with Cruz, Stein observes: "Envy is a part of almost everybody's shadow. Most people loudly deny that they are envious, because that is really a quality that very few people want to or can admit to."[27] Drawing on the work of Melanie Klein and Michael Fordham, Stein deepens his exploration of envy's psychological underpinnings. However, much like his work on shame (discussed in Chapter 11), he does not merely diagnose the problem but also proposes pathways toward liberation.

Stein's Answer to Evil

In another pivotal essay, "Answer to Evil," Stein zeros in on one of the central causes of violence and evil within the human psyche: evil. To my surprise, he not only traces evil to its source but he also presents a response to it in no uncertain terms. "By itself," Stein writes,

> the ego is deficient, riddled with envy, strife, and confusion. But when the ego is united with the Self, its deficiency ceases. Now the ego becomes filled with the Self. When the Self is known, envy and strife come to an end.[28]

How can envy and strife, which seem endemic to the human psyche and our fate on this planet, truly come to an end? Stein offers what could be considered his own philosophical remedy—a panacea for the enduring problem of evil in human nature. While envy is here to stay, Stein argues, it can be diminished through analysis and, at times, reduced to a near-zero state. Similarly, while strife is an inevitable aspect of human experience, it also serves as a constructive process, as seen in political debates and post-Jungian forms of activism.

Yet, if we are riddled with psychological complexes (such as those producing envy and strife), how can we possibly realize the purpose that Providence has intended for us? While we may never completely rid ourselves of these internal complexes, we can at times transcend them. According to Stein, psychological deficiency signals the absence of something good—our potential wholeness, or the fullest realization of the Self. However, the emergence of this wholeness is not a matter of personal will. Rather, it is dictated by a greater force. It is not we who decide when the Self will manifest its numinous potentialities, but destiny itself.

Since evil is a perennial and persistent problem, it can never be eradicated within an individual's process of individuation. Even profound numinous experiences do not mark the end of this struggle, as life continues to unfold. Thus, another factor must be at play in the transformation process. Stein emphasizes the necessity of creating space within the analytic dialogue for the Self to emerge through hidden doorways into the interactive field—a process requiring deep introspection and reverie. Stein explains:

> The ego must be silent and must make space for the Self. This means that the ego must break and abandon its schemes and defenses against the Self. For when the Self comes near to the ego, the defenses become upset, and a crisis ensues. Now the ego must make some hard decisions.[29]

Jung taught that the Self is not inherently good. Thus, the tension between solar and lunar conscience initiates a process of reconciliation—a marriage of contraries— that demands the utmost discrimination and self-honesty in order to relativize notions of good and evil. The Self calls individuals to actualize their fullest potential, yet this presents the ego with a perplexing dilemma: it must simultaneously serve the Self, synthesize opposites, and function harmoniously within society. Crucially, the ego does not determine the timing of this unification process. As Stein observes:

> The Self has a lot of potential, that is, possibilities for being, which are not yet shaped or formed. These potentials are contained within the Self, and may become conscious, receiving a form and a name, when the Self decides the time is right.[30]

One can hear echoes of Stein's earlier work, *Transformation: Emergence of the Self* (1998), in this discussion. However, his thinking appears to have been distilled and refined by the Self in this later work. Setting aside the focus on transformation in the lives of great personalities—previously illustrated through case studies of four historical figures—here, he addresses a broader audience comprising not only his readers, consultees, and patients, but humanity as a whole, envisioning new possibilities for collective awakening. He states: "The Self awakens the ego, and a new consciousness is aroused. The Self performs this awakening function by incarnating a tangible symbol."[31]

What Stein refers to as a tangible symbol is what he previously called the transformative image. This symbol brings knowledge of the Self,

> it brings light, it frees the ego from guilt and bondage to the former complexes.... The ego that is enlightened and connected to the Self should relate to others similar to itself and should help those who want to be similarly enlightened.[32]

Here, Stein speaks of the potential for enlightenment through analysis, distilling his earlier insights into a concentrated and potent alexipharmic—a philosophical antidote to the destructive forces of envy, violence, and hatred that fester in personal and national complexes. He asserts that liberation from these illusions is possible, provided one remains diligent and places faith in the Self as a force capable of delivering the ego from its inherent frailty and frigidity. Stein continues:

> The Self is fragrant and warm. The ego is cold. The ego without the Self is sick and deficient. The Self is like a doctor who comes to heal: when the Self comes, the ego should not hide its deficiency. The doctoring Self will apply the "ointment," which is empathy and understanding. Feeling accepted, the ego will be healed.[33]

This passage reflects Stein's post-Jungian wisdom, distilled from his deep reading of the ancient Gnostic masterpiece *The Gospel of Truth*. I find it intriguing that he speaks of the unifying factor in the psyche as a "doctoring Self."

Solving the Enigma of the Problem of Evil

In his final essay in this volume, "The Shadow and the Problem of Evil," Stein proposes a stage of consciousness he calls the "sixth stage" (I wonder whether he intends this as a progression beyond the fifth stage of the sage):

> We call the awareness of *unus mundus* ('one world'), the awareness of synchronicity. This is the intuitive awareness that the inner figures called archetypes are not limited to the human psyche but correspond to patterns in extra-psychic reality. There is an ontological reality that both are grounded in.[34]

For such transformations in consciousness to occur, Stein argues, the transcendent function—activated through active imagination (the fourth pillar)—is needed.

Notes

1 CW7, 119.
2 CW7, 31.
3 CW7, 120.
4 CW7, 23.
5 CW7, 65.
6 CW7, 24.
7 CW7, 91.
8 CW7, 15.
9 CW7, 16.
10 CW7, 17.
11 CW7, 23.
12 CW7, 30, 31.
13 CW7, 95.
14 CW7, 111.
15 CW7, 120.
16 CW7, 121.
17 CW7, 122.
18 CW7, 130.
19 CW7, 130.
20 CW7, 134.
21 CW7, 135.
22 CW7, 139.
23 CW7, 141.
24 CW7, 147.
25 CW7, 159.
26 CW7, 165.
27 CW7, 180.
28 CW7, 203.
29 CW7, 203.
30 CW7, 203.
31 CW7, 204.
32 CW7, 204.
33 CW7, 204.
34 CW7, 220.

Chapter 9

Collected Writings Volume 8
Psychology and Spirituality

The Dream of Wholeness

Stein begins his essay "The Dream of Wholeness" under the guise of a literary miner panning for nuggets of gold from the history of world religions and folk traditions. He first examines Plato's myth of the original, formless beings who were later split in half, condemned to spend their lives seeking their severed counterparts. This myth provides a partial explanation for the human mating instinct and the pursuit of unity—whether in heterosexual, homosexual, or bisexual relationships—framing it as a fundamental longing for completeness.[1] In Jungian terms, Stein connects this notion to the anima and animus archetypes, associated with the innate drive toward loving union.

Stein explores a vast array of world mythologies, religious traditions, and folk imagery to explore humanity's enduring quest for completion. Across diverse religious traditions, this search is often symbolized through the "golden ring" of union, typically expressed in experiences of erotic fulfillment. Almost invariably, such narratives culminate in depictions of divine union between a god and goddess. Recognizing this archetypal pattern, Stein observes:

> We stand at a moment in Western spiritual history when the Mother-Father God image has a chance of becoming integrated into the heart of our spiritual traditions, into the doctrines of God.... What is emerging is the concept of wholeness, perhaps personified as a Man-Woman Deity, a united Pair, which promises the recovery of the ancient, primordial, archetypal dream of wholeness.[2]

This dream of wholeness cannot be so easily dismissed by the three major patriarchal religions of the Near East, Middle East, and West—Judaism, Islam, and Christianity. The emergence of depth psychology reshaped our understanding of spirituality, prompting the postmodern world-in-transition to seek new guiding images—ones fostering unity and integration with a less rigidly gendered perspective. Today's spiritual "alchemy" is centered on transformation. We stand at a pivotal moment in our conception of creation. The myths that once provided meaning no longer resonate as they once did. As we hunger for new narratives, a pressing

DOI: 10.4324/9781003664024-10

question arises: Who can point the way to the Self in contemporary society? To which mythologies can we safely turn? Stein responds:

> We may all be evolving, psychologically, spiritually, historically according to a transpersonal pattern of development.... This movement reaches back to the Garden of Eden, where it all began, mythologically speaking, and recovers Eve and the Serpent, who represents the chthonic energy of the Goddess and Her worship. Now the Serpent will again have a place in the home, as it had in antiquity, and the painful enmity between spirit and matter, mind and body, heaven and earth, man and woman may be healed and overcome. This is the movement of holistic health and of proper concern for the natural environment in our time. The watchwords here on Balance and Harmony.[3]

Gaia has returned. So too has Donald Trump, who opposes Gaia through his relentless pursuit of new sources of fossil fuel. What makes Stein's 1994 article so compelling, I believe, is its prescient insight into the trajectory of global myth-making during a period of transformation, shortly after the first Gulf War. At the heart of the Jungian journey of individuation lies the search for a soulmate—union with the anima or animus, King or Queen—symbolizing the synthesis of opposites within the Self.

Stein's active imagination in which he envisioned the Cosmic Christ (Love Absolute) contributed to the potential evolution of our species, enabling him to outline a stage of human development transcending the struggles of civilization, with its persistent heartache and sorrow. As he writes: "The centrality of the Quest image will give way to images of the Quiet Center, the Place of Peace, the Self in Repose."[4]

Here, Stein is engaged in not only mythologizing, but also theologizing. This psychologically centered space of quiet, repose, and peace anticipates a new age of humanness. As he writes:

> The Age of Conquest and Evangelization is over; the age of Depth and Wholeness is just beginning. After the age of Yahweh and Yahweh-Sophia, and after the Age of the Father-Son-and-Holy Spirit, we will have the Age of the Centered, Whole Human Being.[5]

Stein envisions this age of wholeness as emerging from Jung's guiding myth of meaning and the evolution of consciousness, as articulated in *Memories, Dreams, Reflections*.[6] However, another way to read this essay is as Stein's own myth—a post-Jungian extension of Jung's hypotheses, formulated three decades ago. Today, we are all miners in search of gold. While Jung's writings—particularly his volumes on psychology and alchemy—offer rich insights, Stein suggests that many more discoveries await each of us, to be unearthed in our own ways.

On Modern Initiation into the Spiritual

Stein begins this essay with a poem by Mark Strand called "My Name," which describes the poet's experience of hearing his name spoken aloud for the first time.

This moment resonates with Stein, who recalls a similar experience during his early 20s when he was grappling with difficult vocational questions, particularly regarding his future studies at Yale. His transformative "calling," the moment that awakened his spiritual identity as "Murray Stein," came through his reading of *Memories, Dreams, Reflections*—an encounter that awakened the God principle within him.

Hearing the "calling" of one's spiritual name, Stein argues, is central to modern initiation rites into psychological reality. This experience coincides with the emergence of vocation, which, as Jung explored in his 1932 essay "The Development of the Personality," pertains to the challenges of personality development and the inner voice. Stein addresses this theme in his second essay in Volume 8 of the *Collected Writings*, titled "On Modern Initiation into the Spiritual." He writes: "Initiation into the spiritual is one of the varieties of religious experience [echoing James and Jung] that today we interpret as psychological."[7] In an earlier essay, Stein examined the sexual instinct and its role in the spiritual unification of masculine and feminine—whether in heterosexual or same-sex relationships. Here, his focus shifts to what might be called the instinct for vocation and its archetypal image or counterpart, recognizing that many individuals experience multiple callings. For Jung, vocation was central to postmodern initiation. On a personal level, I encountered this phenomenon in my own dreams, in which the Self spoke through a muse calling herself "Stefania." A Catholic Italian anima figure, Stefania revealed that she had written a literary novel titled *Destiny*—an experience that echoes Stein's insights on the significance of names. But what are the rites of passage for young people today? Stein tells us:

> The key element of this initiation is the profound experience of being personally addressed by the archetypal. In the poem, the speaker's name is called by a "voice" that emanates from the deep psyche, from the stars, nameless and timeless. What seems to be one's most personal and intimate possession—a name—is instantly transformed into something quite impersonal, belonging to the ages, not to an individual "me." It transcends the individual and transient bearer. The personal is thus lifted to the impersonal, the individual to the sublimely archetypal. Likewise, one's time-limited existence within the frame of human life becomes extended infinitely beyond all space and time. One is immortalized.[8]

To ground his theory, Stein recounts the dream of a retired psychotherapist. For Stein, the dream did not represent initiation into a social or professional identity, nor the adoption of a specialized persona, but rather an initiation into what he calls "the spiritual, which speaks about the deeper meaning of her life's work, a vocation that is not tied to a specific job or profession. At the time of the dream, she was not asking for meaning; meaning simply arrived."[9] Here again, Stein positions vocation at the center of the spiritual quest for meaning.

Stein further writes:

> What a positive outcome of this initiation mainly depends on is an inner openness to the 'call.' This readiness to receive the transcendent Other creatively

may well increase in its painful experiences of rupture and loss of significant others—teachers, mentors, parents or parent figures.[10]

Readers may find it valuable to explore the entire essay, particularly Stein's lengthy analysis of the calling of Martin Buber, centered on the archetype of the *zaddik*, which shaped Buber's "abiding sense of meaning." This final section is especially moving, as it reveals what I perceive as the "doctoring Self" at work in Stein's literary efforts to heal the painful misunderstandings in Jung's professional relationship with Buber. I only wish he had offered a similar restorative approach in his writings on Victor White—a subject whom, to my knowledge, no Jungian has yet restored from the disrepair suffered in his relationship to Jung. Perhaps one day I will take up that task myself.

Making Room for Divinity

According to Stein, Jung's self-concept established a crucial link between analytical psychology and spiritual ideas of transcendence—an area traditionally explored by philosophers, metaphysicians, and theologians but rarely advanced by 20th-century depth psychologists. Stein seeks to bridge that gap, asserting: "This theory will provide the new skin for the new wine pressed out by Jungian psychoanalysis. It is a new, and I will call it a postmodern, vision of the human."[11] What fascinates me here is Stein's emphasis on the "new." What exactly is this "new wine" to which he refers? Where can we find it? He provides an answer in "The Ontological Grounding of the Self."

With his command of the German language, Stein lifts a passage from Jung's *Mysterium Coniunctionis*, identifying a misinterpretation in the Hull translation. To restore Jung's original meaning, he offers a refined translation: Divinity, Divinization, or "'Divineness' *die Göttlichkeit* expresses or shapes or molds (*ausdrückt*) the self in the form of a *coincidentia oppositorum*. As Jung announced in the beginning of Mysterium, the psyche is structured as a polarity."[12]

Stein clarifies for non–German-speaking audiences that the term *Göttlichkeit* does not translate easily into English. He carefully unpacks its meaning as an adjective:

> *göttlich* = divinelike, like a Deity, made of a divine substance. It is not a specific Deity… I believe this is Jung's way of referring to what Paul Tillich called the God beyond God, the Ground of Being, the ultimate Source.[13]

Stein further explains: "In other words, the psychological self is shaped and conditioned by Divinity, *die Göttlichkeit*."[14] However, Stein makes an important distinction: while the Self serves as "the fundamental psychic ground of all images of Deity, is itself grounded in and reflective of Divinity,"[15] it is not identical to the divinity itself. Rather, the Self reflects and is grounded in *die Göttlichkeit*, but the two are not the same. He emphasizes: "Jung is not equating the self with Divinity… the psychological self is shaped and conditioned by Divinity, die Göttlichkeit."[16]

In a complex manner, the Self, divinity, and psyche are inextricably woven into the transparent fabric of the reflecting mind. I would like to remind readers of the dream discussed in Chapter 4, in which a woman envisioned an enormous snake with the head of a woman, from whose serpentine body white orchids grew.[17] This dream exemplified the natural expression of divinity arising from the archetypal ground of the goddess (or divine mother), incarnated in the snake with a woman's face. The connection between this snake-woman figure and transcendence can be empirically understood as a *coincidentia oppositorium*—a synthesis of instinct and spirit. Within her psyche, this image reflected the integration of the lower brain stem's primal instincts with the highest cortical functions of the mind, represented by the white orchid. Through this vision, the Self was becoming conscious of itself as an imprint of *die Göttlichkeit.*

An intriguing omission from Stein's version of this essay—one that appears in *Minding the Self: Jungian Meditations on Contemporary Spirituality*—is his assertion that all God-men or God-women fall short of "full incarnation of the Ground of Being despite theological claims to the contrary."[18] What is absent from the version included in the *Collected Writings* is the idea that all historical figures regarded as divine are merely incarnations of God images, and no individual in history has ever fully embodied the Ground of Being, nor ever will. This notion is fundamental to the sermons of Meister Eckhart.

I will quote in full the passage that moved me most, as I believe it presents a theoretical insight that could be easily overlooked:

An individual can strive to individuate as far as is possible, and in this sense incarnate the self, but no single person can incarnate the Ground of Being completely because it far exceeds the capacities of an individual self. Some humans may approach the state of full incarnation of the self, but none, even the greatest spiritual figures of history like Buddha and Christ, have achieved full incarnation of the Ground of Being despite theological claims to the contrary. All are limited by their times and their cultures. These images of selfhood are only partial representations of the full self and always leave some important elements of the self out of their portraits.[19]

Later in his 2014 text, Stein expands on the distinctions between the Self and the Ground (*Grund* in German) of Being—distinctions I find particularly illuminating. The following passage may be of special interest to more theologically minded readers:

The human task is to incarnate as much of the self, and therefore also of what stands behind the self, which is the Ground of Being, as possible in a single lifetime. This is the task of individuation, and it is what I mean by minding the self. The task of humanity as a whole is to incarnate the Ground of Being as fully as possible on a collective level. This has been the project of the world's religions until modern times, for better or worse.... Perhaps in time individuals can build a structure for a future collective expression of a more complete rendition of the Ground of Being on a collective level, an incarnation of the Divinity on a worldwide collective level. This is a task for the ages and one that can be measured only in eons, long spans of time like the Platonic Years, which occupy 2000 calendar years apiece.[20]

This is one of Stein's most heavily edited essays. In my view, the final version is sure to be of great interest to both theologians and contemporary post-Jungian scholars alike, which is one reason I have included it here. Also, for clinicians, Stein's innovations in analytical psychology may provide valuable insights for teaching his Four Pillars model in a more integrated manner—particularly in relation to the God concept (as distinct from a mere God image) upon which the model is built. While Stein articulates the pillars with clarity, the ground upon which they rest requires further conceptual development.

In the final version of the essay, Stein makes it clear that by "divineness," Jung was not referring to a specific deity, nor did he equate the Self with the Ground of Being or claim that the Self is inherently divine. Rather, Jung was offering a "theologically oriented psychology"—one that left a distinct stamp on the psyche of Florence, Italy, and found expression in its poet laureate. This vision, which emerged amid tremendous political unrest and upheaval, gave rise to a synthesis of good and evil, light and dark, and male and female—as manifested in Dante's *Divine Comedy*. Through his love for Beatrice, Dante became a transmitter of a Christian wisdom greater than any before in the history of the Holy Roman Empire, transforming time itself into an eternal process of transmutation.

Stein's conceptual clarifications align more closely with the Self (in both its lowercase and uppercase forms), when he describes it as a "projection of a psychological force—a living and dynamic factor." This force, he explains, is "the most elemental and all-encompassing force that humans are capable of imaging, conceiving, and projecting," and this equation of force as the "ultimate God image would correspond to the archetype of the self."[21]

Spirituality in the Psychoanalytic Context

Stein begins his essay "Spirituality in the Psychoanalytic Context" with a striking assertion: "Psychoanalysis is the child of modernity."[22] How, then, does this child appear in the postmodern landscape of Jungian psychoanalysis, as envisioned by Stein? From 2014 onward, Stein has consistently articulated its aims as follows:

The ego is not meant to be in charge of the psyche as a whole. This is a spiritual realization in analytic terms. The spirituality that comes about through analysis leans on this realization and the experience of the self.[23]

Stein further elaborates:

> The Self manifests in dreams and visions as a highly ambiguous image full of inner tensions and contradictions that can be resolved only at the level of the archetype per se, which is beyond our knowing, as is Divinity. What we experience of it is always just a piece of it, never the whole.[24]

What Stein introduces here—building upon Jung's basic formula—is the theological dimension of divinity, or divineness, which he extracts from Jung's writings. In addition to his earlier observations, Stein further emphasizes: "The psychic energy field that is generated by relationship between an analyst and analysand is an additional possible entry point into an apprehension of a spiritual dimension."[25] He concludes by asserting: "Analysis is a sustained reflection on the God's script, which becomes manifest as we mind the self. Consciousness of the message inscribed in our souls heals our one-sidedness and neurotic illnesses. The net effect is immense gratitude."[26]

Here again, Stein seamlessly integrates Jungian psychanalysis with spirituality in a manner both theological and psychological. He consistently underscores that the highest aim in the evolution of consciousness is the gratitude and generativity that arise from engaging with the vehicle of active imagination and the transcendent function.

The Search for Meaning

One of Stein's most recent contributions to Jungian psychoanalysis appears in his 2020 essay "The Search for Meaning." In the opening sentence, he fondly recalls reading Victor Frankl's famous book *Man's Search for Meaning* as a high school student in North Dakota—a land deeply connected to the Oglala Sioux vision quest.

The quest for meaning lies at the heart of Jungian psychology, forming the central axis of Jung's myth of meaning. In the second section of the essay, Stein provides a concise overview of Jung's lifelong search for a myth to live by. Here, he highlights a significant passage from *The Red Book* in which Jung asks his soul: "*Gibt es auch einen Übersin?*" Stein translates this as: "Is there also a supreme meaning?" To further illustrate Jung's concept and its relation to individuation, I would like to quote directly from Stein's text. In his conception of the Self as a "caller"—the one who summons us to realize our fullest potential—Stein emphasizes the imperative to individuate as fully as possible, striving toward ultimate wholeness. He writes:

> Without doubt, the sense of vocation is one of the most important sources of a sense of meaning in a person's life. It is a great motivator. Vocation is a calling, and the Caller is the Self. The subject receives a calling from a source beyond itself, an inner source that is irrational. In religious language, the Caller is God. This anchors the subject's personal sense of meaning in supreme meaning.

People do things out of an emergent sense of vocation that often they cannot explain or justify. They say they simply must do them.[27]

The personal sense of meaning is anchored in a supreme (or transpersonal) sense of meaning—emanating from the caller, the Self, or divinity. Thus, personal and transpersonal meaning are inextricably intertwined through an irrational source within the psyche, whether envisioned as god, the goddess, or both. The infinite Ground of Being, the transcendent factor that confers objective meaning to individuals undergoing individuation, is what Jung identified as ultimate meaning—a reality that transcends and can only be discovered through dialogue with the soul. This dialogue, whether with the anima, the animus or something more—a plus, as Jung suggested—serves as the gateway to the Self that calls to us. In Stein's view, this call comes through our spiritual name. He explains: "*Übersin… is* transcendent meaning. It is objective, not subjective." Stein then recalls the dream of a young male analysand who came into proper relationship with the Self. The Self had been constellated early in his childhood, when, at the age of four, he was adopted by a couple who had no children. As an only child, he had always felt special. However, at the age of 30, he was struggling with questions of meaning and vocation, as well as a general loss of motivation. Uncertain about his future, he brought a dream to a session—one Stein found deeply meaningful. I will abbreviate Stein's account of it here:

> He was visiting the magnificent Hagia Sophia in Istanbul, Turkey. He had been visited the holy mosque (once a Greek Orthodox Church) on a trip shortly before the dream. As he was walking into the grand cathedral under the beautiful dome below, suddenly he saw the heavenly scene of the Father God surrounded by other spiritual figures. He saw the Father-presence coming lower in the dome and felt himself spiritually ascending at the same time. As they approached each other, the father looked him in the eye, pointed his finger toward him, and said in a serious and solemn voice that echoed throughout the space between then: "I want you!"

The Self wanted him. The young man awoke with tears in his eyes—tears that were later mirrored in his analyst. The dream must have reminded Stein of his own vision of the Cosmic Christ. At the age of four, the dreamer had felt chosen by his adoptive parents. Now, he was being chosen once again—this time by the Self, the caller, for a mission that only he could fulfill within the transference-countertransference field between himself and his analyst. The calling Self was asking more of him than he had previously given. And now, the figures standing before him were no longer his personal adoptive parents, but figures from a transcendent, transpersonal realm—perhaps God and Sophia, Christ and Wisdom, or Allah.

This dream became a source of the young man's personal myth, with the Hagia Sophia serving as the setting for his ascension—an experience imbued with numinosity for both himself and his analyst. Stein does not reveal which vocation the young man ultimately pursued, but in the context of his search for purpose, the dream offers compelling evidence that he found his way. From a clinical perspective, Stein's case study demonstrates how something numinous was evoked in the transference-countertransference dynamic, with Stein embodying an elder, fatherly/motherly presence. For the patient, this experience likely evoked reminiscences of the healing energies he felt as a four-year-old boy at the time of his adoption. In the analytic process, such regressive experiences hold immense significance. They reconnect individuals—especially those who may feel unchosen by God or the Self—to an "opening" toward something *Über* (above or beyond) themselves. This is akin to the hand of God—an ineffable presence that cannot be fully understood through rational understanding, as it belongs to the realm of the irrational, sacred mystery.

Stein's formulation of the Self as the caller to the called could not have been more powerfully affirmed than through this young man's dream. The moment of shared meaning they experienced in the relational matrix—expressed through their mutual tears—is deeply moving. Readers will recall Stein's three countertransference attitudes in Jungian psychoanalysis: power-oriented, shamanistic, and maieutic. In this case, Stein was clearly fulfilling a maieutic function, providing the psychic space necessary for the Self to give birth to the young man's vocation. Finally, it emerged as a spiritual calling, whether from God or the calling Self. Having worked for 20 years as a Jungian psychoanalyst with adoptive children, I am reminded of cases from early in my career—ones I will never forget for the joy they brought me. The experiences of returning children to their homes after two to three years in residential treatment were profoundly moving. I can still recall calling out a boy's name, my eyes brimming with tears, and saying, "X, you are going home!"—a moment in which the child's joy became utterly contagious.

The important point to understand is that this analytical experience could not have emerged without empathic relatedness, affect attunement, and loving attention—principles that constitute the second pillar of Jungian psychoanalysis. In this sense, Stein functioned as a transformative figure within the analytic relationship, facilitating the healing of the young man's mother-father wound and abandonment trauma. Through his role as a midwife to the patient's calling, Stein embodied both mothering and fathering functions, guiding the young man toward a deeper integration of the Self.

Synchronizing Time and Eternity: A Matter of Practice

Stein's lecture "Synchronizing Time and Eternity: A Matter of Practice," delivered as a keynote address at the joint IAAP/IAJS conference at Yale University in the summer of 2015, marked a transformative moment in his life—one that was apparent to those of us present who were aware of Stein's personal history. Change was in the air. At the age of 72, Stein had been living in Switzerland for well over a decade, having successfully migrated from his "family romance" in the United States. Now, standing at the podium of his beloved alma mater, Stein found himself returned to the very place where a book, *Memories, Dreams, Reflections*, had previously ignited his vocation as a Jungian analyst in 1968. Stein also stood where Jung himself once stood when, in 1937, during his seventh and final visit to the United States, he delivered the famous "Terry lectures" at Yale. The subject of those lectures—"Psychology and Religion"—was the very theme that launched Stein's own career as an international scholar. From a synchronistic perspective, it is remarkable that both Jung and Stein formulated their foundational contributions to analytical psychology on the same ground, at the same institution, separated by nearly eight decades.

Jung's series of four lectures in 1937 marked the penultimate moment of his visit to North America, culminating in what Stein referred to as his "Last Supper"—a farewell gathering with a small group of supporters in New York. It was a hallowed time for the field of analytical psychology, as Jung urged his followers to follow Christ's example and embark on their own "experiments" in individuation. This was precisely what Stein had done decades earlier when, at the age of 26, he ventured to Zürich to forge his own path. He had made his experiment. Now, standing at Yale, he had entered the fifth stage of his life as the "sage of Goldiwil."

The central symbol of his lecture was Wolfgang Pauli's remarkable "World Clock"—an image that so impressed Jung that he shared it with his audience during his fourth and final lecture at Yale. Speaking solemnly, Stein reflected on the significance of synchronicity in analytic practice—the awareness that moments of transcendence can emerge spontaneously, without any discernible cause. The World Clock, as Stein explained (drawing from Jung's interpretation), represents the meeting place of time and eternity within the Self.

In his lecture, Stein explored the nature of synchronistic events in analytic practice, emphasizing that, when we remain open to chance occurrences, we encounter something numinous. He observed that, as human beings, we long to step outside of time, to transcend the constraints of the present, and to enter the eternal moment. If we can experience—even for an instant—a true feeling of timelessness, in which everything unfolds simultaneously, we may encounter a deeper symmetry of meaning from a transpersonal perspective. Such moments of altered perception, he argued, can transform us permanently at the highest levels of our being, even if we appear unchanged on the lower floors of the Self. As Jung asked: "*Gibt es auch einen Übersin?*" ("Is there also a supreme meaning?"). In his keynote address, Stein answered in the affirmative.

In his lecture, Stein distinguished between *kairos* time and *chronos* time, reflecting on the timing of synchronicities in our lives. Why do meaningful chance events occur precisely when we are most open to the Self? Imagine, for a moment, what it might have felt for him to return to Yale—to stand in the very place where the calling Self had first pronounced the letters of his name.

In retrospect, he observed, such moments are critical for sensing our life's many purposes. This is not abstract speculation but empirical reality. And yet, beyond conscious intent, accidents and coincidences may alter our paths irrevocably, placing us on a surer course. Big dreams or visions can shake the very foundations of the psyche, taking our breaths away. Such transformative experiences raise fundamental questions: Might the psyche itself be grounded in metaphysical reality? Could these moments reflect the Ground of Being? Such instants, if one retains a feeling for their numinosity, are never forgotten. Stein refers to these as individuation moments—minutes, hours, or even days of profound transformation. And there is seldom just one. There are many.

I encourage readers to read Stein's full lecture to appreciate the symmetry of the symbolism in Pauli's World Clock and Stein's meditations on its significance alongside Jung's. Though long and sometimes heady, it is an extraordinarily important work for the field of Jungian theory and practice.

In the concluding section, Stein revisits the question of whether the religious function of the psyche has a place in Jungian psychoanalysis. His answer is an unequivocal yes. Yet he does not stop there—he presses further:

> Does the psyche as we understand it and work with it as Jungian analysts include a space for the intersection of time and eternity, for the secular and sacred? How do we walk the fine and often twisting line between ego-building and self-incarnation? Is it our business as Jungian analysts to 'mind the self' and address such questions of ultimate concern?[28]

These are important questions—ones that cannot be glossed over. Stein's most substantive insights are delivered with such grace that I feel compelled to highlight them again here: "Time and eternity are woven tightly together in the fabric of lived individuation, if for no other reason than that synchronicity plays such a vital role in life as concretely experienced. But how do we carry this in consciousness?" He then returns to Pauli's World Clock, describing it as an image "from the Self, from eternity, directed by the 'Master' to us, to assist us as we make our way forward through time."[29]

Here, Stein revisits his earlier reflections on the interplay between eternity and time, reminding us once more of the enigmatic "Master" in his closing sentence. But who was Pauli's inner "Master"—a term that emerged from Jung's analysis of Pauli's "piano lesson" dream. In this moment, Stein is theorizing—seeking a theologically grounded psychology and a psychologically grounded theology—while contemplating the nature of the Self. Not every Jungian feels compelled to unite these disciplines, yet the question still remains: How can dreams—whether Pauli's, Stein's patients', or our own—assist us in building upon the Four Pillars in a way that affirms all beings as rooted in the same ground of experience, heading toward the same destination?

Moreover, what methods might open the doors of perception to the theological dimensions that Jung so often illuminated and that Stein, as both a Protestant and a Jungian, has helped refine? How might we, in our everyday lives and analytic practices, keep these doors to the Self ajar, without foreclosing the possibility that the "Master" (whether understood as God or the Self) who once visited Pauli might also visit us and our patients—provided we give equal consideration to all Four Pillars?

At Yale, Stein left his mark in time for all of eternity. Those of us in attendance, who felt the electricity in the room, witnessed a profound meditation on being and selfhood. Stein reflected on the relationship between psychology and physics, and natural science and theology, as well as their possibility of unification. Ultimately, he confirmed the Self's acausal intentionality in Pauli's life—as perplexing as it may seem to our ego-awareness.

The Mystery of Transcendence–A Dream for our Time

In the 2022 essay "The Mystery of Transcendence—A Dream for our Time," published by Chiron Publications, Stein offers another glimpse into the ineffable mysteries of the hidden hand of the Self through a striking dream image from a female analysand who was also a spiritual practitioner. The dreamer envisioned a five-story house. On the fifth floor, a single flame burned brightly—an image Stein interpreted as a dream for our times—and an inner figure named "Teacher" (akin to Pauli's "Master") delivered a command: "Leave the door open for others to enter." Stein concluded: "This is the basis for the invisible spiritual community that today is becoming global."[30] This invisible spiritual community can be understood as a soul society—a network of post-Jungians contributing to the advancement of the world. In 2024, Stein co-authored a book with this woman (see Chapter 12).

The Marriage of Animus and Anima in the Mystery of Individuation

First published by Chiron Publications in 2022, "The Marriage of Animus and Anima in the Mystery of Individuation" explores the marital union of the animus and anima, as depicted in a series of 20 alchemical woodcuts from the *Rosarium philosophorum*. Jung incorporated the first ten images into "The Psychology of the Transference" to illustrate the relational dynamics of analysis.[31] However, those familiar with Jung's work who have not encountered the final ten images might find themselves wondering—as I did—what became of the rest? Why did Jung omit them, and how might they inform contemporary analytic practice?

Stein's reflections on all 20 images are insightful, but his discussion of the final ten is particularly compelling. His analysis becomes especially fascinating when he turns to image 11, in which the anima and animus—the alchemical marriage couple—acquire wings. Readers of Stein's earlier work may recall the emergence of another winged creature—the butterfly—as a symbol of metamorphosis in his book *Transformation: Emergence of the Self*. Here, however, the imagery is uniquely alchemical.

The imagery in this second series of ten woodcuts suggests a "spiritually advanced state of consciousness."[32] The wings of the couple in the alchemical bath symbolize the emergence of

> an archetypal mind, mind that is in contact with the world of the archetypes. We can think of it as a Platonic mind rather than an Empirical mind. It is what the Greeks called *nous*, the archetypal basis of mind itself.[33]

This framework offers a more contemporary and nuanced template for understanding the transference-countertransference relationship than the one Jung introduced 80 years ago. In discussing the *Syzygy*—the Greek term for "union" or "conjunction"— Stein emphasizes that the spirits of the couple remain distinct yet interwoven, existing as anima and animus as a "single unit, like Siamese twins."[34] He further notes:

> In recent times and with LGBTQ gaining acceptance in many societies, "the combinations can be quite different and rather fluid. They might be animus identified-man and anima-identified-man, or animus-identified woman and anima-identified woman, or animus-identified woman and anima-identified man. Transgender couples and even more permutations. The restoration of the syzygy on the interpersonal level need not be reflective of gender differences.[35]

This is especially important today, as evolving perspectives on sex and gender are transforming clinical practice across cultures.[36] Stein's revisions of Jung's early model of the psychology of the transference are therefore timely and necessary, and his more expansive interpretation of the *Rosarium philosophorum* extends its relevance to all individuals, thereby broadening the metaphors of union within the analytical space. Jung's decision to exclude the final ten images has, in many ways, limited our understanding of psychoanalysis, and particularly that transformative moment when, as Stein suggests, an analytic couple gets their wings. Thus, Stein's revision expands the framework in a more transpersonal dimension.

For instance, in his analysis of image 14, Stein writes:

> There is no movement, even at a cellular level. The neurons are quiet. It is the Void: no sensations, no thoughts, no images. The Spirit, which has departed is flying upward for advanced exposure to the Divine realm of transcendence.[37]

I see his commentary here as highly pertinent to advanced stages of analysis—those representing the solitudes of reverie needed for the deeper awakening of the Self.

Stein's analysis of the final four images is even more transcendent, identifying in image 17 the "triumphant culmination" of the "transformation process, the Solar Rebis, also known as the red Stone."[38] These more spiritualized images may represent the catalysts of higher forms of individuation in clinical practice. Stein describes:

> The third and final passage through death and rebirth, which begins with picture 18 and concludes with picture 20, is so mystical and employs imagery that so strongly suggests the afterlife that I [Murray Stein] am inclined to think of it as a stage of individuation that exceeds this life and extends into the Beyond.

While reflecting on these images, Stein is reminded of some poignant questions raised by aging analysands—particularly those experiencing mental decline or infirmity. Such analysands, he notes, often ask:

> If I should (God forbid!) descend into dementia as I age further, will all that I have gained by way of inner work and individuation in my life just melt away

and disappear? Does any of that survive the deterioration of the body's brain or the death of the body?[39]

In his discussion of image 19, Stein offers a reassuring perspective, revealing his own understanding of the soul or spirit after death:

> The Holy Trinity is placing a crown on the human figure as the sacred words of the sacramental action are spoken (or sung) in the sky above. This is the crown of glory that would have traditionally, according to Catholic doctrine, been given to the faithful bride of Christ, the church.[40]

Stein interprets the final stage of transformation in the *Rosarium philosophorum* as providing a partial answer to the analytic questions surrounding cognitive decline, uncovering further nuggets of wisdom from the transcendent or transpersonal Self. As he explains: "The ultimate gift to the individuating personality is the elevation of identity to the archetypal basis and fundamental essence of the personality with no residue of the temporal remaining." He adds:

> In Picture 19, we see into the Beyond and witness what is happening there. This is the story of Dante's journey into and through the heavenly realms in the third canticle of *The Diving Comedy, Paradiso*. There the poet becomes privy to the transcendent realities and mysteries and is, in turn, transformed by his visionary experiences as he writes, that he could feel the center of his thoughts and desires being guided 'by the Love that moves the sun and the other stars.' He becomes One with divine Love and is no longer the Dante Alighieri who lived in Florence, endured years of exile, and became the famous romantic poet. Internally, he is Divine, as is his immortal poem. The theme of divinization is continued in the final picture in the series, the image of the risen and triumphant Christ.[41]

How does this Christian symbolism relate to the second pillar of Jungian psychoanalysis? "Ultimately," Stein explains,

> there is a birth of transcendence in consciousness that rises above all divisions created by the psyche, and a person enters into a space of supreme Oneness.... These are states of mind beyond all conditioning.... Meditating on the pictures of the *Rosarium philosophorum* has been a way for some people to find their way toward this final goal.[42]

This suggests that the concerns Stein addresses—regarding fears of dementia or Alzheimer's disease—are not only relevant to those approaching the end of life, but also to individuals in the sage or even missionary stages of life, when experiences of transcendence become possible. Engaging with these images through active imagination can render resurrection imagery an experiential reality, provided the archetype of transfiguration is awakened within what Jung referred to as the trans-psyche.

In the "Conclusion" of his essay, Stein writes:

> The analogy, or identity, of the product of the alchemical transformation mystery to the resurrected Christ caused concern among the Church's theologians, who proceeded to declare alchemy a false and misleading teaching, a heresy. In effect, the alchemists were saying the human individuals can attain to the spiritual level of the transcendent Christ.[43]

Further Meditations on the Risen Christ

In his "Foreword" to Alan Asay's book on the witnessing of the Risen Jesus by the disciples he so loved (even Judas!), Stein reflects on the significance of such visionary experiences, particularly those described in the final cantos of Dante's *Paradiso*. He argues that visions of this kind are highly pertinent to analytic work in a relational context and should be positioned within the broader scope of what is possible in analysis. As he writes:

> To my mind, a successful Jungian analysis is one that uncovers this source of love and total acceptance within.... Patients in analysis may find it [self-love or love of the Self] in the therapeutic relationship or in experiences in dreams and active imagination.[44]

It is not always acknowledged that love is the true ointment that heals the psyche when an individual enters a space of supreme Oneness. Such transpersonal experiences are often left unspoken in the analytic setting, as some analysists hesitate to articulate them within the therapeutic relationship. Yet, moments of intersection, when time and eternity touch, are deeply felt. In these rare and profound instances, both patient and analyst may feel touched by the curative powers of love emerging from the depths or heights of the psyche.

Previously, we encountered this kind of agape love in the young man's dream of spiritual ascension in the Hagia Sophia. In that exchange, both analyst and patient were moved to tears—and that, in itself, was enough.

As we near the conclusion, I wish to share something golden—a passage from the second-to-last paragraph of Chapter 12 of this volume:

> Modern depth psychology has mounted a powerful critique on the isolated ego. As never before, we can see its relativity and slender archetypal support. The new dominant arriving is a myth of connectedness to replace the one of separation and control. It is based on a realization of a network of relations that ties all peoples together into one pluralistic unity. It requires almost unimaginable tolerance of differences and acute consciousness of interdependence among all the parts.[45]

Stein leaves us with a vision of pluralistic unity—a conscious awareness of all the parts that constitute the whole within an infinite universe of being. In doing so, he invites us to further reflect on the transmarginal dimensions of Jungian psychoanalysis and what remains possible within its evolving landscape.

Finally, in his Jungian meditations on Zen Buddhist D.T. Suzuki's writings on the "Ox-Herding" pictures, Stein explores a particular image titled "Entering the Marketplace":

> Minding the Self accumulates more psychic substance and permanence in consciousness. As the individuation process runs on, the personality matures around a center that is not only personal but also impersonal... he [the enlightened Sage] seems to bestow synchronistic effects on his environment, so something special emanates from him, but this is subtle and he takes no credit for it.[46]

With these sublime thoughts, I conclude my review of Volume 8 of Stein's *Collected Writings*.

Notes

1 CW8, 1.
2 CW8, 8.
3 CW8, 9–10.
4 CW8, 11.
5 CW8, 11.
6 CW8, 2.
7 CW8, 14.
8 CW8, 14.
9 CW8, 21.
10 CW8, 34.
11 CW8, 43.
12 CW8, 46.
13 CW8, 46, 47.
14 CW8, 47.
15 CW8, 50, 51.
16 CW8, 47.
17 CW3, 230–231.
18 MS, 17.
19 MS, 17.
20 MS, 19, 20.
21 CW8, 49.
22 CW8, 75.
23 CW8, 79.
24 CW8, 82.
25 CW8, 84.
26 CW8, 88.
27 CW8, 100.
28 CW8, 123.
29 CW8, 124.
30 CW8, 213.

31 CW8, 215.
32 CW8, 239.
33 CW8, 240.
34 CW8, 217.
35 CW8, 220–221.
36 Herrmann, S. "Walt Whitman on Religious Liberty: Marriage Equality and the American Cultural Complex." In *Cultural Complexes and the Soul of America: Myth, Psyche, and Politics*, edited by Thomas Singer, 180–196. New York: Routledge, 2020.
37 CW8, 244.
38 CW8, 245.
39 CW8, 247.
40 CW8, 249.
41 CW8, 249–250.
42 CW8, 253.
43 CW8, 252.
44 CW8, 258.
45 MS, 91.
46 MS, 125, 126.

Chapter 10

Outside Inside and All Around

The title of Stein's 2016 book, *Outside Inside and All Around*, reflects his effort "to open wide the doors of our perception of the world, mundane and transcendent, that surround and inhabit us."[1] I include a review of its chapters here because many have not yet appeared in his *Collected Writings*.

In this book, Stein explores how both mundane and transcendent perceptions can be experienced in Jungian psychoanalysis, though the latter are less common without the practice of active imagination, which the book advocates for clinical use. In the opening chapter, Stein examines three pairs of inner/outer distinctions that emerge in different forms of what Jung termed "transgressivity," or transgressive experiences. Such experiences occur when the mundane and the transcendent intersect within the trans-marginal Self-field, allowing the numinous to break through from trans-temporal reality (operating within *kairos*) into the time-bound ego (defined by *chronos*). Stein identifies three primary modalities through which transgressivity manifests in Jungian psychoanalysis: "a) in imagination or reverie, b) in dreams, and c) in synchronicity."[2]

Imagination and reverie serve as gateways to the infinite depths and heights of the Self, as well as the unitary reality, or *unus mundus*. Both techniques enable the Self to perceive the world as a unified whole via the ego-Self axis, facilitating numinous experiences of "Oneness."[3]

In discussing this idea, Stein makes use of a masterful diagram from Erich Neumann's 1952 lecture, "The Psyche and the Transformation of the Reality Planes." This illustration, though often underemphasized in Jungian theory and practice, is revitalized by Stein, who presents it three times (on pages 21, 65, and 258) across consecutive chapters to stress its significance. Integrating this diagram into his own creative theorizing, Stein demonstrates its centrality to his work. A particularly notable aspect of the diagram is its delineation of three fields of knowledge, which Stein describes using Neumann's exact terminology: "a) an ego-field, b) an archetypal-field, and c) a self-field."[4]

What interests Stein most is the "Self-field"—the reality plane on which the cosmic and transcendent intersect with the imminent and finite, and on which synchronicities (holding both objective and subjective validity from a transpersonal

DOI: 10.4324/9781003664024-11

perspective) are seen, sensed, and felt. Stein describes the intersections in this field as revealing

> knowledge that is waiting to be presented to consciousness. This knowledge becomes available in the 'intermediate realm,' when awareness is opened to its presentation. What this requires are two conditions: You have to be in the 'field,' and you have to be open to it. Then field knowledge will present itself.[5]

As evidenced here, Stein has a way of making Neumann, known for his highly abstract theories, feel pragmatic and grounded.

In the section "Dreams as Transgressive," Stein draws on William James's term "extra-marginal" to describe information and insights lying beyond the margins of ego consciousness. To clarify his ideas on transgressive experiences and synchronicity, he reports a highly personal example—a dream his wife, Jan, had while he was preparing notes for a lecture. The account is quite remarkable:

> She was in a bathtub, working on a swimming suit designed for herself. A glass separated her from a shop. She saw the shop owner, an older man, dressed in black in the second part of the dream in a large library. She was an observer in the room while he was about to get married, in preparation for his wedding ceremony, arranging books on the library shelves. He had with him a younger assistant, a man who dressed in green, a very energetic and competent man, whose quick movements and high-spirited energy assisted the older gentleman. The younger man was quickly arranging the scholar's books in order along the shelves, in preparation for the ceremony.

In Jan's dream, there is a correspondence between her animus principle and the two central dream figures: (1) an old man dressed in black who is about to wed and (2) a young man dressed in green, who is assisting the old man in arranging his books before the wedding. The older man is the shop owner, and his shop sells a variety of goods, including food, household items, and pharmaceuticals. In the first sequence, Jan's dream-ego is separated from the shop by a glass pane. She can peer through at the shop owner but is uncertain whether he can see her. Before this scene, the dream begins with Jan's dream-ego in a bathtub, designing a swimsuit for herself. The dream unfolds in three stages before reaching its resolution (lysis): (1) the dreamer in an ego field, alone in her bath, designing her swimsuit; (2) the first aging animus figure, dressed in black, working in an archetypal field—the shop apothecary; and (3) the Self-field, where the dream-ego observes the two animi working together in the library, separated by a glass pane—a symbolic trans-marginal plane. The younger man in green leads the effort to organize the bookshelves in the gentleman's library. Then, Jan wakes up. Stein explains:

> This is an example of transmission over psychic boundaries from my side (Stein's preoccupation with an image for a lecture) to hers (dreaming beside

me at night) and from hers to me the next day by recounting her dream. This was then followed during the day after by a synchronicity: my wife was reading a book and suddenly came upon a passage about "the green man" in world mythology and literature.[6]

Jan's dream, Stein reflects, helped open the doors of his perception in 2016, expanding his vision of the Self from the dimension of time into the timelessness of the Empyrion. Upon hearing about the passage Jan had been reading at the time (on the Green Man), Stein immediately recalled a passage from the Koran that had been the central theme of Jung's Eranos lecture in 1939 (the same year of his vision of the greenish-gold Christ), which Stein also discusses in several essays, as well as in *How and Why We Still Read Jung*, a more recent book edited by Jean Kirsch and Stein. Stein describes that synchronicity experiences began to multiply in the days following Jan's dream, forming "a network of meaning that surrounded us during our 40th wedding anniversary in Venice." This account connects significantly to earlier examples of synchronicity reported by Stein, such as the butterfly-related incidents that occurred around the deaths of close friends, representing instances of *kairos* when the doors of perception opened. Indeed, coupling and synchronicity seem to go hand in hand.

Importantly, I want to draw readers' attention to the word "transmission" in Stein's analysis of Jan's dream. In Eastern traditions, particularly in India, this word is often used to describe direct communication between a teacher and a disciple. Here, however, the transmission is two-way, representing a reciprocal exchange between husband and wife. The Self appears to have been communicating something from an unknown source, manifesting in the space between them—the transpersonal Self. Stein explains:

> Timing is essential in synchronicity, which after all contains the word for time, *chronos*. We felt the Green Man probably with us, as though we had entered into Neumann's third stage of consciousness where ego, archetype and self-fields all come together. This brings a very special feeling of being anchored in the *unus mundus*.[7]

Stein then provides another extra-marginal example of a sacred instinctual coupling, recounting an experience in which a pair of mallard ducks mysteriously waddled across the road before him and his wife, following the funeral of another dear friend. This friend, a Jungian analyst, had lost her husband—also an analyst—several years earlier. As Stein and his wife drove home, reflecting on the couple's passing, the two mallards suddenly appeared, crossing their path. This moment became pregnant with reverie, as three dimensions of psychophysical reality converged: (1) their two ego consciousnesses, (2) the archetypal realm represented by the married couple, and (3) their departed friends, who had entered the Self-field and found material expression in the synchronicity of the two ducks. Forced to pause as the mallards passed, the couple experienced a profound Oneness—an affirmation of togetherness just prior to their 40th wedding anniversary in Venice.

Notably, Dante had visited Venice in August 1321 as an envoy for his distinguished host, Guido Novello da Polenta, undertaking a delicate diplomatic mission to resolve a troublesome political dispute.

Stein writes that the two ducks:

> took their time in a dignified way, crossed the road, and disappeared into the woods on the other side. There was no doubt in our minds that this was a signal from the other side—an inseparable couple in life and an inseparable couple in death. *Imaginatio* instantly told us who they were, and we were in an intermediate realm where psyche and matter came together in a moment of transcendent meaning.... This meaning is nothing more.

However, he does not hesitate to add that it is also "nothing less, than our life is lived both in time and in eternity. And a strong experience of this kind leaves an indelible mark on consciousness, even transforms it."[8] Continuing, he writes:

> These indicate strongly, and I believe persuasively, that as individuals we are far more connected to the world and to the cosmos than we are normally aware of as we go about our daily business. If we can be open to this network of connections continuously, it might be too much to bear; hence, we have defenses for shutting us off and shutting us in. However, if one has a powerful and convincing experience of the *unus mundus*, it will change ego-consciousness permanently. We should not forget, ever, that these connections and links do exist, and from time to time they do inform us that we are anything but isolated and alone in the cosmos.[9]

With this, he concludes his opening inquiry into the mystery of the marriage of opposites in this book, which he dedicates to Jan. It is a touching narrative—almost dreamlike. The absolute knowledge imparted to the couple by the Green Man in the space between them would later unfold into an ever greater vision for Stein. Four years later, in 2020—amid the global shutdown of the COVID-19 pandemic—he would write his essay on the Four Pillars. Around this same time, he would embark on an in-depth reading of Dante for the first time—an experience that would ultimately affirm what his anima already understood about the Self's highest stages of spiritual transformation.

On Psyche's Creativity

Stein opens the chapter titled "On Psyche's Creativity" by recounting a lengthy dream of an analysand that he found particularly inspiring, as it signaled an emerging creative process. To further develop this theme, he introduces an essay by Erich Neumann, "Creative Man and Transformation," commenting,

> Sadly, much of Neumann's work has been overlooked or undervalued by the field of analytical psychology as it has developed since Jung's death. One hopes this

neglect will be rectified now with the publication of the extensive and revealing correspondence between Neumann and Jung, *Analytical Psychology in Exile*.[10]

I could not agree more with this statement.

Neumann was a major theorist in field, yet his contributions have often been overlooked. This is tragic, given the depth and sophistication of his work. Stein gives us hope that our field might come to recognize the significance of Neumann's ideas for theoretical development. He then turns to a second paper by Neumann, "The Place of Creation," based on an Eranos lecture delivered in August 1960, just months before Neumann's untimely death in December of that year. In this essay, Neumann formulated what Stein refers to as a "meta-psychological summit."

Stein then provides an in-depth analysis of Neumann's essay, homing in on the Israeli analyst's seminal idea of a directing agency (DA) in the psyche. According to Neumann, the DA is a force of nature that arises out of the unitary field into a trinity of creation, and can be integrated through the ego-Self axis. He conceptualizes the DA as an Organizing Principle (OP) within the personality that can move individuals toward wholeness by activating the innate human instinct for individuation. We see the DA at work in Jan's dream, where Murray's unconscious transmission to her while she was sleeping had a reciprocal effect when she later recounted the dream to him. As they reflected on the dream together, Jan referenced a book she had been reading about the Green Man in world mythology and literature. They both "felt" that the Green Man was present with them. Neumann would claim that the DA organized this synchronicity.

Within the human personality, the conscious ego recognizes the DA as an agent of the Self—a world-ordering principle. When the ego aligns itself with the Self, forming a connection through the ego-Self axis, it collaborates with the Self's vital principle to foster wholeness. This process reaches its culmination in human creativity, which Stein regards as its supreme expression. He further states, "In the fourth stage, then, the ego is taken up into the trinity of creation and becomes an executive of its creative activities. When the ego does this, it experiences individual life as a destiny."[11] This notion resonates with my work in *William James and C.G. Jung: Doorways to the Self*, in which I describe a similar phenomenon as a "destiny dream."

I find it particularly interesting that Neumann capitalized the words "Organizing Principle," suggesting that individuation entails a transcendent function—one that momentarily opens the doors of perception to an experience of the transcendental Self. Stein provides an excellent illustration of the OP in action, drawing from Harold Bloom's *The Daimon Knows*, in which Bloom reflects: "I have been reading *Moby-Dick* since I fell in love with the book in 1940, a boy of ten."[12] Examples such as this remind me of the continuity of life experiences shaping destiny from an early age. It is remarkable to consider a ten-year-old boy reading Melville—this shows the precocity of Bloom's mind even before adolescence and serves as an example of vocational development in childhood. As Neumann suggested, certain archetypes can be "switched on" through "evocation," and in Bloom's, case,

Moby-Dick functioned as a calling symbol—pulsating with aliveness through its pages. The image of the whale left an indelible impression on the young reader, shaping his intellectual trajectory. Bloom later became Stein's teacher at Yale and one of the most influential literary scholars of all time.

Questions concerning the role of the DA or OP in the constellation of synchronistic events—such as the discovery of a formative book in childhood or Jan's dream of the old man and the verdant figure—are deeply embedded in the interactional field of Jungian psychoanalysis. These moments emerge when psychological openness occurs, as if a door or window has been momentarily unsealed, allowing for ongoing dialogue and analytic exploration into the mystery of transcendence—the interconnectedness of psyche and matter. Stein's example of his wife's dream illustrates how a couple can mutually transmit archetypal material to one another, particularly when the archetype of vocation is constellated within the Self-field, manifesting both internally and externally. Similarly, one might ask: What role did reading a book at age 10 and engaging in poetic reverie play in shaping the mind-matter correlations that ultimately defined Bloom's intellectual destiny? Stein concludes his essay with the assertion that "there is a goal-directed agency moving toward a meaningful destination. We can only look backward, not ahead."[13] The retrospective glance offers an intuitive grasp of meaning, illuminating the significance of dreams, books discovered in latency, and the vibrational energies of dream figures, all of which constitute a psychoid reality that transcends time.

At the Brink of Transformation

In the chapter "At the Brink of Transformation," Stein's tone becomes more emphatic, urgent, and interpersonal as he draws readers into the transpersonal Self-field. Like a seasoned literary dramatist skilled in deep reading, he guides readers into the liminal realm of the Greek god Hermes—a favorite of his since publishing *In Midlife*. Setting the stage for what follows, he poses a heartfelt question: "With what attitude do you, dear reader, step from the brink into an unforeseen (and unforeseeable) future?"[14] Stein then turns to a letter Neumann wrote to Jung on June 14, 1957, in which the Israeli analyst "jumped into the abyss" and was caught and carried by the godhead on "wings of the heart."[15] It is a marvelous chapter—one that must be read in full to appreciate its profound depth. At the time of writing, Stein captured the momentum of the Neumann revival as it was unfolding across Israel, Europe, and the United States.

The Neumann-Jung letters are a joy to read. Having read all of Neumann's books as a young man, I find Stein's reflections on his theories both illuminating and deeply moving. Neumann remains one of the great mavericks of the Jungian field, and the time has not yet come for the further evolution and synthesis of his thought. Stein, however, has taken an important step in this direction by pointing us toward a future destination. The Green Man's energies are essential for organizing such an ambitious undertaking, but the books already exist, waiting for their assimilation into a synthesis—an empirical-metaphysical masterpiece that has yet to be born.

What I mean here is that there is a timing of events in the DA that works in concert with the OP to orchestrate synchronicities during moments of supreme meaning. We saw this earlier in Stein's essay "*Dante's* Divine Comedy: *A Journey of Transformation*," written for the conference in Ravenna, in 2021. Five years previously, Stein had described that synchronicity experiences began to multiply around a shared "network of meaning" that surrounded him and Jan during their 40th wedding anniversary in Venice. During the two events in Italy, there appears to have been an OP at play. The DA and OP appear to have been working in tandem to miraculously interconnect the timing of many of the happenings in Stein's evolving sense of vocation—to study Protestant theology at Yale, to marriage, to his career as an analytical researcher, writer, and international scholar. Faith has been present in carrying Stein to where he is.

Cultural Trauma, Violence, and Transformation

Stein opens his essay entitled "Cultural Trauma, Violence, and Transformation" with the question: "Can some of us become wounded healers of cultural trauma?"[16] He returns once again to Richard Wilhelm's story of the Rainmaker, which I explored in Chapter 3. Here, he challenges readers further: "Can Jungian psychotherapists become Rainmakers? I know of no other psychology that has a better theory for it. And this can even be carried out even from the remoteness of the study and the lecture hall."[17] What would it mean for the world if this were possible? The Self demands that we take an active role in the unfolding of the world play, through sacred action. To embody the archetype of the Rainmaker, we must first cultivate inner unity. This requires the solitude of the little hut on the hill where we can align ourselves with the Tao.

Turbulence in the Individuation of Humankind

Stein concludes his book with an "Enterview"—a reflective dialogue—with Rob Henderson, titled "Turbulence in the Individuation of Humankind." Here, he reaffirms his alignment with Jung and Neumann in postulating that a DA underlies human creativity, guiding us toward more advanced states of human consciousness. This belief fosters Stein's enduring optimism. He envisions new possibilities for the world, despite the prevailing atmosphere of pessimism in global politics, ongoing conflict in the Middle East, and the economic and environmental crises that have intensified since the industrial age. Stein recalls:

> I grew up with the fear of imminent atomic cataclysm. So maybe I got used to living with images of the end of the world. Global warming is not the end of the world, as far as I can tell. It may be the end of the way we have been used to living in some ways, but human ingenuity is amazing and will find solutions. The will to live and survive will prevail.[18]

He then makes a striking assertion:

> It would be great if we all considered ourselves therapists of the world! After all, are we not? So what should we do? First, it is necessary to recognize that our personal views and attitudes do make a difference on the world around us.[19]

In these reflections, Stein extends his psychological-theoretical exploration of the Healing Self (or Rainmaker) in the human psyche. He continues:

> As therapists of culture and the world, the best thing we can do is to work on ourselves. But at a deep level. This is not so much personal work (which of course is also essential for a strong ego), but inner work that touches archetypal levels of the psyche. Synchronicity follows. Psychic wholeness and balance are contagious. Jungian analysts don't have specific goals. They have faith in the potential of the self to bring about wholeness in their patients. So their aim is to bring about a condition in the analytic setting where the Self has a chance to manifest and be heard. This must take place on an archetypal, i.e., global level.[20]

Here, Stein is addressing not merely Jungian analysts and psychotherapists, but all readers—anyone willing to engage deeply with his work and Jung's, approaching them with openness to the psyche. What he accomplishes is a reversal of what Jung termed "psychic infection" prior to the outbreak of World War II, when insanity erupted on a massive scale. Notably, that was the same year in which Jung was meditating on the Green Man archetype within alchemy, Christianity, and Sufism. Stein suggests that, through the individuation of humankind—one individual at a time, within small groups that evolve into communities of cultural healers—the momentum of transformation can become infectious, influencing the body politic in a constructive, rather than destructive, manner. The idea that Jungian psycho-analysts can serve as Rainmakers or cultural healers through their own inner work can be traced back to Jung, himself, as well as to Richard Wilhelm, whose work built a crucial bridge between East and West. This is the bridge we must continue to construct. To support it, we require the Four Pillars.

Notes

1 OIAA, 10.
2 OIAA, 15.
3 OIAA, 18.
4 OIAA, 21.
5 OIAA, 22.
6 OIAA, 28–30.
7 OIAA, 30, 31.
8 OIAA, 33.
9 OIAA, 35.
10 OIAA, 118.

11 OIAA, 125.
12 OIAA, 130.
13 OIAA, 134.
14 OIAA, 135.
15 OIAA, 136.
16 OIAA, 285.
17 OIAA, 290.
18 OIAA, 300.
19 OIAA, 301.
20 OIAA, 302.

Chapter 11

"The Four Modalities of Temporality and the Problem of Shame"

Words, Jung taught us, can trigger complex psychological responses, and shame is certainly one of them. In this chapter, I review "The Four Modalities of Temporality and the Problem of Shame," which appears in Volume 4 of Stein's *Collected Writings* and was first published as a book chapter in 2017.

When shame appears in excess in psychoanalytic treatment, the play instinct can, at times, serve as a liberating force, alleviating the burden of this dreadful emotion. When this happens, pathways to the Self may open, allowing shame to be nullified. Stein conceptualizes this phenomenon as "achronicity"—a term he coined to describe states of mind in which shame is reduced to nothingness, akin to the untouched snow atop Mount Kilimanjaro. In such moments, when the Self is awakened within us, time ceases to exist, and shame dissolves into sheer nothingness—into the whiteness of the void. This phenomenon holds significant clinical relevance, as shame often manifests as a persistent and repetitive affective complex, resembling a neurosis with an unrelenting narrative. In therapeutic settings, it can sometimes feel as though a patient is buried beneath an avalanche of shame, making it nearly impossible to excavate both analyst and patient from its suffocating weight. Poets, writers, and artists have long understood methods for escaping shame's violent grasp, often achieving liberation through deep reverie and engagement with the creative process, in dialogue with the muse. Jung himself employed a similar approach in *The Red Book*, while Stein has his own methods, just as I have mine. For Stein, these methods are mythopoetic. He enjoys telling stories.

In this precious essay, Stein revisits a childhood memory to illustrate his notion of achronicity. The event in question took place when he was four or five years old, on Easter Sunday in either 1947 or 1948—ironically, a moment in time he seems to have partially lost track of! I previously recounted this story in the "Introduction" to this volume, but I will briefly restate it here, given its profound psychological and theological significance. Stein recalls that, on a Sunday morning before church, his pastor gave him a lesson in time. Holding a small clock roughly the size of his palm, his father demonstrated how the hands could be moved along the face. The small hand, he explained, showed the hour, while the large hand indicated the minute. Understanding these instructions, Stein proudly shared his new-found knowledge with his Sunday School friends (without any intention of evoking

DOI: 10.4324/9781003664024-12

envy). This moment marked a significant breakthrough in his learning—a deeply meaningful encounter with time that he has never forgotten, due to the synchronicity involved: the lesson occurred on Easter, the day of the Resurrection. Over time, it became a foundational narrative in Stein's life, shaping his reflections on the mysteries of time, transference, and psychological transformation. Since that day, Stein has regarded time as his friend. He rarely loses track of it and insists that he is almost never late for meetings. Of course, he acknowledges that he is not perfect, and occasional lapses occur. Nevertheless, a strong sense of shame keeps his steps in check, almost as precisely as a Swiss train! Perhaps by coincidence, his earliest memory of experiencing shame also dates back to this same period.[1]

Please indulge me for a moment as I engage in a brief reverie: In Chicago, Stein crossed paths with June Singer, who was affiliated with the Institute of Transpersonal Psychology in Palo Alto, California. At the time, I was coming of age as a Jungian psychotherapist, working with children in the Bay Area at Lincoln Child Center. There, I led group processes twice a week, on Tuesdays and Thursdays. My experiences in this setting taught me a great deal about shame and envy as they manifested in the children I treated. Therefore, I find Stein's memory particularly compelling, as it speaks to a crucial challenge in analytical work: helping patients find a path to liberation from shame.

For Stein, the clock naturally symbolizes time, or chronicity. As a child, however, the clock was not merely a tool for timekeeping but also a plaything—a gateway into the Self-field where shame ceases to matter. I have observed a similar phenomenon in my own work with children: during sandplay, their experience of shame often transforms into joy. Through play with the clock, Stein was led into the world of mathematics, where, in my reverie, his mother may have played a role in furthering his understanding of numbers, alongside his pastor father. Moreover, Stein's enthusiastic decision to share his newfound skill of reading time with his friends at Sunday School may have been encouraged by the extroverted tendencies of his father and grandmother.

In my vocational dream research at John F. Kennedy University, where I earned my Master of Science in Clinical Psychology in 1986, I developed the hypothesis of the vocational "nuclear symbol." This concept refers to a symbol of the Self with deep vocational significance, emerging in early childhood (around age two) and developing throughout latency (ages 4–11). In my thesis, I hypothesized that such symbols typically become constellated in a child's psyche between the ages of four and seven, though in some cases, the process may extend into later childhood (ages 9–11) or early adolescence.[2] For Stein, the clock appears to have functioned as what I called a nuclear symbol, emerging within the relational field between him and his father through play, and further reinforced by his mother's example of healthy introversion and introspection, which encouraged his precocious thinking. What makes this event particularly significant in the context of his life and writings is that it took place on the day of Christ's Resurrection. Here, Providence, not predestination, was at work.

Stein defines achronicity as a state of cosmic reverie unburdened by shame. He articulates this idea in his thought-provoking paper, stating: "My approach will be more analytical and abstract… to suggest that four basic modalities of temporality play a role in human consciousness in various ways and at different stages of life: achronicity, chronicity, synchronicity and dischronicity."[3] To clarify this abstract neologism, Stein incorporates several diagrams that, while impressive—reminiscent of Jung's diagrams in *Aion*—are challenging to understand. Nevertheless, their meaning resonates on an intuitive level.

Marie-Louise von Franz played a pivotal role in inspiring Stein's theoretical inquiries into the mysteries of time, as well as his fascination with Wolfgang Pauli's dreams of the piano lesson and World Clock, upon which Stein meditated during his IAAP/IAJS lecture in 2015 at Yale. To be sure, the archetype of the timekeeper was activated in him at the age four or five, when he was first learning simple arithmetic. From a developmental perspective, this milestone was encouraged by his father, yet it may have been the story of Jesus at Easter that truly deepened his engagement. In his biblical lectures, Stein amplifies the Bible as if it were a dream, momentarily transcending temporal constraints. Writing, he suggests, is itself a means of annulling time—and with it, shame.

Around the midpoint of this essay, Stein further elaborates on achronicity, describing it as follows:

> [It is] a kind of negative mode of temporality, a zero in time, a beginning point in myth and psychological development. This is experienced as timelessness and outside of time frames. Before the number one, which might represent chronicity, there is the number zero, achronicity. Achronicity refers to the absence in consciousness of the sense of objective time ("real time"). All take place in the present tense…. This is experienced by infants, sleepers, daydreamers, deep readers, meditators and mystics, and aged and demented, creative people at work, in short by all of us…. Achronicity is pretemporal, infinite, and boundless. It is a no-time temporality…. Divinity (singular and plural) resides within achronictic temporality. This is an eternal present.[4]

The trans-temporal state of achronicity is often experienced by children when they are immersed in transformative play. Stein extends this concept to the realm of spiritual transcendence, moving beyond the linear constraints of clock time through the vertical dimension of achronicity and synchronicity, which he presents as twin phenomena. He illustrates how we, too, can experience moments of liberation from shame, stating: "synchronicity in-itself is shame free."[5] But how is this possible? Stein cautions against the illusion that we—or our patients—can ever fully escape from temporality and shame. Such a belief, he argues, would be misguided and potentially harmful. Yet, his theoretical framework offers a pragmatic and illuminating perspective for clinicians. In this 33-page paper, he weaves together numerous strands of insight. I strongly encourage readers to engage with it deeply.

I believe that the clock was Stein's nuclear symbol, similar to Einstein's compass—gifted to the future physicist and mathematician by his father at the age of four. Just as Einstein never forgot the moment he watched his compass point north—the direction of his destiny—Stein, too, was profoundly shaped by his symbolic clock.

Stein's insights on shame and its transcendence can be extended to other toxic emotions and complexes, which can be temporarily overcome through spiritual practice, play, or the production of the transcendent function. Engaging this function through inner dialogue with the Self invites a simultaneous experience of the four modalities of time—both horizontal and vertical—where they converge at the zero-point of the crossbeams. As Stein notes: "Our reflection on this high degree of integration of the four modalities and the contents they bring with them into the fabric of temporality will border on the ontological and theological."[6]

Thus, as Jungians, we cannot exclude theology from our education. Competency as an analyst requires at least some understanding of ontology and its recapitulation of childhood experiences. There is a cyclical nature to time, corresponding with numerical patterns. As Stein observes, 30 years separated his first and final ventures to Zürich before he ultimately meandered into Grossmünster church.

To understand the relationship between numbers and time, we must have the right teachers to guide us. On this subject, I have learned a great deal from von Franz, Pauli, and Stein—especially from a Protestant perspective. Reflecting on my own upbringing, I recall that it was likely my German Lutheran grandmother who first taught me to tell time at about the same age as Stein. As a child psychotherapist, I can easily imagine myself as a young boy in Stein's father's parish, listening to the young Stein express pride in his newfound ability to tell time. Likewise, I can reimagine my years at Lincoln, working with children to help them transmute their shame through sandplay therapy.

So what, then, is the Christian solution to the problem of shame, and how might this key inform analytical practice, helping therapists unlock doorways to the Self? Stein offers an answer:

> The Christian solution to the problem of shame, takes form in the possibility of making an identification with the Christ figure. The stain is washed clean in the symbol…. Following shortly upon the Ascension of Christ, the descent of the Holy Spirit on the day of Pentecost and the reception of the spirit into human consciousness created a new spiritual center in the psyche of the believers…. The Christians, as they now were called no longer lived out of a chronicity-dominated ego but out of a transcendent spiritual identity associated with Christ.[7]

He continues:

> Many mystical traditions, such as Cabbala, Hasidism, Sufism, yoga, Zen Buddhism and others, have made identical moves toward transcending temporality even if only momentarily. This is a goal of individuation as conceived by Jung

and those following him in depth psychology. All arrive at the position sym-bolized by Pauli's "Ring *i*," a place beyond sheer temporality and shame and characterized by compassion, grace, and a sense of wholeness realized.... In that sense, shame is "ontological," that is to say, it is archetypal, and therefore built into the structure of human experience.[8]

"Ontology recapitulates ontogeny" is a psychoanalytic axiom. As Stein suggests, "Symbols [such as his own clock] are the key to discovering and unlocking the treasure chests of the unconscious."[9]

In analytic work, the reception of the spirit into human consciousness can estab-lish a new spiritual center in the psyche, enabling clients to transcend shame and temporarily free themselves from the grip of their complexes. In this essay, Stein creates an imaginative space in which he moves toward higher vistas of spiritual understanding in the Self, offering new conceptual tools to illuminate pathways to individuation. As Jungians, we recognize Jung as our ancestor analyst. Stein, however, follows his own muse, offering insights that serve as a medicine for the psyche. His *Collected Writings* extend these insights to a broader community, embracing all faiths without discrimination—an effort also demonstrated by Jung.

By way of synchronicity, I realized I was on the right track with my reverie in this chapter when, at an analyst dinner meeting, John Beebe, in his characteris-tic eloquence, began discussing the film *The Clock* starring Judy Garland. Later, watching it with my wife, we noticed that the couple in the film meets twice beneath the clock in New York, symbolizing the affirmation of their bond. This resolved my puzzle as to why my psyche had led me to revisit this memory twice in this book—once in the "Introduction" and again near the end. Indeed, time never stops when one is having fun!

Reflecting on Stein's act of sharing his newfound understanding with his friends, I cannot help but wonder whether it may have evoked feelings of envy or shame in some of them. As the pastor's son, he might have been a quicker learner than his peers—some of whom may have struggled with the same lesson. Yet, in this imagined scenario, which completes my reveries, I envision Stein's generous spirit guiding them—helping them learn to read the hands of the clock without sham-ing them with his pride. On Easter, while his more introverted mother taught the children not to identify solely with their chronicity-dominated egos, but rather to cultivate an awareness of their transcendent spiritual identity in Christ, Stein may have embodied that lesson in practice. This vision reflects my fantasy of what a true Christian community should ideally be—a vision shaped by my later studies, since I never attended Sunday School as a child, nor did I know anything about theol-ogy before reading Jung and Meister Eckhart. Thank God for Eckhart! I cannot imagine grasping Jung or Stein without him. Nearly 700 years ago, at the time that Dante was composing his *Divine Comedy* in Italy, Eckhart taught his listeners how to enter the prayer of quiet—to dwell in deep meditation on a Word of scripture, like a mantra in the eternal now. In such moments of pure perception, the doorways of awareness open to transcendence, revealing our eternal existence—whether envisioned as the Heavenly Rose or the thousand-petaled lotus. Here, time dissolves, and the world of nature pulses with consciousness and bliss.

Notes

1 CW4, 275.
2 Herrmann, *Nuclear Symbols*.
3 CW4, 266.
4 CW4, 268, 270, 271.
5 CW4, 279.
6 CW4, 291.
7 CW4, 296.
8 CW4, 297.
9 CW4, 299.

Chapter 12

Ways to the Self

Five Conversations

This chapter focuses on Stein's most recent book, co-authored with the artist Diane Stanley in 2024. My focus in this review is on Stein's contributions as they pertain to Jungian psychoanalysis, though I encourage readers to partake fully of the book's rich bouquet.

Chapter 1, "Ways to the Self: Psychedelics, Active Imagination, Dreams and Jungian Psychoanalysis," opens with a dialogue between Stein and Stanley on the role of psychedelics, and whether such experiences can be meaningfully compared to those encountered in analysis. Stein admits that he has never taken psychedelics, himself. While he cannot directly equate active imagination and dreams with psychedelic experiences, he recalls that reading *Memories, Dreams, Reflections* at Yale in 1968 had a "kind of psychedelic effect" on his mind, expanding his consciousness in a way that evokes that transformative potential of psychedelics. For Stanley, however, the distinction is clear. While psychedelics had a profound impact on her youth, she considers dreams her royal road to the Self. She likens Lysergic acid diethylamide (LSD) to a helicopter ride into the stratosphere—an experience that, while expansive, lacks the deeper integrative benefits she finds through her artwork and Jungian analysis.[1]

After listening to Stanley's experiences, Stein reflects: "LSD affects the neurons and the sense of perception. It affects sensation, whereas active imagination doesn't, or at least not to the same intensity. Active imagination is mentally induced; psychedelic experiences are chemically induced."[2] He then recalls his experience of transcendent love that emerged during an active imagination in 1994 in Chicago, at a time of personal crisis. Struggling with "a strong wind of doubt about the sustainability of love over the course of time," he encountered a vision that transformed his understanding. As described in a previous chapter, he "saw" Jesus Christ in the skies, and:

> the thought came to me —it was more than a thought, it was a revelation—that in Christ time and eternity are fused permanently, and that this signifies that "love never fails" because the timebound experience of love is joined to the eternal source of love, so it can never vanish or be extinguished. It is an eternal flame. I can't tell you what a sense of relief this gave me. It made me a true

DOI: 10.4324/9781003664024-13

believer. It was like Dante's experience. Since then, I have had no doubt that love can ever fail, and I have to say that it also gave me a whole new take on what it means to be a Christian. It brought a new consciousness for me.[3]

Stein then recalls another transformative moment—the breathless experience of watching a butterfly dance at Saint Peter's Square in Rome.[4] Expanding on the butterfly as a symbol associated with death, he writes: "My experience of the butterfly as a symbol was not in active imagination. Not at all. It was in broad daylight and while wide awake. I've had several similar synchronistic experiences around death."[5]

In "Conversation Two: The Problem of Integration," Stein and Stanley discuss the notion of "transmission" in the East, with Stein hypothesizing that, at a very deep level in the analytic relationship, communication between two individuals involves a "transmission or union of energies." He asks: "Don't the Chinese say that when the student is ready, the teacher will appear? If you are engaged seriously in intent, and touch upon the archetypal level, something constellates and then the doors start opening."[6] These pathways align with what the authors refer to in the book's title as "ways of the Self." Interestingly, Stein hesitates to disclose the insights from his dreams that have led him to his supra-personal "secret" or his myth of Supreme Meaning. He is not yet prepared to unveil them.[7] One can only hope he will do so in time—perhaps within the next few years. I pray that this revelation does not arrive posthumously, much like the final 13 cantos of the *Paradiso*, which the people of Venice longed for until they were said to have been miraculously found by Dante's son following a dream transmission from Dante himself, in eternity.

The dialogue gains momentum when Stein asks Stanley, "What do people do with their great visions?"—a question central to Jungian analysis. Stein appears to caution Stanley against prematurely revealing the "diamond within," advising her to safeguard her awareness so as to prevent harm. Keeping the doors to the Self open is essential, yet exposing such inner treasures may invite ridicule, envy, or scorn. He offers a final warning—to Stanley and readers alike—urging them to "be careful."[8]

In Chapter 3, "Pictures from Analysis," Stein explores Stanley's impressive artwork. His interpretations of her paintings are particularly incisive, and it becomes evident that he is engaging with her at a very high level.[9] As their conversation deepens, Stein references Harold Bloom's *The Anxiety of Influence* with respect to poets, summarizing its central idea in a single sentence: "They [poets] are constantly looking over their shoulder at what their predecessors have done, either secretly quoting them or working against their influence for the sake of something 'new' and 'creative.'"[10]

In "Conversation Four: Of Two Minds in One," the dialogue shifts toward the concept of Oneness, or non-duality. Stein observes that Eastern traditions have a much deeper appreciation for what he terms the "non-dual dualistic mind."[11] The term "liberation" is also mentioned, prompting Stein to comment that the word is "not in the psychology dictionary," nor used "very often by psychoanalysts." He asserts:

> What I see, however, is a possibility for people to experience a degree of liberation from the grip of their complexes, if they do the work in analysis. If they work on their dreams, reflect on their emotional states of mind, do active imagination, and so forth, they develop a different kind of relationship to themselves and to the world around them. They become freer.[12]

Stein defines liberation from complexes as follows: "One lives in two states of mind. You know, there is a liberated part of us and a not-so-liberated part of us. We move back and forth between them. The complexes are never totally dissolved."[13] He reflects briefly on Stanley's remark that presentations on active imagination are exceedingly rare in the field, reminding her:

> But it's made a comeback since the publication of *The Red Book* in 2009. This caught people's attention. For Jung, active imagination was the Royal Road to individuation. Without it, it's not possible to arrive at the destination. When teachings get institutionalized, they always lose something of the original genius and spirit of the visionary founder. This has been happening Analytical Psychology as well.[14]

The book is infused with both wit and insight, as Stein and Stanley engage in deep, thought-provoking exchange.

What interests me most in "Conversation Five: Liberation: Limits and Prospects," is Stein's explicit assertion:

> Without numinous experience, it is probably not possible to take those further steps. Without it, you can get bogged down with the same analysis of the same complexes over and over again. That's the reason Jung left the Freudian way of working.... There is a danger in some psychotherapies, that they simply repeat the narratives, which in fact deepens the neurosis.[15]

The discussion centers on Jung's late conversations with the Zen master Shin'ichi Hisamatsu in 1958. Reflecting on this exchange, Stein remarks:

> I do believe that moments of such total liberation [*satori* in Zen] are possible, and that Jung himself did have that experience. Jung was old and physically weak at the time of that interview. He was two years or so from his death. He had a lot of amazing psychological experiences. Among these was a release from temporality into a space where nothing really matters, where there are no longer the effects of gravity.[16]

Here, Stein is referring to Jung's near-death experience during his hospital stay in 1944 following a severe heart attack—an experience Jung recounted in spectacular detail in *Memories, Dreams, Reflections*. As the dialogue unfolds, it becomes increasingly evident that liberation extends beyond the ego; the anima, animus, and Self are also released, together forming a healing agent—a quaternity or mandala of instinctual-spiritual wholeness. This integration enables the deepest possible liberation, achieved through Eros or divine love. Both ego and Self must embody a paradoxical balance of vulnerability and strength to attain such a liberated state, which may be equated with *satori* in Zen, or liberty and freedom in Dantean terms.

Stein focuses on the primary means by which individuation occurs, both within and beyond analysis: through the affirmation and acceptance of one's "destiny." He explains: "That's individuation."[17] Elaborating further, he writes:

> At the more developed stages of individuation, the ego gives itself over to the Self and accepts that the Self ultimately determines the fundamental direction of one's life. You can call this 'destiny.' Everyone has a specific destiny... Ultimately, what determines our destiny is not the ego's so-called free choices. If we become conscious of this, we begin to pay attention to what the Self is up to. That means, for instance, when a synchronicity happens one takes notice of it, extracts the meaning from it, and follows up on the meaning.[18]

In the book's concluding pages, Stein embarks on a seven-page meditation on Jung's achievements. Reflecting on Jung's enduring legacy, he tells Stanley:

> I think he will be read through the ages.... His writings will not fade. Not all of his writings are at high level, but the great ones are. That type of creativity depends on being liberated from the ego's narrow boundaries of the spirit of the times. If you have the key to that type of liberation and can use it to open the drawers fixed on the high walls of the Self, and let come into you what is there, to make itself known, then you too will experience that level of creativity. People will notice that you are different—that you have something special, something extra that is difficult to account for on the basis of your background, studies and cultural background.[19]

It is my prediction that the same will be said of Stein's greatest writings, which I hope I have successfully conveyed for readers' enjoyment and appreciation in this book.

Notes

1 WTS, 9.
2 WTS, 10.
3 WTS, 17–18.
4 WTS, 24.
5 WTS, 25.
6 WTS, 48.

 7 WTS, 52.
 8 WTS, 54.
 9 WTS, 71.
10 WTS, 59.
11 WTS, 111.
12 WTS, 123.
13 WTS, 124.
14 WTS, 126.
15 WTS, 132.
16 WTS, 134.
17 WTS, 141.
18 WTS, 143.
19 WTS, 146–147.

Chapter 13

The Plays

Late Works

Around 1996, Stein had his astrological chart read by Liz Greene, who was living in Zürich at the time. During the divination session, as she studied his chart through a cloud of thick cigarette smoke, she paused, took a breath of fresh air, and, with the seasoned wit and wisdom of a shaman-seeress, declared: "You're going to write plays in your old age." This prediction caught Stein off guard. At the age of 73, he had never considered becoming a playwright. Yet, he tucked her words away in the back of his mind as a possibility worth serious reflection. In time, writing, stage managing, and performing Jungian plays would become a means for him to enact an archetypal role—the dramatist—at the behest of the Self. This creative endeavor would hold deep literary, theological, and psychological significance, not only for Stein but also for the audiences who would witness these performances. Through playwriting, he would ultimately integrate his three central callings—English, theology, and Jungian psychology—culminating in a final flourish of expression, structured across seven successive acts.

As William Wordsworth famously wrote in his poem "My Heart leaps Up," "The Child is father of the Man." Stein recalls fondly that his mother, Jeanette, had written plays for church when he was a boy, and he had performed them before the congregation. Greene's foresight thus resonated with distant yet formative memories, awakening a sense of synchronicity and possibility. As the sage of Goldiwil, Stein found himself in transit toward new evolutions of consciousness, accompanied by further numinous experiences and synchronistic events. The internalized roles of his childhood were ready for transformation—becoming more playful, whimsical, and joyful—as his youthful Self, in turn, fathered him.

Fourteen years after the horoscope reading, Stein and his wife relocated to Switzerland, and by 2010, Stein had become president of the International School of Analytical Psychology Zurich (ISAPZURICH). Around this time, *The Jung-White Letters,* edited by Ann Lammers, had just been published. Inspired by this correspondence, Stein considered the possibility of staging a performance of the letters. By then, the friendship between Jung and White had gained recognition as a significant intellectual exchange, representing a meeting of two distinct worldviews: one of a strictly scientific medical doctor who regarded God as a psychological complex, and one of a Thomist theologian seeking to develop a meta-theory

DOI: 10.4324/9781003664024-14

integrating empiricism with Catholic metaphysics. Together, they envisioned their perspectives as equal pillars of an East-West Bridge—a project Jung had begun co-constructing with Richard Wilhelm but had left incomplete. To be sure, Jung's speculations about the God image did not always align with Jewish, Catholic, Protestant, or Islamic theology. He was well aware of this tension and, in a letter to White on May 21, 1948, warned that his forthcoming book, *Aion*, would be a most "shocking and difficult book."[1] Indeed, it was. While *Aion* is not about God in the theological sense, for Stein, it is. The book explores Jung's research into the phenomenology of the empirical God image (or Self), touching upon a transcendental concept: the experience of totality, encompassing both conscious and unconscious contents, which Jung believed could only be described in antinomian terms.[2] The work draws extensively from the writings of Meister Eckhart.

On June 1, 1948, White wrote to Jung from New York, informing him that the first of his three tours along the West Coast of California to promote Jung's work had been a "huge success." He had funded the trip by delivering introductory lectures on analytical psychology at various Catholic colleges and institutions, steadily establishing himself as a leading Jungian educator for clerics and theologians. During his travels, White addressed the Analytical Psychology Club in San Francisco, where he received a warm reception at the home of the late distinguished analyst Dr. Joseph L. Henderson. He spoke enthusiastically about "the problem of the Catholic analyst,"[3] spreading what he saw as the good news—the happy marriage he and Jung had fostered between Dominican theology and analytical psychology. For a time, their collaboration appeared to be a harmonious union, their friendship evolving in intellectual depth and mutual admiration. However, much like Jung's earlier relationship with Freud, this partnership gradually cooled. The warm energies of Eros that once propelled their exchanges began to dissipate over a growing divergence centered on the perplexing problem of evil. In 2010, Stein was beginning to imagine how he might dramatize this intellectual and personal rift, crafting a play about a friendship that ended not through fault, but through the workings of fate.

After Ann Lammers published her book in 2010, Stein's first foray into staging a dramatic performance of the *Jung-White Letters* brought Liz Greene's oracle-like prediction from a slow simmer to a rapid boil. He had previously seen a similar production in Chicago, where Lee Roloff had staged the *Freud-Jung Letters*. Inspired by this precedent, Stein invited Paul Brutsche and John Hill to collaborate, selecting key letters for the performance. Brutsche agreed to play Jung, while Hill took on the role of White. Their staged reading at ISAPZURICH received great acclaim. Encouraged by this success, they turned their attention to *The Red Book*, selecting seven scenes for dramatization. Once again, Brutsche played Jung, while Hill took on several roles (Elijah, Izdubar, Philemon) and Dariane Pictet portrayed both Salome and Jung's soul. This production proved an even greater success, with performances across Europe, Russia, and China.

Stein had long been intrigued about a little-known meeting between Jung and Rabbi Leo Baeck at a hotel in Zürich in 1946. No notes were taken, nothing was written about the encounter, and neither Baeck nor Jung spoke of it afterward. It remained a deep secret. However, it is believed that, during this private conversation, Jung confided to Baeck in German: *"Ich bin ausgeruscht"* ("I slipped off the path"). Likely, he was referring to his controversial involvement with the National Socialist movement in the early 1930s—an issue I first heard about at a private conversation over lunch in Palo Alto with Tom Kirsch, before conducting further research. I was relieved to hear from Tom about Jung's confession of remorse.

Following the success of the Jung-White play, Stein began to wonder: *What might have been said during that secret meeting?* The idea for a new play took shape, but he soon encountered a challenge—he was unsure how a Rabbi would speak. For a moment, he was stuck. Then, in a striking synchronicity, he met Henry Abramovitch during a trip to Israel at the Jewish analyst's invitation. As they walked along the summit of Masada,[4] Abramovitch told Stein that he had also attended Yale, where he had studied anthropology and been very interested in theater. In that moment, on sacred Jewish ground, Stein turned to him and declared: "You are the man!" Indeed, Abramovitch proved the ideal collaborator—a friend and fellow actor who could give voice to Rabbi Baeck. Enthusiastic about the project, he and Stein co-wrote *The Analyst and the Rabbi.* The play is available for viewing on YouTube and was published by Chiron Publications, accompanied by commentary from both the playwrights and the actors.

Since then, Abramovitch and Stein have continued their collaboration, producing *My Lunch with Thomas*, *Speaking of Friendship*, and *Eranos.* They are now finalizing the script for *Twilight at Bollingen*, a play centered on Jung's final years. Each of these works is written and performed as a conversation, bringing active imagination onto the public stage. The dramatic tension lies in the situation and the dynamic exchanges among characters.

Reflecting on this creative journey, Stein remarked in an email exchange the day after the Winter Solstice in December 2024—when the days began turning toward new light—that all seven plays ultimately grew out of Liz Greene's unexpected comment over 25 years ago. The seed she had planted with her astrological reading had matured into a flourishing tree of creativity, bearing seven varieties of ripe fruit for audiences to experience.

Significantly, Stein's recollection that his mother had written plays for church when he was a boy—and that he had performed them before his father's congregation—strongly reinforces my argument about the enduring power of the nuclear symbols of childhood to shape and transform consciousness throughout the seasons of life. These church plays were likely religious in nature, interweaving Hebrew and Christian themes from the Old and New Testaments, based on the King James Bible. This was part of the role Jeanette played, as both the preacher's wife and the mother of an emerging star.

A Retrospective Look at Stein's Life and Writings Since Yale

Reflecting on his life over the past several years, Stein recently contributed a piece to the 60th-anniversary Yale yearbook for his Timothy Dwight College class of

1965. In it, he meditates on his fundamental values—personally, professionally as a Jungian psychoanalyst, and as an American citizen, despite having lived in Switzerland for the past 22 years. In the concluding section, which Stein granted me permission to quote, he asks: "What did the four years in Yale College contribute to establishing fundamental values for my life?" In response, he invokes three ancestral figures who shaped his understanding of these values:

> William Sloane Coffin, Jr., College Chaplain and preacher extraordinaire, on the values of social justice and service; Harold Bloom, Gnostic genius of imaginative literature, on the values of deep reading and writing; and Hans Frei, mystic philosopher and theologian, on the value of the spiritual life. I think of them as the Big Three. There were many others—classmates, teachers, the college Master of TD (the renowned Dante scholar, Thomas Bergin)—who contributed to the realization of fundamental values such as *Lux et Veritas* and 'for God, for country and for Yale' (in that order), and they too appear from time to time in fond memories, in their writings, in footnotes and references. All together, they cluster as a cloud of witnesses that surrounds my daily life today in the foothills of the Alps. The fundamental values of social justice and service, deep reading and writing, and the spiritual life have held steady through the sixty years since graduation.

As we have seen, after Yale, Stein's interests shifted increasingly toward Jungian psychoanalysis. This path did nothing to contradict his fundamental values but instead deepened his understanding of "the complexity of living them out on a practical level." The fundamental value of Jungian work—individuation, or becoming who and what one is born to be—has remained central to his interests for the six decades since his graduation.

Throughout his many years of teaching, writing, and sharing Jungian perspectives worldwide, the fundamental values embodied by Yale's "Big Three" (Coffin, Bloom, and Frei) have continued to guide him: "Coffin's galvanizing sermons from the pulpit of Battel Chapel, always ritually backed up by the King, President of the University, on social justice and the nobility of living for service and not for self, echo still in my mind." Stein continues:

> the sound of Bloom's impassioned shamanic chanting of the great poems of the Western canon has sustained my dedication to the notion of 'deep reading,' which has become a mantra, and writing as an expression of the heart and not only the mind. Frei's brilliant lectures on finding the spiritual path through the barren wasteland of godless modernity have continued to resonate with the mysteries of the soul as discovered in my life after Yale.

One lesson Stein learned early in his freshman year—after receiving a humiliatingly low grade on a paper for his English class—was that:

> writing is a craft to be practiced and honed: One part inspiration and many parts perspiration. The course on the History of the English Language taught

by Marie Borroff, my only female professor while at Yale, contributed a sense of levels of linguistic discourse and remains a memorable highlight for bringing the English language to light as a multi-textured resource for expression of thought and feeling.

I just discovered—while reading this document two days before Christmas—that Stein's *Collected Writings* now total nine volumes, not eight! He anticipates adding three or four more, bringing the final collection to around 14 volumes. I eagerly look forward to what's to come. Reflecting on this journey, Stein regards his English major as "the structural backbone of this body of work"—a foundation that has supported his lifelong exploration of language and meaning.

Now at 81 and "writing against the clock," as Bloom once told him during his 80s, Stein still finds writing both a pleasure and a source of deep satisfaction. Lately, his collaborative plays with his fellow Yalee Henry Abramovitch—ranging from short, two-person dialogues to multi-character pieces—have been particularly meaningful. These works can be viewed on YouTube, with links available on Stein's website, murraystein.com.

Stein's journey has come full circle. Raised in Canada as the son of an immigrant Protestant pastor and a Baptist mother, he never considered applying to Ivy League colleges while living in South and North Dakota. It was a college counselor at Denby High School in Detroit who encouraged him to risk "putting a message in a bottle and casting it into the flood of applications headed for Yale in the Fall of 1960." To his overwhelming surprise, he received an admission letter along with a full work-study scholarship. His years at Yale ultimately cost his parents nothing—a gift for which he remains deeply grateful. "It was an awesome opportunity to enter the halls of a great center of learning, and the pleasures and joys experienced there remain vividly memorable," he reflects. "For the gift of a Yale education and the fundamental values represented by the Big Three, I will remain deeply grateful."

Finale

Perhaps, the most formidable mind among the Big Three, Harold Bloom wrote in *The Anxiety of Influence*: "Shamans return to primordial chaos, in their terrible and total initiations, in order to make fresh creation possible; but in societies no longer primitive such returns are rare."[5] Stein is one of those rare ones—a shaman-ancestor par excellence. The self-sacrifices and achievements of the early Jungians, along with the contributions of the post-Jungians, now offer strong assurance of our field's survival. Stein has played his part in this legacy and played it exceptionally well. If we, as Jungians, can follow Stein's lead in finding the corpse during our midlife passage and burying the dead in our initiation journeys into primal chaos, we may fulfill our shamanic debts to those who came before us. In doing so, we may honor our living ancestors with our own birth dues and enact dramatic performances of resurrection for the living.

Notes

1 Lammers, A. *The Jung-White Letters*, edited by Ann Conrad Lammers and Adrian Cunningham, with consulting editor Murray Stein. London & New York: Routledge (Philemon Series), 2007, 119.
2 Jung, *Collected Works* 9(ii), 116.
3 Lammers, *The Jung-White Letters*, 121.
4 Masada, an ancient fortification in Israel where the first Jewish-Roman War ended in 72–73 AD, is situated atop an isolated plateau resembling a mesa at the eastern edge of the Judean Desert, overlooking the Dead Sea. The mythic narrative of Masada became a powerful national symbol in the early years of Israel's statehood after 1948. I interpret it as a representation of the transcendent function constellated within the imaginative space between Murray and Henry. As such, Masada serves as a symbolic site of healing for the Jungian field in the post-Jung era.
5 Bloom, H. *The Anxiety of Influence: A Theory of Poetry*. New York: Oxford University Press, 1973/1997, 60.

Chapter 14

Collected Writings Volume 9

Jungian Studies

Stein begins Volume 9 of his *Collected Writings* with an essay titled "Jung's Vision of the Nature of the Psyche and Analytic Practice." In this piece, he offers a succinct summation of the central aim of Jungian psychoanalysis: the healing of the psyche through the pursuit of human wholeness. In the opening lines—first published in 1998, the same year his masterpiece *Transformation: Emergence of the Self* was released 26 years ago—Stein writes:

> A wit once proclaimed that the art of the physician is to entertain the patient while nature heals. This may be as true for analysis as it is for medicine... Today most experienced analysts of all theoretical persuasions would agree that they are not healers of psyche but at best only allies of the healing processes that are to be found within it. All but the most inflated clinicians recognize their limitations of skill and technique in the therapeutic process. What actually heals in psychotherapy remains a mystery. Perhaps it is a certain kind of love.[1]

Here, I will begin with a brief survey of some newly encountered passages from the first three chapters—lines I have not previously come across but that resonate with my interests. Following this, I will provide an overview of some significant insights from Part Two of this volume, focused on Jung's *The Red Book*. Since half of the volume is dedicated to *The Red Book*, I encourage readers to explore it further on their own. In my concluding statements, I will offer at least a glimpse of Stein's finale, in which his expertise on this vast subject shines forth with his characteristic depth and eloquence.

Chapter 1 takes us deep into the enigmatic journey toward the Self. Stein writes:

> Jung's reliance on 'nature' to supply the healing forces is not some sort of woolly mysticism but a physician's recognition that human art and science have their limitations. The analyst is not omnipotent and certainly requires the cooperation of nature if healing is to occur.[2]

DOI: 10.4324/9781003664024-15

He continues:

> Yet the practiced skill and masterful technique of the trained analyst are also important in analysis, and in some cases, they are even crucial. Otherwise, training would be unnecessary and training institutes an egregious waste of energy. While there may be "natural therapists" and healing personalities, the difficult analytic cases require a great deal of expertise and skill. This seems to have been true since time immemorial, as evidenced by shamanic healers, who were and are also highly trained technicians. Hurtful experiences in early life prevent nature's healing processes from having much effect. It is often the case that the pathways by which nature does its healing are blocked and need to be opened and cleared of obstacles. Often, weak bridges need to be built up into solid, workable psychic structures, and in some cases a whole new psychic infrastructure must be constructed if nature is to have a chance to work its healing effects. Faulty and malignant conscious attitudes and developments, acquired usually through traumatic and hurtful experiences in early life, prevent nature's healing processes from having much effect.[3]

A little further into the opening chapter, following an overview of Jung's views on the nature of the psyche—and how they diverge from those of Freud and Klein, particularly regarding the "death instinct" or *thanatos* principle—Stein inserts two sentences that resonate with the thematic motif I have been tracing. With an ear attuned to the leitmotiv of "pathways," he references in the extended passage quoted above: "This mindbody totality is what Jung conceived of as the self. The self is the God principle, as it were, and the ego is the human reality principle."[4] Previously, Stein described synchronicity as the "God principle." Here, it becomes evident that the Self and synchronicity are deeply interwoven. In my review of the next two essays, I will seek to further elaborate these concepts, reflecting on the significance of literary interlocutors in Jung's intellectual life. Following Stein's lead, I will focus particularly on Freud and Victor White. But first, let us hear some more from Stein about the Self. He writes:

> The ego's consciousness is privileged within the psychic universe because of its unique link to the self. Being a complex, however, means that the ego is also deeply constituted by trauma. In fact, Jung theorizes that the ego comes into being through the 'collisions' that inevitably take place between an individual and the world. He was familiar with Otto Rank's notion of the centrality of the birth trauma for ego development, and while he did not give this early experience quite the weight that Rank did, he would concede that traumata suffered at birth have a fundamental constituting force in ego formation.[5]

Given Stein's own experience—having endured a forceps delivery as an 11-pound baby—it is evident that he writes from direct personal experience. He continues:

> The deep connection to the self at the ego's core makes it a paradoxical psychic object. On the one hand, it is the seat of anxiety and pain, receiving its personal birth and awakening through trauma. On the other hand, it is divine and godlike because of its identity as the self. The ego is the place where time and eternity meet most intimately and crucially. The ego is at once the incarnation of the self in the time space continuum and the fragile resister of existential anxiety. Clustered around this central bipolar core at the heart of the ego are associations that make up a person's remembered history and personal identity. Experiences of self with mother, with father, and with other significant figures in the surrounding world are introjected and woven into the fabric of consciousness and ego identity. These can be supportive and life enhancing associations, or they can be debilitating and toxic ones. Analysis attempts to separate the ego from the pathological associations trapped into the structure of the ego complex and to recover and support the beneficent ones.[6]

Furthermore, he writes:

> The ego develops, according to Jung, through suffering collisions with the environment. These collisions, if they are not too severe and injurious, bring challenges rather than debilitating traumas. If the ego responds positively to the challenges posed by the environment, it develops strength and mastery and begins to show increasing autonomy. It gains self-confidence and adapts more and more effectively and forcefully to the world around. For this reason, some analysts will, after having established a sound working relationship with an analysand whose ego is relatively sound and healthy, deliberately create tension in the relationship in order to facilitate ego strengthening.[7]

The chapter continues to reveal insights into the art and science of analysis, including the ways in which analysts, at crucial moments, challenge analysands in an attempt to fortify their egos. But what about relationships beyond the analytical setting? Stein's early education as a literary scholar, prior to his decision to attend Yale Divinity School, provided him with precisely the foundation needed to later apply his analytical lens to a domain of Jungian scholarship that has been deeply significant to me for 44 years: Jung's relationship with Victor White. White's books, *God and the Unconscious* and *Soul and Psyche*, which I first encountered and cherished during my time at the University of California, Santa Cruz, remain central to this enduring interest.

Jung as a Preacher

Chapter 2, "C.G. Jung as Writer in Dialogue," stands out as the crème de la crème in this regard. I was pleasantly surprised to discover that Stein had originally published this piece in the first printed edition for the Guild for Pastoral Psychology in 2005. In Volume 9 of the *Collected Writings*, it appears in slightly modified form. The opening paragraph is particularly inspiring. He writes:

> There exists numerous images of Carl Gustav Jung: scientist, physician, prophet, mystic, artist. Each one lures somebody to claim its centrality. None of them is definitive or exhaustive of its reality. The whole man always proves to be greater than the sum of his parts. And yet each of these pieces is needed to complete the full portrait. I wonder if we pay enough attention to Jung the writer. To me, it seems this prominent feature of his life has been neglected or overlooked in many of the studies now available on his life and work.[8]

Stein's essay not only explores Jung as a writer, but it also introduces readers to another archetypal persona—one Jung assumed only once, when he penned his most divinely inspired work, "Answer to Job": the persona of the preacher.

Stein begins by exploring Jung's relationship with Freud—a well-trodden subject in Jungian scholarship. Given the extensive literature on this topic, I encourage readers to consider Stein's unique contribution to the conversation. However, what has received comparatively little attention—until recently, I believe—is Jung's relationship with the Dominican theologian Victor White. Stein devotes significant attention to White in the second part of Chapter 2. While many of the ideas he presents are spelled out clearly enough in his other eight volumes (reviewed in previous chapters), here, he focuses on an aspect of Jung's intellectual development that may be less familiar to most readers. The emergence of these insights feels particularly encouraging.

To fully grasp Jung in all his vast complexity as a man, we must approach his relationships with the utmost care through deep, attentive reading—an approach that Stein both recommends and exemplifies. Jung considered his intellectual and personal dialogues with White deeply significant, until their ideological divergence resulted in a painful rupture. Their parting, which was traumatic for both, was one of Jung's great "collisions." Yet, echoing Stein's earlier discussion on ego strengthening, the confrontation may have been precisely the challenge Jung needed for the further evolution of his vocation, once nature had set it in motion.

Stein rightly observes:

> Often, he was inspired as a writer, as an idea would take hold of him and give him words to infect others with the same spirit. Some said he was charismatic as a lecturer. I believe he was. He could have been a great preacher.[9]

A preacher! The archetype of the preacher was clearly at play in Jung's psyche when he landed his great "whale," as he described it in a letter to his secretary, referring to "Answer to Job." Stein affectionately notes: "Among Jung's most thoughtful letters are those he wrote to White."[10]

Stein discusses the divisive topic of evil, which led to the temporary rupture of Jung and White's friendship, in depth. Then, he issues this decisive statement:

> Evil actively opposes the good, and the two principles are locked in an eternal struggle for the upper hand. If they were to be united in a single God figure, moreover, this monotheism would need to conceive of God as combining both good and evil in one Being. White, steeped in classical philosophy and Thomistic theology and deeply influenced by Roman Catholic doctrine, could not accompany Jung down this path.[11]

Indeed, for White, the notion of a God embodying both good and evil would have been a catastrophic theological deviation—one wholly incompatible with his position as a Blackfriar, a member of the Dominican Order. Trained in the tradition of St. Dominick to guard against heresy as a theological watchdog of the Vatican, White could not reconcile Jung's vision with the tenets of his faith. Jung, fully aware of this, nonetheless remained unwavering in his insistence on driving home his argument. When "Answer to Job" was published, White was incensed and, in response, transgressed the delicate line of friendship. Yet, despite this breach, Stein continues his compassionate analysis of their friendship, emphasizing its deep significance for Jung's intellectual evolution. He credits White as a catalyst for one of Jung's most extraordinary works of imaginative thought:

> One may well argue that the writing of *Answer to Job* is a product of the Jung-White relationship. White was the catalyst for this incandescent piece of writing, just as Freud was the stimulus for Jung's earlier works, *Wandlungen und Symbole der Libido* (The Psychology of the Unconscious in the English translation) and *Psychological Types*.[12]

Stein's finely attuned ear for sermons, shaped by his attendance at his father's churches and later at Yale's Battel Chapel, allowed him to solve a key part of a puzzle that many Jungian scholars have overlooked. He observes: "In much of his writing, one can sense the firm intellectual commitment to scientific method and the barely checked sounds of another kind of writer, a poet or preacher. This comes strongly to the fore in his letters."[13] Indeed, the preacher archetype was woven into Jung's correspondence with White for well over five years before he composed "Answer to Job." White, in many ways, helped awaken this latent aspect of Jung's psyche—an archetype that had lain dormant since early childhood. It emerges with increasing intensity in their exchange, building from its inception in White's first letter to Jung, to its moment of apotheosis before their eventual rupture.

Stein expands this theme in the next chapter, "Of Text and Context," first published in 2007. Writing with the cadence of a poet, he observes: "Some people said he was charismatic as a lecturer. In an earlier age or a different cultural context, he could have been a brilliant preacher, like his grandfather Preiswerk, who held forth from the big Cathedral pulpit in Basel."[14] I think this is as true of Jung as it is of Stein.

I will briefly add that, beyond Jung's maternal grandfather Samuel Preiswerk—whose Zwinglian preaching Jung had heard as a boy—a far more resonant voice of an ancestral preacher was present in the Protestant psyche of Europe. This voice originated in the very region from which Stein's paternal ancestors (and my own) hailed in Thüringen. It was none other than the voice of Meister Eckhart, whom Jung had read in his youth and had given him a feeling for the true power of the living God.

In this chapter, Stein repeatedly describes the archetype of the preacher in Jung's writing, observing:

> In much of his writing, one feels both the firm intellectual commitment to scientific method and the barely checked sounds of another kind of writer in the background, sometimes a poet or a preacher, certainly a passionate author and a creative personality.[15]

Jung's reading of the Bible—which, as we have seen, Stein has critiqued and corrected in his various works—is here described as a "misreading." Relying on Bloom's theory of poetry, Stein writes: "In effect, he [Jung] rewrites the supreme fiction of Christendom, the Bible. In Jung's *Answer to Job*, we find what Harold Bloom would call a 'strong misreading' of the Bible, which creates the possibility of a great poem."[16] "Answer to Job" is, indeed, a poem—one sung by an inspired preacher. Whether it constitutes theology, psychology, or a combination of both in a singular, unitary channel has been explored at length by Stein, as described in previous chapters.

Jung's Collision with White

Stein's metaphor of a "collision" with reality—through which trauma strengthens the ego in the service of individuation—certainly applies to Jung's own ego consciousness following his fierce wrestling with White over the problem of evil. This struggle culminated in an overwhelming encounter with the superior force of the Self, which, as Jung experienced it, authored "Answer to Job" with a transcendent power—giving him a voice beyond his own that, in the end, wounded him with love. Nowhere else in Jung's writings does the psychological God image emerge with such spiritual vigor and existential urgency. Here, the dark side of the God image—the shadow side of the Self—erupts with the force of an "earthquake" or tidal wave. Writing as a 77-year-old, Jung fired arrows of justice at the very source that wounded him in the most sensitive part of his being: the integrity of his vocation as both a natural scientist and the son of a theologian.

In his grappling with the issue of evil, Jung's emotions were tested as profoundly as his intellect—his feelings as much as his thinking. He allowed his emotional subjectivity to speak, not merely from a place of Christian brotherly piety (which he had felt reciprocated by White, whose letters often ended with "I love you, C.G"), but in an uninhibited and impious manner. In "Answer to Job," Jung wrote with the fervor of a preacher, proclaiming the science of analytical psychology as though listening to a stream of divine music.

This outburst of religious emotion is one of the most powerful pieces of prose ever written by a psychologist—its tone resembling less an abstract scientific treatise on individuation and more a shamanistic-prophetic text. Following Stein's lead, we can see that Jung's most profound sermon was delivered through the archetype of the preacher: the Self-as-preacher in Jung. He took his aim at the shadow of the God image—the source of his wounded friendship with White. As we know, this theme, fed by a Christian cultural complex, was shaped by Jung's Zwinglian heritage. Yet, the emotional depth of "Answer to Job" surpasses even the voices that influenced him most: his grandfather Samuel Preiswerk and the mystic Meister Eckhart. Jung's voice here is unmistakably ministerial.

As Job's first advocate in Küsnacht, Jung stated that he waited 40 years before writing "Answer to Job." When he finally did, the work flowed out ceaselessly and effortlessly, as though carried by an unrelenting current of elegiac verse driven by a force of love and violence within the psyche. White's challenge struck Jung at his most vulnerable spot, compelling him, as Stein observes, to seek an internal remedy. This process involved a shamanic countertransference through which he endured and confronted what he perceived as Christianity's ailments, as well as those within White, himself. Through this struggle, a maieutic function was activated, allowing for the emergence of a broader conceptualization—a new God image surpassing all previous ones. Jung perceived this image from a standpoint that transcended time, milieu, and historical constraints—rooting it instead in the collective psyche of the here-and-now. From this transcendent Ground of Being, he claimed, the God images of history derive their distinct cultural forms and expressions.

Through his dialogues with the watchdog of the Dominican Order—who sniffed out Jung's supposed heresy—Jung endured a violent collision of opposites within the God complex. After 40 long years of suffering, he finally reached the point at which he could articulate a significant portion of his new myth, as later expressed in *Memories, Dreams, Reflections*. Looking back, this 40-year span began around 1910–1911—a period marked by Jung's painful estrangement from Freud and his second encounter with William James in America. "I entirely agree that for unprepared readers *Job* is a hard nut to crack," Jung wrote in a late letter. "Anyone who finds in the problem of Job—which William James also tackled—too much scorn, irony, and suchlike rubbish had better leave the book alone." In the footnote to this statement, Jung cited a famous passage from Lecture XVIII of James's *The Varieties of Religious Experience*:

> It's a plain historic fact that they [Kantian idealists] never have converted anyone who has found in the moral conception of the world, as he experienced it, reasons for doubting that a good God can have framed it.... No! the book of Job went over this whole matter once and for all definitively.[17]

Stein offers the final work on White's impact:

> What the stimulating relationship with Victor White contributed was the spark that ignited the passion so hotly expressed in *Answer to Job*. It is as though Victor White brought the author in Jung up to a state of high excitement. What Jung initially greeted as a white raven when White appeared on the scene turned out to be *un homme inspirateur!*[18]

In conclusion, I appreciate Stein's essays on Victor White, which represent a significant step toward a more nuanced and positive understanding of this important friendship in Jung's life.

Liber Novus

The second part of Volume 9, dedicated to *Liber Novus*, comprises the essays "*The Red Book*," "What Is *The Red Book* for Analytical Psychology?" "How to Read *The Red Book*, and Why: The Story of a Modern Man's Search for His Soul," "Systema munditotius: A Psychogram," "*The Red Book* as a Journey to Individuation," and "Acts of Imagination: Creation of the (Inner) World."

Now, as promised in my opening remarks, we arrive at the climax—Stein's remarkable insights into Jung's *Liber Novus*. In his essay "*The Red Book*," Stein examines Jung's self-created God image, Abraxas, as presented in "Seven Sermons to the Dead":

> In the extensive correspondence with Father Victor White between 1945 and 1960, in which the problem of evil and various doctrines of God were thoroughly discussed, there are no references to Abraxas, although Jung frequently proclaims his disgust with the Christian doctrine of *privatio boni*. Jung may not have found an answer to the problem of evil in Abraxas, but he still wanted to hold out for a new God image that would somehow include archetypal shadow, a.k.a. absolute evil, within the God image.[19]

I appreciate that Stein consistently uses the term "God image" when discussing Jung's visionary work throughout most of this volume. In particular, he demonstrates how Jung's intense engagement with White—spanning their 15-year correspondence—helped him move toward an answer to the problem of evil within the God image. This paradox of opposites, however, was only clarified—in my view—by Stein's own "Answer to Evil."

In the essay "What is *The Red Book* for Analytical Psychology," Stein asks:

> So, what is *The Red Book* for analytical psychology now that it has arrived and after so many of Jung's writings have by now been already published? Does it belong in the canon? Is it a seminal work for analytical psychology to be placed beside Jung's other major works, or is it to be taken as the equivalent of

a writer's diary and sketchbook, akin to Leonardo's Notebooks, which shows the early workings of a brilliant mind as the creator prepares for his more serious scientific contributions to the world? Conversely, one can ask: Are Jung's later writings no more than an explication of this monumental symbolic work to make it more accessible for modern readers and thinkers? Perhaps it is both.[20]

In the same essay, in a section titled "The Transmission of Spirit in Tradition," he discusses Jung's "Zofingia lecture" from January 1899:

What is surprising as we read this essay is Jung's explicitly positive regard for the term "metaphysical." In all of his later psychological writings, he would eschew anything having to do with "metaphysical" terminology, saying repeatedly that he is speaking only as a psychologist and not as a theologian. However, what he actually did, subtly, with his later psychological theory was to find a way around speaking about transcendence as "metaphysical" while retaining much of the sense of what this term conveys. For "metaphysical" he substituted the term "archetypal," and for "the supernatural world of ghosts, gods and angels" he used the concept of "the unconscious." In this way, he discovered a channel of communication whereby numinous figures and powers can be transmitted from one generation to another without metaphysical or supernatural agency. This is similar to what science has done by explaining the creation of the universe, electromagnetic force, gravity, the nature of light, and so forth without reference to a supernatural God.[21]

I have not yet read Jung's "Zofingia lectures." However, while exploring this section in Stein's book, I was struck by the timing—Jung delivered these lectures around the same period that he encountered William James's *Principles of Psychology*. In this work, published in 1890, James proposed a fourth level of the self: the "metaphysical self." This connection is highly significant in tracing the foundational influences on Jung's psychology, preceding the humor, magic, practical sense, and wisdom that would later emerge during his period of writing *The Red Book* (1913–1928).

I will now conclude with a final quote from Stein's essay "How to Read *The Red Book*, and Why: The Story of a Modern Man's Search for His Soul":

Jung titled his work *Liber Novus*. With this astonishing title, the book asserts its priority over the biblical predecessor. It is displacing (usurping?) the authority of the two biblical Testaments, Old and New, and replacing them with a Testament for the new era of human consciousness to come. The work is offered as a text for the beginning of a new Aeon, the Age of Aquarius. It could be called the Age of Phanes if we follow Jung's lead. In this respect, it stands beside, or surpasses, Nietzsche's Thus Spoke Zarathustra as a book for the future of the human spirit.[22]

Conclusion

As we've seen in this book, the Self is an inborn spiritual potential that must be developed as fully as one is capable. What leads us to wholeness is according to Stein the *transformative image* that brings us the greatest joy, peace, and meaning in life. Jungian psychoanalysts can learn to awaken this image in their analytic practices by dialoguing with the archetype of the "inner analyst," or analyst within. Stein's strengths as a theologian have enabled him to correct for some of Jung's relative weaknesses in theology in order to arrive at a more precise specificity about the nature of the Christ image, and the problem of evil that Jung left incomplete in his writings. In Stein's works, Jung's hypotheses about the Self are disseminated toward a larger radius of communion, where all faiths are welcomed into the fold, East and West, North and South, without any unnecessary dualisms. In *The Bible as Dream,* Stein charted a new way forward for theology and analytical psychology to become more unitary, integrative, or non-dual. In so doing, he completed Jung for purposes of neo-Jungian studies, which we are promoting in this series. In Stein's Chicago lectures, there was a future still awaiting him that he could not see clearly enough on American soil. Once on Swiss soil, in Zürich, his instincts became rooted in the land of his maternal ancestors and he outstripped his forerunners by striding steadily toward his own separate identity, as an independent researcher and neo-Jungian theorist.

We've seen his many innovations in this volume, where Stein's ideas were applied to the analytic process in a practical, grounded way. What Stein revealed is how transformations take place not only in patients in analysis, but also in artists, scientists, and national poets, such as Rilke in Germany, and Dante in Italy. Following in the footsteps of Dante, in pursuit of the ultimate, Stein beckons us onwards and points us to the way to the Heavenly Rose.

Stein's literary, analytic, and theological identity—his whole being—is unique to him and his personal history: from Canada to North Dakota, to New Haven to Zürich, Chicago to Goldiwil Switzerland. His 82 years reflects one consistent character. There is no other Jungian life quite like Stein. He is a highly individualized Jungian analyst, a Canadian-American-Swiss original.

As Stein continues to achieve a greater and more lasting impact on our Jungian and post-Jungian culture during his halcyon days, my prediction is that the field of analysis will begin to see the centrality of *Transformation* more than ever before. Stein gave us access to the banquet of the living in nine blue and white volumes of his *Collected Writings* that are stronger than death. His words will live on as we age, in search of new vistas of discovery.

If Jung was the analyst of the Swiss sublime, Stein was his minister, apostle, and teacher of a new neo-Jungian doctrine where personal theology, the Word, was made flesh in a fresh incarnation, like the Ox-herding picture of the Sage re-entering the marketplace toward a potentially awakened spiritual democracy. As we've seen, some of Stein's lectures, such as "On Reading the Bible Psychologically," were compiled from talks he delivered in 1989, at the Catholic Seminary in

Mundelein, Illinois, not far from where the new Pope, Leo XIV, attended seminary at Catholic Theological Union in Chicago's Hyde Park neighborhood. I see this as a synchronicity for our field, one we can all celebrate! Today the Sage of Goldiwil is being superseded by the World-Seer, who is in touch with the Self and can transmit its radiance to others through the *spiritus rector* of our own vocations, in any faith. The Alps beckon him, as they did Jung; to re-imagine psychology perhaps a few steps further than Jung postulated: for post-modernity. This is a victory for Stein, the neo-Jungian writer and analyst-theologian, whose life we've been honoring herein.

Notes

1 CW9, 1.
2 CW9, 1, 2.
3 CW9, 2.
4 CW9, 16.
5 CW9, 16, 17.
6 CW9, 17, 18.
7 CW9, 20.
8 CW9, 29.
9 CW9, 30.
10 CW9, 34.
11 CW9, 35, 36.
12 CW9, 36.
13 CW9, 36.
14 CW9, 40.
15 CW9, 58.
16 CW9, 62.
17 *C.G. Jung Letters,* 2, 330.
18 CW9, 66.
19 CW9, 175.
20 CW9, 182.
21 CW9, 186.
22 CW9, 214.

List of Abbreviations Used in the Bibliography and Footnotes

CW   Stein, M. *The Collected Writings of Murray Stein.* 9 vols. Edited
        by Steven Buser and Leonard Cruz. Ashville, NC: Chiron
        Publications, 2019–2024. References to individual volumes are
        listed by title in the endnotes.

MDR   Jung, C.G. *Memories, Dreams, Reflections.* Recorded and edited by
        Aniela Jaffé. Translated by Richard and Clara Winston. New York:
        Vintage Books, 1961.

MS   Stein, M. *Minding the Self: Jungian Meditations on Contemporary
        Spirituality.* London and New York: Routledge, 2014.

OIAA   Stein, M. *Outside Inside and All Around And Other Essays in Jungian
        Psychology.* Ashville, NC: Chiron Publications, 2017.

RB   Jung, C.G. *The Red Book.* Edited with an introduction by Sonu
        Shamdasani. New York: W. W. Norton & Co., 2009.

WTS   Stein, M. *Ways to the Self: Five Conversations.* Ashville, NC: Chiron
        Publications, 2024.

Bibliography

Bloom, H. 1973/1997. *The Anxiety of Influence: A Theory of Poetry.* New York: Oxford University Press, 60.

Henderson, J., and M. Oakes. 1963. *The Wisdom of the Serpent: The Myths of Death, Rebirth, and Resurrection.* Princeton, NJ: Princeton University Press.

Henderson, J. 1964. "Ancient Myths and Modern Man." In *Man and His Symbols*, edited by C. G. Jung, 104–157. Garden City, NY: Doubleday & Co.

Herrmann, S. 1998. "Murray Stein: The Transformative Image." *The San Francisco Jung Institute Library Journal* 17 (1): 17–39.

Herrmann, S. 2003. "Melville's Vision of Evil." *The San Francisco Jung Institute Library Journal* 22 (3): 14–36.

Herrmann, S. 2005. "Melville's Vision of Evil," expanded edition for the International Association for Analytical Psychology (IAAP). Accessed at iaap.org ("Articles—Psyche and Culture").

Herrmann, S. 2009. "Colloquy with the Inner Friend: Jung's Religious Feeling for Islam." *Jung Journal: Culture and Psyche* 3 (4): 123–132.

Herrmann, S. 2010. *Walt Whitman: Shamanism, Spiritual Democracy, and the World Soul.* Durham, NC: Eloquent Books.

Herrmann, S. 2014. *Spiritual Democracy: The Wisdom of Early American Visionaries for the Journey Forward.* Foreword by John Beebe. Berkeley, CA: North Atlantic Books (Sacred Activism Series).

Herrmann, S. 2018. *Emily Dickinson: A Medicine Woman for Our Times.* Cheyenne, WY: Fisher King Press.

Herrmann, S. 2020a. *William James and C.G. Jung: Doorways to the Self.* Oberlin, OH: Analytical Psychology Press.

Herrmann, S. 2020b. "The Hypothesis of Psychic Antibodies: The Fight of the Kingsnake and the Rattlesnake." *Jung Journal: Culture & Psyche* 14 (4): 1–15.

Herrmann, S. 2020c. "Walt Whitman on Religious Liberty: Marriage Equality and the American Cultural Complex." In *Cultural Complexes and the Soul of America: Myth, Psyche, and Politics*, edited by Thomas Singer, 180–196. New York: Routledge.

Herrmann, S. 2022. *Swami Vivekananda and C.G. Jung: Yoga in the West.* USA/Singapore: Strategic Books Publishing and Rights Co.

Herrmann, S. 2024a. *Meister Eckhart and C.G. Jung: On the Vocation of the Self.* Bloomington, IN: iUniverse Publishing.

Herrmann, S. 2024b. *Vocational Dreams: Calling Archetypes and Nuclear Symbols.* USA/ Singapore: Strategic Books Publishing and Rights Co.

Kirsch, J., and M. Stein. 2013. *How and Why We Still Read Jung.* London & New York: Routledge.

Kirsch, T. 2000. *The Jungians: A Comparative and Historical Perspective.* London & Philadelphia, PA: Routledge.

Kirsch, T. 2014. *A Jungian Life.* Carmel, CA: Fisher King Press.

Lammers, A. 2007. *The Jung-White Letters,* edited by Ann Conrad Lammers and Adrian Cunningham, with consulting editor Murray Stein. London & New York: Routledge (Philemon Series).

Stein, M. 1982/1995. "The Aims and Goal of Jungian Analysis." In *Jungian Analysis,* edited by Murray Stein. Chicago & LA Salle, IL: Open Court.

Stein, M. 1983. *In Midlife: A Jungian Perspective.* Dallas, TX: Spring Publications.

Stein, M. 1985. *Jung's Treatment of Christianity: The Psychotherapy of a Religious Tradition.* Wilmette, IL: Chiron Publications.

Stein, M. 1992. "Power, Shamanism, and Maieutics in the Countertransference." In *Transference-Countertransference,* edited by Nathan Schwartz-Salant and Murray Stein, 67–87. Wilmette, IL: Chiron Publications.

Stein, M. 1993. *Solar Conscience / Lunar Conscience.* Wilmette, IL: Chiron Publications.

Stein, M. 1995a. "Introduction" to *Encountering Jung on Evil.* Princeton, NJ: Princeton University Press.

Stein, M. 1995b. "Organizational Life as Spiritual Practice." In *Psyche at Work: Workplace Applications of Jungian Analytical Psychology,* edited by Murray Stein & John Hollwitz, 1–18. Wilmette, IL: Chiron Publications.

Stein, M. 1996. *Practicing Wholeness: Analytical Psychology and Jungian Thought.* New York: Continuum (Chiron Publications).

Stein, M. 1998a. *Jung's Map of the Soul.* La Salle, IL: Open Court.

Stein, M. 1998b. *Transformation: Emergence of the Self.* College Station: Texas A & M University Press.

Stein, M. 2014. *Minding the Self: Jungian Meditations on Contemporary Spirituality.* London & New York: Routledge.

Stein, M. 2015. "A Lecture for the End of Time—Concerning Rebirth." In *How and Why We Still Read Jung,* edited by Jean Kirsch and Murray Stein, 26–45. London & New York: Routledge.

Stein, M. 2017. *Outside Inside and All Around and Other Essays in Jungian Psychology.* Ashville, NC: Chiron Publications.

Stein, M. 2019. *Individuation: The Collected Writings of Murray Stein, Volume 1.* Ashville, NC: Chiron Publications.

Stein, M. 2021. *Transformations: The Collected Writings of Murray Stein, Volume 3.* Ashville, NC: Chiron Publications.

Stein, M. 2022a. *The Practice of Jungian Psychoanalysis: The Collected Writings of Murray Stein, Volume 4.* Ashville, NC: Chiron Publications.

Stein, M. 2022b. *Analytical Psychology and Religion: The Collected Writings of Murray Stein, Volume 6.* Ashville, NC: Chiron Publications.

Stein, M. 2023a. *Analytical Psychology and Christianity: The Collected Writings of Murray Stein, Volume 5.* Ashville, NC: Chiron Publications.

Stein, M. 2023b. *The Problem of Evil: The Collected Writings of Murray Stein, Volume 7.* Ashville, NC: Chiron Publications.

Stein, M. 2024a. *Psychology and Spirituality: The Collected Writings of Murray Stein, Volume 8.* Ashville, NC: Chiron Publications.

Stein, M. 2024b. *The Collected Writings of Murray Stein, Volume 9.* Ashville, NC: Chiron Publications.

Stein, M. 2024c. *Ways to the Self: Five Conversations.* Ashville, NC: Chiron Publications.

Index

For Product Safety Concerns and Information please contact our EU
representative GPSR@taylorandfrancis.com
Taylor & Francis Verlag GmbH, Kaufingerstraße 24, 80331 München, Germany